NEWARK
The Nation's Unhealthiest City
1832–1895

NEWARK
The Nation's Unhealthiest City 1832 – 1895

STUART GALISHOFF

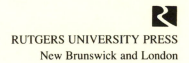

RUTGERS UNIVERSITY PRESS
New Brunswick and London

Parts of this book have appeared previously, as follows:
"Cholera in Newark, New Jersey," by Stuart Galishoff, in *Journal of the History of Medicine* 35 (1970):438–448.

"Triumph and Failure: The American Response to the Urban Water Supply Problem, 1860–1923," by Stuart Galishoff, in *Pollution and Reform in American Cities, 1870–1930*, ed. Martin V. Melosi. Copyright © 1980 by the University of Texas Press.

"Safeguarding the Public Health: Newark, 1895–1918," Stuart Galishoff. Copyright © 1975 by Stuart Galishoff. Used by permission of Greenwood Press.

Jacket photo: "A Bit of Germantown," from M. Lamb, *Sketch of Newark, N.J.* Courtesy Newark Public Library.

Publication of this book has been made possible, in part, by a grant from the New Jersey Historical Commission, Department of State, Grant-in-Aid Program

Library of Congress Cataloging-in-Publication Data

Galishoff, Stuart.
    The nation's unhealthiest city.

    Includes index.
    1. Public health—New Jersey—Newark—History—19th century. 2. Sanitation—New Jersey—Newark—History—19th century. 3. Newark (N.J.)—History.
I. Title.
RA448.N73G335   1988   614.4'274932   87-16355
ISBN 0-8135-1281-6

                            British Cataloging-in-Publication information available

To Fran

CONTENTS

LIST OF ILLUSTRATIONS

MAPS

FIGURE

LIST OF TABLES

PREFACE

IN THE LATE 1960s, WHEN I BEGAN MY STUDY OF Newark's sanitary and public health history, I thought I would need at most five to seven years to complete the work. Today I am amazed that it took two volumes and twenty years for me to attain my goal. I have learned that scholarship must often take a back seat to the imperatives of life. A job took me far from my source materials. New research opportunities that I could not resist presented themselves. Most important of all, my son's illness forced me to rethink my priorities. An old Hasidic saying expresses it best: man plans and God laughs. The delay, however, may have been beneficial, for it gave me time to think about some of the historiographical issues in urban public health history that have been raised in recent years. Furthermore, a considerable body of literature on the history of urban sanitation and public health now exists, and it has enabled me to put Newark's experience in a national context.

Many persons have helped to make this a better book. Joseph O. Baylen, Timothy J. Crimmins, and Martin Kaufman read various parts of the manuscript and showed me where it could be improved. Joel A. Tarr generously shared with me his vast knowledge of the history of sewerage and wastewater treatment. Charles Cummings and his talented and dedicated staff at the Newark Public Library, New Jersey Reference Division, found research materials that I did not know existed and acted as unpaid research assistants when I needed to know the first name of a Newark official or the exact title of a publication. Any errors of fact, interpretation, or style are, of course, my own. There are no words I can use to describe my gratitude to my wife, Fran, for making this work possible. She never lost faith in its value, or in me, during the many years when it appeared it might never be completed.

Sections of Chapter 3, "Cholera," were previously published in *Journal of the History of Medicine and Allied Sciences* 35 (1970):438–448, and are reproduced with its permission. Material contained in Chapter 2, "Public Health, Drainage, and Water Supply," and Chapter

6, "Sewerage," first appeared in *Societas—a Journal of Social History* 6 (Spring 1976):121–138, which ceased publication in 1978. A segment of Chapter 4, "An Age of Giants," is taken from Stuart Galishoff, *Safeguarding the Public Health, 1895–1918* (Westport, Conn.: Greenwood Press, 1975), 3–11, copyright © 1975 by Stuart Galishoff, and is reprinted by permission of the publisher. Excerpts from Chapter 9, "Water Supply," were previously published in Martin V. Melosi, ed., *Pollution and Reform in American Cities, 1870–1930* (Austin: University of Texas Press, 1980), 35–57, copyright © 1980 by the University of Texas Press, and are reprinted by permission of the publisher.

NEWARK
The Nation's Unhealthiest City
1832–1895

INTRODUCTION

THE HISTORY OF PUBLIC HEALTH IS THE STORY OF SOCIety's endeavors to protect its members against the hazards of group living. Since the beginning of civilization the human race has been confronted with two discrete but related problems: sanitation and disease prevention. As cities came into being, waste disposal and control of acute, communicable diseases became major concerns. Cities are particularly vulnerable to two types of epidemics—those transmitted by fecalized water supplies, such as cholera, typhoid fever, and dysentery; and those spread by person-to-person contact, including influenza, smallpox, and diphtheria. But until recently, sanitation and disease prevention were not subjects of extensive lawmaking; nor was there a need to establish government agencies armed with summary police powers to protect the public health.

In small, homogeneous communities, such as existed in colonial America, a dense network of primary group relationships, operating through the force of public opinion, governed people's conduct and guaranteed the maintenance of social order. In a society closely bound by ties of kinship, race, language, and religion, citizens could usually be depended upon to observe community standards of acceptable public behavior. Individuals who failed to abide by community mores were punished by methods designed to shame wrongdoers into reforming their ways. Thus homeowners who failed to clean their privies or allowed garbage to accumulate in front of their homes were ostracized by their neighbors or were asked to account for their behavior at a town meeting or in church. In towns and small cities, where people worked and lived in close proximity and fear of public censure deterred antisocial behavior, few persons dared to abridge community norms of municipal sanitation.[1]

As society became more complex and heterogeneous, older methods of social control weakened. Beginning in the 1840s and 1850s, large numbers of Irish and German immigrants began arriving in American cities. When these newcomers, most of whom were Catholic or foreign speaking, rejected the customs and leadership of the native Anglo-Saxon Protestants, conflicts developed between the two groups. At the same time, the spectacular growth of cities led to a worsening of sanitary conditions and higher death rates. Native-born Americans blamed the immigrants for this decline and called upon local government to restore order in the cities. Laws were passed to enforce sanitation and boards of health were established to control the spread of communicable diseases. When restrictive ordinances proved incapable of preventing a further deterioration of living conditions, municipal governments responded by undertaking the building of sanitary infrastructures. Sewers were laid, public water supplies were developed, and the city assumed responsibility for garbage removal. Public health thus became one of the leading questions in the new urban-industrial society that emerged in the mid-nineteenth century.[2]

The insalubrity of American cities during the nineteenth century and the worsening sanitary conditions occasioned by industrialization, immigration, and rapid growth are graphically revealed in Newark's public health history. Once noted for its handsome thoroughfares and majestic elms, Newark became a vast cesspool of human and animal excrement and industrial wastes. As privies, stables, slaughterhouses, tenements, and smokestacks multiplied, the shadow cast by sickness and premature death lengthened. From 1832, when it suffered its first major epidemic, to 1895, when a bacteriological laboratory was established by the board of health, signaling the start of a healthier era in the city's history, communicable diseases were rampant. Epidemics of cholera aroused the most concern, but it was the silent endemic diseases, notably tuberculosis, pneumonia, and the diarrheal diseases, that caused the greatest mortality.

While much research still needs to be done, on the basis of the extant historical studies[3] and contemporary surveys,[4] Newark's experience with disease and sanitation during the nineteenth century appears to have been very similar to that of other American cities. Given the propensity of cities to emulate one another in all manner of things, it would be surprising were it otherwise.

Nineteenth-century American cities shared a common culture. The principal determinants of public health—sanitation, nutrition, housing conditions, medical theory and practice, governmental actions, and social values—varied little from city to city. Thus the battle against epidemic diseases was fought along the same lines and with much the same results all across the United States. Similarly, Americans believed in the virtues of individualism, limited government, and rapid economic growth, and thought that air and water were inexhaustible natural resources to be used and abused as businessmen and municipalities saw fit, all of which hindered the development of effective public health programs.

But cities also competed with one another economically and hence were compelled to adopt sanitary improvements that made them more desirable places to work and live. A city's success depended to a considerable degree on its ability to project an image of progressiveness and modernity. Business leaders were especially concerned about local sanitary conditions, since their fortunes were linked to their city's ability to attract new residents and industries. Local chambers of commerce and boards of trade throughout the nation pressured municipal governments to build expensive sanitary public works. Consequently, cities quickly seized upon innovations that improved the public health or provided sanitary amenities lest their rivals gain an advantage. The adoption of planned water supplies and sewerage provide cases in point.[5]

By the second half of the nineteenth century, American cities had outgrown the cisterns, wells, and springs that furnished most of the nation's drinking water. As the domestic sources of water used by individual homeowners dried up or became polluted, cities had to develop public supplies. To do this they brought in water by gravity from impounded mountain streams or, more commonly, by pumping it from nearby rivers and lakes. In the years 1860–1896 the number of public water supplies increased from 136 to 3,196, of which a little more than half, including nearly all of the largest ones, were municipally owned. Tragically, population growth and industrialization led to increased pollution of surface waters, with the result that most communities drank their own sewerage or that of their neighbors upstream. Typhoid fever and dysentery became endemic and urban mortality rates remained abysmally high. A few cities in the 1870s operated filtration plants, but they were designed to improve only the water's appearance and were ineffectual against pathogenic microorganisms. In the following decades, scientists discovered new methods of water purification that prevented most waterborne diseases, and cities began to treat their water supplies. In 1880 only thirty thousand Americans drank filtered water. By 1923 the only water that was not being either filtered or chlorinated was groundwater, which underwent natural purification in its passage through the earth, and the water obtained from a few impounded streams of exceptional purity.[6]

The adoption of sewerage provides a similar story. At the time of the Civil War, cities had at best only a few underground sewers and some large drains for removing surface waters. In the following decades public water supplies and indoor bathroom appliances came into general use, adding to the dangers presented by the city's dependence on privies and cesspools. English engineers had developed the principles of water-carriage sewerage some time earlier, and in the 1870s American cities initiated extensive programs of sewer construction. At first sewers were poorly built and were opposed by many because of the public nuisances they frequently created. Gradually, municipal engineers gained control of the work, established plumbing standards, and built integrated sewer systems. By 1920, public sewers served 84 percent of the residents of the nation's eighty-three largest cities.[7]

The urban poor sometimes supported public health reforms but often did not, depending on whether they perceived the reform to be in their interest. They usually supported the acquisition of a larger, more dependable water supply, since it improved their lives in so many ways. At first they were less certain about the benefits of sewerage and almost always strenuously opposed the efforts of local health officials to require costly renovations of their homes. Though it was an article of faith among middle-class reformers that filth caused disease, the poor saw that persons who lived in squalor often enjoyed good health while many who resided in clean, meticulously maintained houses fell prey to pestilential diseases. Since the poor frequently did not have money to purchase the food and coal they needed, they were unwilling to pay for protection against a distant, uncertain hazard.

In the bibliography to one of his more recent works, the noted urban historian Sam Bass Warner, Jr., observes

> If modern urban history is to present the background to the environment of today's cities, it must produce inclusive studies of the many elements that determine the health and survival of city dwellers. Such histories would treat cities of varying sizes and economic structures as particular ecologies within which changing interventions by health institutions, medical science, sanitary engineering, and regulatory policies are assessed in terms of changes in the health and well-being of their populations. I know of no urban history that undertakes this task for a modern period.[8]

For the last decade I have been attempting to fill this void in my studies of Newark and Atlanta. Whereas other public health histories are primarily chronicles of the local board of health, my studies seek to embrace all public policies and actions that had an impact on morbidity and mortality rates. Thus much of this book deals with sanitary services that were outside the jurisdiction of the health department. In particular I have emphasized the development of a public water supply and sewerage, the period's two most important sanitary advances and the only course of preventive or therapeutic medicine that significantly reduced urban mortality in the nineteenth century.[9]

Since the adequate board, the engineers in charge of sewerage, and the board of health did not act in concert, I have used a topical organization instead of the more traditional chronological approach. But though these agencies functioned independently of one another, their activities were informed by a common purpose. Health officials and sanitary engineers proceeded on the assumption that filth was responsible for disease and cleaning up the environment would reduce urban mortality. The belief that disease resulted from miasmas emitted by decaying organic matter held sway in the United States until the 1890s, when it was superseded by the germ theory of disease. Hence the topics and the time frame of the book form a logical unit. The study's primary foci are the development of sanitary services, the work of the Newark Board of Health, and, more generally, the control of epidemic diseases. For purposes of completeness, and because my previous book[10] pays it little attention—concentrating instead on the new directions in public health brought about by the advent of bacteriology—I have carried forward the history of sewerage and garbage disposal in Newark to 1918.

Historians of medicine generally agree that the contribution of modern medicine to the decline in mortality rates in the Western world has been much smaller than most people believe. The life expectancy of persons in the West, especially children, has increased mainly because living conditions have improved. Fewer Americans today go hungry or lack essential vitamins and minerals in their diets and, therefore, have greater resistance to disease than their ancestors. We are also less exposed to pathogenic microorganisms because of sanitary and hygienic improvements in our environment, such as pasteurization, refrigeration, chlorination, and water-carriage sewerage. Thomas McKeown maintains that pasteurization, water purification, and sanitary means of waste disposal account for about 20 percent of the total reduction of mortality that has occurred in England over the last 150 years. Mainly we live longer because nutritious foods are plentiful, inexpensive, and available all year round.[11]

The decline in urban death rates in England has been continuous since the first half of the eighteenth century except for a brief period during the early nineteenth century, when a large part of the rural population had to relocate in cities to find work. Undernourished, ill housed, and dependent on polluted wells and filthy communal privies, the urban poor succumbed in great numbers to tuberculosis, typhus, pneumonia, diarrheal diseases, and the acute, infectious ailments of childhood. Urban mortality rates in British cities rose during the 1830s and 1840s and then began to decline again in the late nineteenth century as sanitary reforms were made and both housing and food supplies were improved. American urban mortality rates followed a similar course, rising during the 1840s and 1850s as a result of industrialization and the arrival of thousands of impoverished immigrants and declining after the Civil War as living conditions got better.[12]

While the sanitary and public health experiences of American cities were alike in their broad outlines, there were important variances in detail resulting from differences in size, location, financial resources, and ethnic composition. For example, New York City had to grapple with the tenement house evil many years before any other community, owing to its great size and large immigrant population. Yellow fever devastated southern cities throughout the nineteenth century, but disappeared in the North after the 1820s. The local topography greatly affected decisions regarding water supply and sewerage. New York City had to go to the mountains forty miles away for its water, whereas the Great Lakes cities could easily tap an almost inexhaustible supply. Brooklyn, Chicago, and Jersey City started building integrated sewer systems in the 1850s, but Baltimore relied on its deep ravines to carry the bodily wastes of its citizens into Chesapeake Bay until the second decade of the twentieth century.[13]

These differences, however, do not alter the basic sameness of experience. American cities everywhere responded to the growing mountains of filth in their midst by developing sanitary infrastructures based on massive engineering undertakings. In every city, capital-intensive technologies for cleansing the environment were substituted for labor-intensive methods, and the locus of responsibility for water supply and waste removal shifted from the homeowner to the municipal government. Some cities may have been slow to build sewer systems, but all of them eventually abandoned the use of privies and night soil removal for water-carriage sewerage.[14]

In instances where Newark's public health development appears to have been singular I have noted it in the text or in a note. Where I have not drawn comparisons to other cities it may be assumed that I found Newark's experience to parallel that of other nineteenth-century American cities that underwent rapid growth and industrialization.

I A VILLAGE BECOMES A CITY

T HE CITY OF NEWARK IS LOCATED ON THE WESTERN shore of the Passaic River and Newark Bay. It is New Jersey's leading city, with a population of nearly 350,000, and is the hub of one of the nation's larger metropolitan areas. Despite having evolved in the shadow of its towering neighbor across the Hudson River, Newark has achieved eminence in its own right as a financial and industrial center and cannot be considered a mere satellite of New York.

In 1918 Newark's population reached 435,000 as a result of the boom created by military preparations for America's entry into World War I. Since then the flight of business and population to the suburbs, heightened by the city's extremely small land area, has caused a steep reversal in its fortunes, to the point that it is frequently portrayed as a symbol of the nation's urban malaise. But in the nineteenth century, Newark was noted for another claim: in 1860 it was the largest industrially based city in the United States. At a time when commerce was king, 73.5 percent of Newark's labor force were engaged in manufacturing. On the eve of the Civil War, Newark ranked seventh in the nation in the value of its manufacturers and eleventh in population.[1]

A group of Puritans in search of a Christian Zion founded Newark in 1666. Originally from Milford and Branford, Connecticut, they had been moved by conscience to leave their recently built homes and seek haven in the wilderness. The decision was made following the absorption of their communities in 1664 by Connecticut Colony. With annexation came a loss of freedom and the threat that outside authorities would force them into less devout ways. And when that year Connecticut adopted the "Half-Way Covenant," extending church membership to persons who led upright lives and whose parents were church members but who themselves had not experienced the gift of grace, pious Puritans began planning their departure. Fearing contamination from ungodly neighbors, they chose the tranquil west bank of the lower Passaic River to reestablish their Bible commonwealth.[2]

Eighteenth-century Newark was a pretty town of well-built, spacious homes where little or no poverty existed. The community had been laid out in the manner of a New England town. Dominating the landscape were the commons, or town-owned greens, the church spires, and the stately homes along Broad and Market streets, already Newark's best-known thoroughfares. The town's cleanliness and orderly street pattern seemed to reflect the comfortable, smug parochialism of its inhabitants.

Newark remained a small town for the duration of the colonial period. Though only nine miles west of New York, the two cities were separated by three sizable rivers—the Hudson, the Hackensack, and the Passaic—and by large areas of tidal swampland. Four miles to the west of Newark the Orange Mountains formed a barrier to transportation, while southward stretched more meadowland.[3]

Martha Lamb, in a magazine article published in 1876, described Revolutionary Newark as a rather nondescript country town, which "had acquired little fame, save for its shoes, its fever and ague, and its sweet cider."[4] Michael Crevecoeur, who passed through in 1801, gave Newark a more favorable review, calling it "the most beautiful village on the continent."[5] He was particularly impressed by Broad Street. Along this wide, two-mile-long thoroughfare prosperous citizens had built numerous brick and stone houses separated from each other by gardens and orchards. Newark's population by then had grown to about twelve hundred persons.

Most Newarkers were farmers who worked in the fields during the day and returned to their village homes at night. To augment their incomes, many farmers developed craft skills, especially shoemaking, which they worked at during the idle winter months. Laboring in the traditional artisan manner, local craftsmen produced goods by hand in their own homes or in the small workshops scattered throughout the community. But whereas the artisans of other towns produced their wares almost entirely for local consumption, Newark craftsmen were able to tap a national market. Newark's proximity to New York City afforded it easy access to southern markets. Sailing ships carried the goods of Newark artisans to New York harbor, where they were re-loaded onto packet vessels engaged in the coastal leg of New York's triangular cotton trade with England and the South. Newark was to become "the workshop of the South." A much smaller amount of manufactured goods was shipped west through the Erie Canal. By 1826 over one-third of Newark's work force were shoemakers. The presence of persons skilled in leather craft attracted other industries in which related skills were needed, such as harness and saddle making. Newark's days as a peaceful, somnolent town were numbered.[6]

Even during the period when Newark was small and isolated, the town's Puritan elders could no more accept the change that came with the Enlightenment than prevent the eroding of religious zeal that was occurring from within. The heavenly city contemplated by Newark clergymen was replaced inexorably by a secular vision of wealth and comfort. Town leaders who had once prized Newark's isolation now came to regard it as a hindrance, for the path to riches could not be traveled without transportation links to the outside world. The first step was taken in 1795, when bridges were laid across the Passaic and Hackensack rivers. In 1832 the completion of the Morris Canal brought the iron mines of Morris County, New Jersey, and the coalfields of Pennsylvania within each reach of Newark. Steamboat and railroad connections with Philadelphia and New York City were secured shortly thereafter.

Newark leaders realized that they could not compete with the great Atlantic seaports at their back for the trade of the western hinterland. Unlike most American cities, Newark early tied its destiny to the craft and industrial skills of its artisans. A wide variety of goods were made in Newark, including shoes, saddles, hats, carriages, harnesses, and jewelry, most of which were exported to southern markets. The development of new technology, especially the use of steam power to drive machinery, set the stage for the appearance of the factory system of production. In the years 1830–1860 Newark's population rose from 11,000 to 72,000, a more than sixfold increase. Newark was booming![7]

Industrialization and urbanization also brought less desirable changes. As real estate values climbed and housing became scarce, the living conditions of the common folk deteriorated. The laboring poor were huddled together in crowded quarters above factories or were squeezed into the fringes of the meadows bordering the Passaic River and Newark Bay. This low-lying, malaria-infested area, known first as "Down Neck" and later as "Ironbound," became the center of Newark's poorest immigrant settlers.[8]

The Irish were foremost among Newark's immigrant poor. First brought to Newark in the 1820s to build the Morris Canal, they came in droves in the following decades driven by abject poverty and British mistreatment. Though widely dispersed in clusters throughout the city, the Irish exhibited a preference for the lightly populated wards bordering the meadows. Shunned by the original settlers because of its mosquitoes, humidity, and poor drainage, the meadows offered these downtrodden and despised Catholic newcomers inexpensive homesites located a comfortable distance from unfriendly Protestant areas of town.[9]

In the late 1840s and 1850s the Irish were joined by German immigrants, including many refugees from the unsuccessful revolutions of 1848 in central Europe. The Germans settled mainly in the "Hill" area, the wooded piedmont region lying to the west and northwest of downtown Newark in what became the Sixth Ward. Here they recreated a German village, complete with beer gardens, singing societies, and turnvereins.[10] However, aside from these few immigrant enclaves, there were no large, ethnically segregated districts. The necessity of workers to be within walking distance of their jobs dictated a mixed land use pattern of homes and businesses, which forestalled the development of sharply differentiated neighborhoods. Ray Ralph, who has made the most intensive study of nineteenth-century Newark residential patterns, concurs with other urban historians that "only in the later part of the century when urban transportation improved did extensive segregation of cities occur on a large scale according to nationality, race, and economic class."[11]

The alien cultures of the Irish and German immigrants strained the tolerance of the city's Anglo-Saxon, Protestant residents. Natives reacted to the presence of these often non-English-speaking, mainly Catholic immigrants by demanding conformity to the Yankee and Puritan traditions of their ancestors. Battle lines were drawn over the German custom of visiting beer gardens on Sunday afternoon, aid to parochial schools, and the alleged rowdyism of the newcomers.[12]

The most intense native-immigrant conflict developed over demands of the Catholic clergy that the government of Newark provide financial assistance for parochial schools. The issue became acutely important with the creation of a citywide public school system in the 1850s. Protestants opposed public aid to parochial education both on principle and because it threatened the survival of the infant public schools, which were desperately in need of more money.[13] Moreover, public education was regarded as a means of exerting social control over the immigrants. The *Newark Daily Mercury*, a leading Whig paper, asserted bluntly that the "masses from abroad must be forced to assimilate to our institutions, and not to engraft upon them habits and customs not congenial to freedom."[14]

Occasionally the conflict between native-born Americans and immigrants escalated into physical confrontation. The most serious incident occurred on September 5, 1854, when the American Protestant Association Lodge of New Jersey staged a parade to commemorate the convening of the First Contintental Congress. Several thousand APA lodge members from surrounding areas arrived in Newark that morning with patriotic streamers and banners in a display of Protestant solidarity. Other marchers demonstrated their sympathy with the association's principles by carrying Bibles or, more sinisterly, by displaying pistols in their belts. As the parade proceeded down William Street past a German Catholic church, fighting erupted between the marchers and a crowd of Irish onlookers. Shots were fired and one Irishman was killed. St. Mary's Catholic Church on the corner of William and High streets was ransacked by the marchers and its organ and all its chairs and doors were destroyed. More violence would likely have occurred had not Catholic clergymen quickly intervened and dampened the desire for revenge among their parishioners. Though the exact cause of the riot is in dispute, its roots lay in the religious and ethnic bigotry of the times.[15]

Newark's first form of government was modeled closely on the New England town pattern. Problems requiring public action were discussed at the annual town meeting, with special meetings called when necessary. Two concerns that had to be addressed repeatedly were voting on bounties for killing marauding wolves and impounding stray hogs and cattle. Community affairs requiring constant attention were handled by committees appointed at the annual meeting. The limited scope of public responsibility can be seen in the fact that there were only two standing committees, one for the maintenance of the streets and the other for the care of the poor.[16]

With the population growth, the town-meeting form of government became impractical. In 1832 a federation of four wards, each organized as a separate township, was established. Sectional rivalries rendered the government impotent, and in 1836 the townspeople voted to incorporate Newark as a city. A weak mayor-council form of government was established. The common council gained increased powers in public health but remained dependent upon the state legislature for authority to finance capital improvements.[17]

In the decades preceding the Civil War Newark's government was dominated by a small elite of men of property and high social standing. Its first two mayors, elected in 1836 and 1837, were lawyers, patrician heirs of longtime resident Puritan families. As industry assumed greater significance, the influence of the Puritan aristocracy declined. Newark's succeeding mayors were drawn almost exclusively from the ranks of its leading businessmen. These businessmen-politicians formed an interlocking directorate that controlled the city's affairs. Together they dominated public officeholding, set the city's economic course, and ran its charitable and social agencies.[18]

Newark's officeholders prided themselves on the honesty and frugality of their administrations. Thus in 1857 the *Newark Daily Advertiser* exulted that while other cities were complaining of "corrupt and extravagent rulers . . . our own can boast entire exemption from the evil. No lucrative contracts are given to partisan favorites, no extravagant salaries deplete the city treasury, and no wholesale corruption marks the proceedings of the common council."[19] But as the *Newark Daily Mercury* was to note on several occasions, this was largely achieved by neglecting vital public services and by ignoring the needs of the poor.

The belief that the most important function of government was the promotion of business led to a narrowly circumscribed public policy that largely ignored health and social welfare concerns. What few municipal services existed were mainly provided through the efforts of private individuals and voluntary groups of citizens. Hence for nearly two decades following its incorporation in 1836, Newark depended on a feeble night watch and amateurish volunteer fire companies for its safety. The establishment of full-time police and fire departments in the 1850s came about only because of the pressure exerted by businessmen who wanted better protection and lower insurance premiums for their property. The first systematic effort to light the streets was not attempted until 1847 and was limited to public buildings in the central business district. Moreover, no long-range planning went into the establishment of municipal services. City officials sought to limit municipal services to what could no longer be provided by voluntary effort and were concerned only with meeting current needs at the lowest cost.[20]

Working-class people suffered the most from the city's unwillingness to finance public improvements. In the decades preceding the Civil War the city did virtually nothing to make the living conditions of the poor more tolerable. The absence of parks in the community provides a case in point. At the time parks were believed to have an important health benefit because of the oxygen produced by trees and were sometimes referred to as the "lungs" of a city. This and the enjoyment they afforded citizens made them an adornment for any city. But the land that would have to be set aside for the parks could be sold at great profit and when developed would generate tax revenues, and neither individual property owners nor the city government was willing to make any financial sacrifices for the common good. Other than the commons established by the original settlers in 1666 and Lincoln Park, a small jewel located on the southern end of Broad Street, Newark was without parks. And even in these two spaces the government had failed to provide benches, fountains, and other amenities, as furnished in Philadelphia and Boston, though the cost of these improvements was minuscule. The *Newark Daily Mercury* estimated that to provide seating in Newark's parks would cost a maximum of $500.[21]

A few voices were raised in support of public parks. The *Newark Daily Mercury* lambasted the citizenry for caring only about the value

of their property and "the amount that can be made by a lucky speculation in real estate. There should be outlets established where health
might be preserved and invigorated and where amid toil and mechanical labor the eye might occasionally meet the green grass and the old
familiar forest trees."[22] The *Mercury* urged that the government act
quickly to establish public squares in the rapidly growing Fifth Ward
before further development of the area made it impossible. Four years
passed without any new parks being opened, during which time thousands of immigrants made Newark their home. In 1853 the editor of the
Mercury again appealed to the city government for relief: "In a few
years our population will have doubled, crowding our mechanics and
laboring men into these outer wards, and it is therefore the more necessary that immediate steps should be taken to secure the great advantages resulting from public parks to the health and welfare of those who
most require them."[23] Still nothing was done, leaving large areas of
Newark without parks.

The *Newark Daily Advertiser* also expressed alarm about the lack
of safe, sanitary housing for workers. A severe housing shortage
brought on by the doubling of Newark's population in the years
1843–1853 caused the *Mercury* to fear that unscrupulous property
owners might try to take advantage of the situation by compacting tenements onto building lots. The *Mercury* warned that it was essential not
"to crowd too great a number of buildings into too small a space . . .
where the victims of a selfish economy should live and swelter in their
own pollution and where the pure air of Heaven should never be permitted to enter."[24] Stating that there was still time to avoid this tragedy, it called upon Newark's capitalists to invest in limited dividend
housing for laborers.[25] But the *Mercury*'s call went unheeded, since
no investors were willing to forgo the opportunity to make a large
financial gain in order to help ameliorate the living conditions of the
poor.

The city's failure to provide decent housing for workers left them at
the mercy of gouging landlords. A survey made in 1860 disclosed that
the poor paid in rent from 15 to 70 percent of the cost of their "loath-
some apartments," while better houses rented for 7 to 15 percent of
their value. Decaying barns, carriage houses, warehouses, breweries,

and other old, dilapidated structures were converted into housing for the Irish and German newcomers, who had no choice but to take whatever landlords offered. Those who could not even afford these mean lodgings rented cellars and basements or occupied squatters' shacks on the outskirts of the community.[26]

Most Newarkers were ignorant of the degradation that existed in their midst. The *Newark Daily Advertiser* stated that the reports of the district physicians, who attended the indigent in their homes, "would startle the public." The dwellings of the black and impoverished foreign populations, especially, were said to contain scenes of squalor, drunkenness, and debauchery. In one of the poorer neighborhoods of Newark, families lived in shanties measuring ten feet by ten feet. The ground outside the buildings was covered with revolting filth, while inside morbidity ran amok. The inhabitants of the shanties were described as covered with festering sores, the manifestations of scrofulous, cutaneous, and contagious diseases, which the *Advertiser* unsympathetically attributed to the occupants' immorality.[27]

Not all Newarkers equated sickness with immorality. The mid-nineteenth century was a time of transition in Western attitudes toward sickness, and while some persons continued to relate illness to personal indiscretions, most adopted the modern view that disease was a product of substandard environmental conditions. It was in this light that Isaac A. Nichols, Newark's health officer, wrote in 1858, "It is a melancholy truth founded upon evidence ony too strong and overwhelming, that it is the lives of the poorer classes, who inhabit the densely scattered districts of our large cities, that are so liable to be shortened by a variety of causes."[28] The report of the board of health for 1860 concentrated on the growing tenement house evil and warned that Newark's reputation for salubrity was threatened. The report also voiced concern about the sacrifice of health caused by ill-lighted, ill-ventilated, and overcrowded apartments. It noted that there was an average occupancy of two persons per room and that each tenement was inhabited from cellar to garret. Finally, it gave eloquent testimony to "the palid, feeble, wasted form and effeminate squalid sickly children of these abodes."[29]

The board of health's fear that wretched housing would produce sickly children was validated in a report of the Newark Medical Associ-

ation on the city's mortality for 1860. Of the 2,175 deaths that occurred
that year, 1,363, or 63 percent, were among children under five years
of age. These deaths, the report stated, were mostly among children
born of foreign parentage and could be attributed to poor nursing, badly
constructed dwellings, and other causes related to their conditions of
life.[30]

Despite the appearance of crowded tenements and Newark's incorporation in 1836, the city retained many of the characteristics of an
overgrown village. Pigs roamed the streets in search of garbage, sheep
grazed on the meadows, and the waterways that traversed the city carried off its sewage in full view for all to see. Broad Street, the main
thoroughfare, resembled a "muddy shallow river" whenever rains
swelled the streams that originated in the hills to the west. Other major
arteries also frequently became impassable because of the deep ruts left
by wagon wheels in the unpaved streets.[31]

Still, assuming a positive correlation between filth and illness, Newark's sanitary state compared favorably to that of other American cities. Newark's cumulative death rate per 1,000 population for the years
1841 through 1855 was 18.66,[32] significantly below that of the nation's
largest cities. The corresponding rate for New York City, Philadelphia,
Boston, and New Orleans for the second quarter of the nineteenth century was 30.2, and while all vital statistics for this period must be used
with extreme caution, broadly speaking there is no reason to believe
they do not provide proximate mortality trends.[33] Newark's slow
growth during its first two centuries of existence permitted an orderly
development of land resources, which made for a more comfortable
mode of life than in cities that had experienced rapid urban development. The 1852 city directory reported that the population explosion of
the years 1832–1852 notwithstanding, Newark was less congested than
many smaller communities. The directory pointed to the width of the
streets, the spaciousness of the commons, and the abundance of trees as
evidence of the city's cheerfulness and salubrity.

Newark's shade trees were its glory. On hot summer days most pedestrians did not have to walk far to find shelter from the sun. Shade
trees lined the principal thoroughfares and parks and nestled up against

the factories, smothering the smoke of forges and muffling the sounds of engine whistles in their thick foliage. "The city is almost embowered with green," exclaimed one visitor. "It is said there is not a street in all Newark that is not adorned with shade trees. . . . New Haven, the 'city of the elms,' has not within its borders so many elms as Newark." The people of Newark had all the more reason to be proud of their magnificent elms for they were not indigenous to the area, having been planted by individual householders for the most part.[34]

Newark residents were more fortunate than the inhabitants of larger cities in that the food supply was close at hand. Vegetables were grown in backyard gardens, and fresh meat was provided by local slaughterhouses. Moreover, the livestock sent to the slaughterhouses were fattened under the watchful eyes of townspeople, in some instances in their own corrals. Because there were few middlemen in Newark's food industry, adulteration was seldom a problem. The existence of pasturage within the city assured a close supply of fresh, wholesome milk. While New Yorkers in the 1840s and 1850s struggled to rid their city of "swill milk" (milk obtained from cows fed on distillery wastes) and milk adulterated with water, chalk, and molasses, Newarkers consumed milk that was sweet and pure.[35] Problems of food and water supply, liquid and solid waste disposal, and congestion and dirt, which made the country's great seaports hothouses of morbidity during the early and mid-nineteenth century, did not reach the critical stage in Newark until after the Civil War.

The steepest rises in the mortality curve were occasioned by epidemics of cholera in 1832, 1849, and 1854. After a near absence of some thirty or forty years, smallpox reappeared in the 1840s and periodically swept off large numbers of persons. But if epidemic diseases were responsible for the high peaks in the death rate curve, endemic diseases caused the most fatalities. Tuberculosis, diseases of infancy, and respiratory diseases were the major causes of death. Surprisingly these diseases aroused little concern. Being of everyday occurrence, they were not as feared as the unpredictable visits of cholera and smallpox. Familiarity led to a casual acceptance of these undercurrents of death. Malaria and infectious diseases of childhood were also present.[36] Malaria was rightly believed to be indigenous to the Newark area because of its marshes, and the disease may have hampered the city's growth.[37]

The vital statistics of the period must be handled with care, since omissions were frequent and the cause of death often misdiagnosed. In the majority of instances the death certificate was signed by a church sexton or by an undertaker who, not having a medical background, either had to omit or guess the cause of death. In 1837 persons having charge of vaults and burial grounds were required to furnish the city clerk with monthly lists of interments. This ordinance was superseded in 1848 by a state statute stipulating the compulsory recording of births, marriages, and deaths. The task was assigned to town and municipal clerks, who reported to the secretary of state. In 1858, to effect compliance with the law, Newark forbade interment without a death certificate signed by a physician or a coroner and stating the age, sex, residence, occupation, place of birth, and cause of death of the deceased. But laws regulating the collection of vital statistics were poorly enforced, and consequently the records of the period are incomplete.[38]

The collection of vital statistics was closely tied to public supervision of interments. During the colonial period, the dead were laid to rest in churchyard burial plots. In the face of savage onslaughts of yellow fever during the early years of the Republic, public supervision of funerals was begun. Because it was believed that corpses were sources of contagion, the interment of persons who had died from pestilential diseases suddenly became a serious public health matter. To prevent corpses from poisoning the air with their emanations, cemeteries were required to locate a safe distance away—at least a mile—from population centers. In cases of yellow fever deaths special precautions were taken, the bodies being placed in airtight coffins deep beneath the ground.

About two and a third acres of downtown Newark were occupied by the Old Burying Ground, the final resting place for the original settlers and their descendants for several generations. In 1828, to prevent overcrowding at the cemetery, Newark officials authorized the purchase of a burial place in the eastern end of town. Residents were given the opportunity to move the graves of their families to the new cemetery without expense, but few persons could bring themselves to disturb the remains of their loved ones. In the following decades the Old Burying Ground fell into disrepair. The grass and shrubbery were trampled under, the grounds were encroached upon, and the headstones were scattered, broken, and defaced. Municipal and state legislation failed to halt the desecration until 1857, when a new charter was promulgated authorizing the common council to regulate burials. Acting under this power in 1858, the common council prohibited additional interments within the Old Burying Ground and forbade the establishment of new cemeteries within the Watch and Lamp District.[39]

In the mid-nineteenth century rural cemeteries located on the city's fringe became a feature of the urban landscape. The cemeteries did more than provide a peaceful setting for persons who wished to be buried where their gravesites would not be disturbed by urban development. "Designed according to the romantic conventions of English landscape gardening," they were intended to provide a sanctuary from the maelstrom of daily life, a place of spiritual and aesthetic repose, where citizens could refresh themselves before returning to face the challenges of city life. Built to serve both the living and the dead, the cemeteries were visited by thousands of middle-class Americans on weekends and holidays. The cemetery's shade walks, forest groves, and cultivated flowering shrubbery served as a romantic counterpoint to the frenzied commercialism of American society.[40]

The rural cemetery movement gained much of its impetus from urban population pressures. With population growth, downtown real estate became too valuable for churches to set aside land for cemeteries. Moreover, public officials were concerned that the interment of persons with acute infectious diseases posed a danger to the community. Since the graveyards often could not be maintained properly, and the churches would soon have no room for further burials, it was usually not difficult to persuade city dwellers to put their loved ones to rest in rural cemeteries.

At the same time that some churches were being persuaded to move their burial plots to the suburbs, the private rural cemetery captured the imagination of affluent city dwellers. The movement brought together urban residents who wanted to escape periodically to an idyllic pas-

toral setting and transportation companies that needed passengers
for their suburban lines. Philadelphia alone had about twenty such
cemeteries.[41]

By the mid-1850s Newark was served by two private cemeteries that
doubled as parks. Mount Pleasant Cemetery, in the outlying northern
regions of the city, was opened in 1844. The cemetery occupied about
forty acres of hilly terrain overlooking the Passaic River and was
widely used by picnickers from Newark and other nearby urban centers. Deprived of the use of public parks that were never built, affluent city dwellers found a substitute in the pastoral environs of rural
cemeteries.[42]

Fairmount Cemetery, located about two miles to the west of Broad
and Market streets, was opened in 1855. The *Newark Daily Mercury*
reported that the land had been purchased from the First Presbyterian
Church by some of Newark's most influential and respected citizens. A
few days prior to its dedication, the *Mercury* described the natural
beauty of the area and the many improvements, including flowerbeds,
footpaths, a lake, and several thousand ornamental and shade trees,
that were planned for the site.[43] The *Mercury* commented that "when
the grading and other improvements . . . are finished, the cemetery will
form a quiet and fitting place of final repose for the dead, and an attractive resort for the living."[44] Two years later it boasted that "no city of
our size can present more attractive cemeteries than we."[45]

The municipal government paid more attention to the dead than it
did the sick and infirm. The sick poor in Newark were treated shabbily.
In the years preceding Newark's incorporation, the medical care of
prisoners and the indigent was provided without charge to the town by
Dr. J. B. Goble, who was given the title "resident physician." In 1837
the office of resident physician was replaced by salaried district physicians who served on a part-time basis.[46]

A decrepit old almshouse located on the edge of the meadows, where
its ignominy could not trouble the conscience of the community, housed
the incapacitated. From a health standpoint, a worse site could not have
been chosen. Damp, humid, and thick with mosquitoes, some species of
which transmitted malaria, the almshouse was a nursery of sickness
and death. Intended to provide indoor relief for the poor, the almshouse

was in reality a dumping ground for the community's handicapped, dependent, and deviant members, a place where orphans, widows, the infirm, the feebleminded, and other luckless souls were indiscriminately herded together with drunkards and criminals, often two or more to a bed.[47]

The high morbidity and mortality rates at the almshouse became a public issue in the 1850s. In 1851 there were twenty-six deaths at the almshouse, which during any given month that year housed about fifty-five persons. "This would appear to be a very large proportion for the average number of inmates," the *Newark Daily Advertiser* commented matter-of-factly, "but we must remember that most of the inmates, or at least of the adults, would not be there at all were it not for the fact that disease had rendered them unable to take care of themselves."[48] The *Advertiser* also noted that three-quarters of the inmates were "foreigners," and that probably best explains why the *Advertiser* was not more alarmed about the institution's high death rate.

In November 1855 the common council received a report that the inmates of the almshouse were suffering extensively from intermittent fevers. The report attributed the high incidence of sickness to overcrowding and the almshouse's unhealthy location. The almshouse physician, Dr. George S. Ward, who had had the job for less than a year, was asked to investigate and to make recommendations.[49]

A little over a month later Ward made his report. There had been seventy-four inmates at the almshouse that year, of whom sixty-two had come down with intermittent fever (malaria). That the disease was not attributable to the weakened constitutions of the inmates, as some councilmen suggested, but rather to exposure to miasma that arose from adjacent swamps seemed clear to Ward. He noted that all but one member of the superintendent's family had been prostrated by repeated attacks of the disease, though they had enjoyed good health before coming to the almshouse. He stated further that it would be impossible to cure the sick so long as they remained in their present surroundings.

Ward also commented on the small rooms, bad ventilation, and lack of facilities for isolating the sick. He stated that at a minimum the almshouse needed two rooms for the sick, segregated by sex, of fifteen to twenty beds each. Moreover, he worried about the effect of exposing children to persons who were chronically ill or of poor character. The lives of twenty-six children hung in the balance.

Ward went on to say that his dissatisfaction had increased since going to New York City, where he had visited the excellently managed almshouses and hospitals on Blackwell's and Randalls islands. He argued that by not moving the almshouse to a healthier site, the Newark Common Council was in the long run being economically foolish, since so long as the inmates remained where they were they would be too ill to ever support themselves. Ward concluded by asking for an almshouse "to which we can point with pride—one as dissimilar as possible from the present *abortion*, and of which it may be said, that it is questionable as its being charity to send our paupers thither."[50]

Ward's outspoken views were not received favorably by the city's political leaders. Mayor Horace J. Poinier announced his opposition to removing the almshouse and repeated the argument that the fevers were the consequence of the poor health of the inmates. If the almshouse's location was at fault, asked Poinier, why weren't more inhabitants of the area bedridden with fevers? He conceded, however, that the building in which the inmates were housed was inadequate and contributed to their morbidity. He argued that enlargement of the building and other structural renovations were all that was necessary to make the almshouse safe.[51]

Despite the mayor's opposition, the supporters of a new location refused to give up without a fight. In June 1857 the superintendent voiced his concern about the incidence of fevers in the institution and strongly urged the selection of another site. A letter from a newspaper correspondent who signed himself "Health" challenged the mayor's logic. The removal of the almshouse had been recommended by past and present poor and alms committees, by the superintendent, and by most Newark physicians. That some residents of the meadows area were not seriously afflicted by malaria he attributed to their naturally robust health and successful acclimatization to the area's diseases over a period of years.[52]

The matter came to a head at the July 1 meeting of the common council, when the Committee on Poor and Alms asked for authority to purchase a twenty-acre site costing $6,500 for a new almshouse. The opposition was led by Alderman Owen McFarland, who maintained, despite the mass of contradictory evidence, that no healthier locale could be found than the meadows. As for the ill health of the superintendent, McFarland remarked pointedly that it would be cheaper to appoint another superintendent than to move the almshouse. Another alderman conceded that the marshes generated disease but said the city did not have the money to relocate the almshouse. After further debate the request for a new almshouse was turned down by a vote of 21 to 4. *The Newark Daily Mercury* commented prophetically that in light of its overwhelming defeat the relocation of the almshouse would not be brought up again for some time to come.[53]

Following an epidemic of cholera in 1849 in which some of the stricken were sent to the almshouse, resulting in numerous deaths among the inmates, a small frame cabin located nearby was set aside for use as a pesthouse. Those unfortunate enough to be sent here received the worst treatment of any of Newark's poor. Victims of epidemic diseases were moved from their sickbeds to the pesthouse with scarcely a thought given to their welfare. The cabin lacked the most rudimentary sanitary facilities, making cleanliness impossible and robbing the occupants of any modicum of privacy or dignity. Maintenance of the building was haphazard, as was medical supervision. The medical attendants (nurses), upon whose ministrations the sick were almost entirely dependent, were recruited from the dregs of society. The almost criminal quality of nursing care was revealed in the large numbers of persons who died unattended from cholera because the medical attendants feared contracting the disease from their patients. A new pesthouse made of brick was built after the Civil War, but the reforms made then proved to be of short duration.[54]

Most indigent urban residents in antebellum America were treated in dispensaries and almshouses. Only a few large cities had general hospitals. "Hospitals . . . were designed to serve the respectable poor, to treat their acute and curable conditions, mental diseases, and obstetrical cases."[55] Almshouses cared for the "undeserving poor" and chronic and incurable patients. By 1860 there were about sixty urban dispensaries in the United States. The dispensaries offered free medical care for the "worthy poor" and provided clinical training for the young physicians who volunteered their services. The medical care given to the poor included vaccination, tooth extractions, consultations, medications, and home visits.[56]

Though special health committees and boards of health were established in Newark during the cholera epidemics of 1832 and 1854,[57] a permanent public health body did not come into existence until several years later. By provision of the city charter of 1857, the common council was authorized "to establish a board of health, to define its powers and duties, and to provide for the protection and maintenance of the health of the city."[58] One year later, on March 19, 1858, an ordinance establishing the Newark Board of Health was enacted. The board was composed of the mayor, the members of the Common Council Committee on Public Health, and the health physician. The health physician was appointed by the common council and served without pay. The board of health was given the power to inquire into and abate nuisances, to isolate persons with pestilential diseases, and to remove, disinfect, and destroy infected household belongings. Provision was also made in the same ordinance for the care of the sick poor. A dispensary was established in the offices of the board of health, and district physicians were appointed to administer to the indigent.[59] Subsequent municipal legislation and charter revision gave the board of health jurisdiction over the construction and maintenance of cesspools, the keeping and slaughtering of animals, the removal of night soil, and the sale of food.[60]

For over a decade the Newark Board of Health was better known for its dispensations of medical charity than for its public health work. The board's preoccupation with medical care may be partly explained by the city's lack of facilities for treating the sick poor. For a scandalously long time Newarkers in need of hospital treatment were compelled to go to New York City to find it. Until the establishment of a city hospital in 1882, the district physicians and the dispensary provided the only municipally sponsored medical services available to the poor.

Newark's urgent need of expanded medical facilities for the sick poor was attested to by the heavy demands placed on the dispensary and the district physicians. During its first year of operation the dispensary cared for over 1,100 patients, or about 2 percent of Newark's population. Of these, 337 were vaccinated, 57 were treated for bronchitis, 16 for pulmonary catarrh, 22 for conjunctivitis, 44 for constipation, 39 for cough, 33 for diarrhea, 46 for dyspepsia, 34 for intermittent fever, 32 for gastric derangement, 26 for phthisis, 31 for rheumatism, 22 for ulcers, and 22 for worms. Somewhat surprisingly, a little more than half of the patients were of American nativity. Persons born in Ireland, who made up about 16 percent of the population, constituted nearly 30 percent of the dispensary's clientele, whereas the equally numerous but more prosperous Germans made up just 7 percent. In addition to the work of the dispensary, the six district physicians attended 1,082 cases and the apothecary filled 4,115 prescriptions.[61]

With the bridging of the Hackensack and Passaic rivers in 1795, an era of rustic tranquility ended in Newark. The rapid urbanization that ensued caused many changes in the community's ways of doing things, not least of all in public health. For over 150 years following its settlement in 1666, Newark had been a small, homogeneous community in which informal social mechanisms had operated to insure public hygiene. But with the arrival of large numbers of Catholic and non-English-speaking peoples, Newark's Puritan mold was shattered and it became necessary to try to achieve through laws what previously social pressure had accomplished. Moreover, as Newark grew the community's ad hoc methods of dealing with acute, communicable diseases proved increasingly ineffectual. In place of hastily organized cleanup campaigns and the appointment of emergency health boards during epidemics, public health work would have to be organized on a continuous basis if Newarkers were to be protected against unnecessary sickness and premature death.

2 PUBLIC HEALTH, DRAINAGE, AND WATER SUPPLY

LONG BEFORE PUBLIC HEALTH BECAME INSTITUTION-alized, communities were confronted with the problem of protecting themselves against epidemic diseases. In 1807 a Newark resident wrote to the *Sentinel of Freedom* about a strange malady that was sweeping the town. He attributed the epidemic to filth, stagnant pools, and dead animals that, in the furnace of the August sun, were decomposing and emitting poisonous vapors. He assigned most of the blame for the town's unsanitary condition to local slaughterhouses that used the streets as garbage receptacles.[1]

Throughout history people have lived in close proximity to livestock and domestic animals. While this intimacy has been a source of aid and comfort to men and women, it has also complicated their lives. Dogs carry fleas and transmit rabies. Pigs and cattle running loose in urban communities have a habit of rooting up gardens and trampling down fences, and their excreta are a magnet for flies.

The presence each spring of packs of wild dogs running freely through the city was an ominous portent, since scarcely a year passed without a rabies scare. The frenzied anguish of the spasmodic, crazed rabies victim sent a shiver throughout the community. At such times overwrought residents were apt to kill rabid and nonrabid dogs alike.

The city attempted to prevent the community from being overrun with dogs by taxing them. Beginning in 1836, male dogs were taxed at the rate of two dollars for the first cur and five dollars for each additional one; the corresponding rates for bitches were ten dollars and five dollars. In addition, the running of dogs at large was prohibited. Dog owners were required to put a collar on their pets with their names and residences plainly inscribed. Collarless dogs and dogs that attacked persons or other animals could be killed on sight. Finally, the mayor was authorized, when public good required it, to destroy all dogs running at large.[2]

The city's first canine ordinance was superseded by a weaker law passed in 1849, which lowered the tax on dogs to one dollar for males and three dollars for females. Whereas before all dogs running at large could be killed, the new law exempted dogs with securely fastened wire muzzles. The law did grant the city one new power for dealing with canines during a rabies outbreak or when the presence of large numbers of wild dogs threatened public safety. During such times the common council was authorized to establish dog pounds and to impound all unmuzzled dogs running at large. As an incentive for the work, a fifty-cent reward was offered for every captured dog. There was a two-dollar charge for redeeming dogs at the pound, a fine that pet lovers hastened to pay, since canines not claimed within forty-eight hours were to be killed.[3]

Partly because of the law's weakening, but mainly because of lax enforcement, the canine problem became more troublesome in the early 1850s. Several persons died each year from rabies, and in 1857 the *Newark Daily Mercury* commented that there were enough dogs "running into everyone's way, and snapping and growling at anybody who displeases them, to give the whole community the hydrophobia."[4] By then the dog menace had become so alarming that a group of citizens decided to take matters into their own hands.

On April 14, 1857, the *Newark Daily Mercury* reported that 150 dogs in widely scattered parts of the city had been poisoned. When the *Mercury* subsequently reported that the deaths might have been caused by some sort of distemper, an anonymous communication was sent to the paper professing to give the true story of what had happened. The writer began by apologizing to dog owners for having killed so many of their favorite animals but justified it on the grounds of "the greatest good to the greatest number." He described how he had resolved to kill every mutt in the city after having been severely bitten by a large dog about a month earlier. Finding about a dozen persons of similar thinking, they had organized themselves into a canine-killing society and had resolved not to end their slaughter until Newark was rid of wild dogs. "We intend to carry out our object despite all threats or offers of

reward for our detection, being satisfied that nine-tenths of the community bid us God speed."⁵ He added that the society had already raised
two hundred dollars in subscriptions.

He went on to say that for the past twelve years the mayors of Newark had issued annual proclamations authorizing the killing of all dogs
running at large, to little effect. "It may be argued that these laws have
reference to the season of the year when *rabid* dogs are prevalent; but
we contend that we have not commenced operations any too soon, as
within the past two weeks two individuals in one family in our city
were bitten by a favorite dog which died on last Sunday . . . with the
symptoms of hydrophobia. Let your readers imagine the unpleasant an-
ticipations which these unfortunte individuals must now be laboring
under."⁶ He closed the letter by inviting persons who wished to assist
the society to address their communications care of "Dog," Newark
Post Office.

The association carried out its work by leaving poisoned meat
around the city. In one instance, however, a young boy became seriously ill after eating some of the tainted meat. On April 18 the *Mercury*
published a letter from one of the officers of the group, which now
called itself the Newark Dog Poisoners Association, stating that many
persons had inquired about the organization. He announced that certain
specified streets would soon be cleared of dogs by the association's
"committee on administration." This action had been decided upon following a complaint from a new member that for the last three months
he had been obliged to carry a revolver at night while on these streets.
He was particularly afraid of a large black-and-yellow spotted dog,
which the association authorized him to destroy personally.⁷

By the end of April incidents of dog poisoning had almost ceased,
though the *Mercury* reported that the number of unmuzzled dogs running at large had not significantly diminished. Why the association
stopped short of its goal is unknown. The fact that its members were
never apprehended indicates they probably had substantial support in
the community. Thus the *Mercury*, though it still regarded the association's actions as cruel and criminal, now suggested that if it had any
surplus funds it could better devote itself to the elimination of tomcats,

whose piercing yells prevented people from sleeping, since it presumed no one would complain about their extermination.[8]

The canine menace reached the crisis stage again in July 1857, leading the common council to establish a pound in the vicinity of Canal and Mulberry streets. The *Mercury* encouraged citizens to assist in rounding up the animals by stating that the work paid better than catching fugitive slaves and was infinitely more respectable. One boy caught twenty-four unmuzzled dogs the first day the pound was opened, which, at fifty cents a piece, netted him twelve dollars.[9]

The use of bounties, which in the past had been employed to destroy wild animals that preyed on livestock, occasioned some unpleasant scenes. The work was usually undertaken by boys and by idlers who stole from one another and fought for possession of the animals. Some boys were detected removing muzzles from dogs and there were several cases in which dogs had been snatched from the residences of their owners. Still, the stipend achieved its objective. In the first two days it was offered 170 dogs were impounded, leaving the central wards free of unmuzzled dogs. So successful was the pound that a second pound was established in the outlying Sixth Ward.[10]

Not everyone approved of the city's methods of dealing with the dog menace. Irish and German residents who had their dogs taken to the pound began threatening to withhold their canine taxes. Other citizens were disturbed at the wholesale slaughter of the animals and the methods by which they were killed. At one pound the dogs were shot and at the other they were drowned.[11] Residents living near the downtown pound protested the loudest. In a letter signed "many sufferers" they complained bitterly about the pound's location: "Situated as it is in a thickly settled neighborhood only fifteen feet from some dwelling, the stench arising from it endangers the health of us all. Then the barking and howling of from fifty to eighty dogs, shut up in a small building, together with the lashes and imprecations of those having them in charge, is enough to make humanity blush. Night is rendered hideous and sleep is out of the question."[12] Their complaints, however, were ignored, and the pounds kept busy for the remainder of the summer. In all some 2,464 dogs were killed.[13]

Despite these efforts, the city failed to realize any permanent benefits from its canine war. In February 1858 the editor of the *Mercury* commented disgustedly that for every dog that had been killed, a dozen puppies had taken its place.[14] The city's bungling of the problem caused tempers to flare and led to several altercations. In 1859 a mob in the Sixth Ward bent on destroying the local dog pound had to be dispersed by the police. There were several incidents that summer in which young boys who had picked up dogs in the streets had been chased and threatened by the owners of the animals; a couple of the boys had been beaten.[15] In the spring of 1860 a correspondent to the *Mercury* commented that in past years the city had put off acting until it was too late. It had waited until there were three or four cases of rabies, thereby condemning perhaps a dozen or more persons to "pass through unequaled torture, and die the worst of all deaths."[16]

WHILE MOST OF NEWARK'S PUBLIC HEALTH ORDInances were rooted in a fear of pestilence, a few were based on a broader conception of the public welfare. Regulations governing the sale and purchase of food fall into the latter category. A survival of eighteenth-century English mercantalist practices, the sale of food was closely supervised to guarantee quality and to prevent fraud. Market regulations forbidding the sale of unwholesome or spoiled foods were primarily intended to protect the consumer's purse rather than his health, for there was no knowledge of specific food infections. The marketplace was the hub of the preindustrial city. It was here—and in the taverns—that business and politics were discussed and gossip and social pleasantries exchanged. And it was here that the daily necessities of life were purchased.

The charter and the ordinances of the city gave the common council the power to operate public markets and to license food venders. The sale of food was limited to the markets where licensed butchers and fishmongers were required to lease market stalls from the city. Market officials were responsible for the removal of dirt and filth, the examination of foodstuffs, the regulation of traffic, the checking of measures and scales, and the exclusion of persons conspiring to raise prices. The sale of stale, unwholesome, and diseased food was prohibited and carried a stiff fine. Though next to impossible to keep the stalls constantly "sweet-smelling," the sanitary condition of the markets elicited few complaints.[17]

Newark's public markets were unable to meet the demands created by the sudden spurt in population growth beginning about 1830. Even more damaging to the future of the markets was the changed attitude toward monopoly and government regulation that came about during the Jacksonian era. Jacksonian democracy placed a premium on individualism and egalitarianism. It strove for the exposure of banking, medicine, and business to the stimulus of unfettered competition. Governmental attempts to set standards for medicine and to control banking were viewed as a conspiracy on the part of the wealthy to monopolize these lucrative fields by creating meaningless but difficult obstacles for the sons of poor artisans and yeoman farmers. The struggle to open up the economy culminated in the destruction of the Second Bank of the United States, long regarded by Jacksonians as the citadel of unholy power and special privilege. Similarly, regulation of private enterprise was discarded and in its place was substituted the rules of laissez faire and caveat emptor.

In Newark protection of the consumer in the public markets weakened. In 1838 the sale of pork was permitted outside of the markets between October 1 and February 15. Similar allowances were made in 1843 and 1845 for the sale of meat and fish; the 1845 law also authorized the bulk sale from wagons of flour, grain, potatoes, and horse feed. As restrictions on the sale of food were lifted the public markets declined in importance and their maintenance deteriorated. The vendors in the public markets became wholesalers, and as the public stopped buying its food there, the municipal authorities became lax in their sanitary policing of the markets.[18]

THE OUTSTANDING PUBLIC HEALTH MATTER CONFRONTing Newark during its early years of urban existence was the abysmal condition of the streets. As was true of most antebellum cities, Newark's streets were littered with household and commercial wastes.

Many streets became seas of liquid filth during periods of heavy rainfall. Oyster shells and the carcasses of dead animals clogged Newark's
gutters and sidewalks. Broad Street was described as "a liquid paradise
for city scavengers, alias swine." Standing ditch water and stagnant
pools, the results of faulty excavation and poor drainage, were a common sight.[19]

During its first two centuries of existence, Newark expanded slowly
along the axis formed by Broad and Market streets. Two blocks to the
west of Broad Street there was a steep hillside (on the site of present-
day High Street), the first of a series of ridges that extend to the Orange
Mountains. From this elevated section several streams crossed the
Newark plain before descending into the sea. Swelled by storms, they
spilled over their banks, turning the filthy, unpaved streets into liquid
mud. Because of the city's failure to pave its thoroughfares and to provide sewerage, the natural drainage afforded by Newark's topography
was lost. Newark's well-watered streets soon became a nuisance and a
serious health hazard.[20]

Residents complained repeatedly about the wretchedness of the city
streets, but to no avail. During heavy rains large sections of Newark
became quagmires of mud and filth. The area beween Broad and High
streets north and south of the Morris Canal and districts in the vicinity
of New Jersey Railroad Avenue suffered great damage and inconvenience from the lack of adequate drainage. Residents of these areas
could expect from four to eight downpours a year that would flood the
cellars and lower stories of their homes and businesses. In some sections the water table was so high as to preclude the construction of cellars. The open ditches and rivulets that traversed the districts, and that
afforded their only drainage, carried off the neighborhoods' filth, causing them to become little more than elongated cesspools.[21]

The seeming intractability of Newark's drainage problem evinced a
gallows humor. Following a January thaw that submerged Broad Street
in liquid muck for several days, the *Newark Daily Advertiser* observed
that enterprising citizens were seen navigating the street with a scow.[22]
The editor of the *Newark Daily Mercury* remarked facetiously that
"Broad Street . . . is in its glory and mud is rampant in its joyousness.
What would Newark be without its mud?"[23] On another occasion, the

Advertiser reported that strong ropes had to be used to extricate a mule caught in the mud. A few days later it solemnly recorded the death of the mule from injuries sustained in its rescue. Dry weather, while it provided relief from muddy streets, brought with it clouds of dust. Dry summer winds stirred up the dirt on the unpaved streets covering persons from head to foot with the city's filth. Wagon wheels ground horse dung into a fine powder, which blew into the mouths and nostrils of pedestrians, causing fits of coughing and sneezing.[24]

The city had ample powers to rectify the situation. Under the provisions of the charter of 1836 the common council was authorized to clean and keep in repair the streets and highways and to order the leveling, grading, and paving, flagging, or graveling of public thoroughfares. The financing of street improvements was provided for through general taxation and property assessments, and the city surveyor and street commissioner were charged with executing the work. But because of the expense involved and the desire for economy in government, the paving of the streets was continually postponed.[25]

Until the 1850s there was no improvement in the maintenance of city streets. Despite greater and greater accumulations of street dirt (consisting mainly of garbage, rubbish, and manure), gutters and streets were cleaned only twice a year. An ordinance compelling property owners to keep streets abutting their parcels free of obstructions was ignored. Similarly, drainage plans and surveys commissioned by the common council developed must from nonuse. A supplement to the city charter of 1848 authorized the construction of underground sewers, the cost to be assessed either in whole or in part on the property owners who benefited by them. But nothing was done for another four years, during which time the flooding problem became worse as construction of new buildings diminished the absorptive powers of the earth and heightened the danger from rapid runoff of storm water.[26]

Common sewers—open drains that ran down the center of the street—were intended to remove the surface waters of the city. More often than not, however, the drains were poorly constructed and became clogged with wood shavings, rotted straw, and other debris, preventing the water they carried from draining freely. Unsightly and malodorous, they were held responsible for the sickness that abounded in their environs. In any case, surface drainage of storm waters was suitable only for a small town that had easy access to large waterways.[27]

The futility of relying on open drains to remove water from a city of Newark's size was demonstrated in 1850 when the common council appropriated twenty thousand dollars for digging a ditch through the central wards. Anticipating the outcome, the editor of the *Newark Daily Mercury* denounced the ditch as "a public nuisance into which all kinds of filth will be thrown." The ditch, he opined, "exemplified another of those half-way measures that has marked our city policy." He argued that the only sensible solution was to construct an underground sewer system and urged the common council to "cast aside all petty ideas of economy" that stood in the way of the work.[28]

The *Mercury*'s opposition to the ditch was soon vindicated. In the years following its completion the ditch was encroached upon by numerous buildings, severely constricting its flow. Consequently, every time it rained heavily the water in the ditch backed up, flooding nearby homes and gardens. During one storm a man nearly drowned when his cellar suddenly became inundated. In addition, a brook that flowed behind the currier shops near the center of town threw into the ditch a mountain of animal carcasses, giving rise to a grievous nuisance.[29] In 1854 the Common Council Committee on Sewerage and Drainage reported that the ditch was filled with the wastes from the leatherworking shops of the vicinity. "Add to this the dead dogs, cats, etc. (which cause a stench that language is inadequate to describe), and only those who have experienced the . . . odor can fully appreciate its vileness."[30]

At the time, in a number of English cities natural watercourses were being arched over and enclosed in brick. Built with flat bottoms and sides, and washed only by a feeble current, the sewers quickly became clogged with filth and therefore had to be constructed of immense size to permit men to periodically enter and clean them. The filth was removed from the sewers by windlass and pail and was left on the ground to be collected by the scavengers' carts. The plan apparently appealed to some Newarkers, for in 1852 a resolution was adopted by the Newark Common Council to widen, deepen, and enclose one of the city's larger streams. Fearing the creation of a permanent nuisance in their midst, neighborhood people remonstrated and the plan was abandoned.[31]

Many individuals built street drains from their homes to the common sewers. The drains, which were used to remove basement water, household wastes, and occasionally excreta, were the cause of some of Newark's worst nuisances. In the winter they froze and burst, causing the formation of sheets of polluted ice. In the summer they emitted sickening stenches, drew flies, and provided breeding places for mosquitoes.[32]

Two unusually heavy squalls, one occurring in 1843 and the other in 1853, revealed the city's precarious sanitary position. Besides tearing up sidewalks and weakening foundations, the floods left in their wake large numbers of stagnant pools. It was feared that the "exhalations" from the pools would generate malaria. Since the *anopheles* mosquito was ubiquitous in Newark, there was reason to be concerned. In addition there was the danger that fecal containers weakened by the storm would seep their contents into yards and cellars, thereby becoming a source of discomfort and disease.

The flooding was particularly bad in the central business district and the marshy Down Neck area. Because of its watery subsoil, lots reclaimed from the meadows had poor drainage. The land had been raised with garbage and subsequently had sunk. Throughout Newark lots and watercourses had been filled without regard to drainage. Even under the best of circumstances the residents of Down Neck were bedeviled with pools of stagnant water and damp and flooded cellars. The body of water left lying upon the ground by the 1853 storm was so great that in many areas cellars remained flooded for several days.[33]

Increased sickness in Newark affirmed the need for street improvements and better sanitation. After a seventeen-year absence, the dreaded scourge of cholera reappeared in 1849. Scattered cases occurred every year from 1850 to 1853, and in 1854 it struck more savagely than ever before. Since cholera was regarded as a "filth disease," there were urgent demands for sanitary reform.[34] In the winter of 1851–1852, the city was beset by a pestilential fever. The fever was mistakenly thought to be malarial, though symptoms descriptive of typhoid fever, influenza, and typhus were also recorded. J. Henry Clark, a prominent Newark physician, traced the origin of the fever to odors arising from the meadows. While nothing could be done about the meadows, Clark warned that the existence of filth and stagnant ponds within the community was equally as dangerous and might easily spark an epidemic.[35]

The deplorable condition of the city streets was forcibly impressed upon the city fathers during a visit by the Hungarian patriot Lajos Kossuth on April 21, 1852. The event was marred by a spring torrent and by a demonstration of citizens angered by their government's indifference to their appeals for municipal improvements. An ingenious plot was hatched. Just as the mayor started to welcome Kossuth and his procession from a portable platform in front of city hall, a boat dragged by horses appeared, and a trumpet proclaimed the arrival of "King Mud" and his royal retinue. The mayor's speech was drowned out, and the mud that rolled away from the boat's bow nearly reached the assembled dignitaries. A wagon crammed with curious onlookers collapsed, dumping twenty-five residents into the ooze. The city luminary who was leading the procession landed in the mud when his mount bolted. A humorous account stated that "Kossuth was informed these events were not on the regular program."[36]

By the time of Kossuth's memorable visit Newark's harassed citizens had had their fill of mud and low comedy. At first it was proposed to alter all street grades to conform to a single grade.[37] When this remedy appeared to be unfeasible, a citizen's committee was formed to investigate the problem. The committee, which presented its recommendations to the common council in July 1852, found great neglect everywhere in keeping the gutters clean and unobstructed. It reported that "in many streets the gutters are filled with dirt and filth to the top of the curbstones, so that the water has no passage; . . . consequently, the streets are filled in wet weather with mud and water. This is the chief cause of the wretched condition of many of our streets."[38] The committee proposed that the streets be paved or macadamized. It also suggested that the Morris Canal be lowered so that it could be utilized for drainage, ignoring the likelihood that the canal, like the city ditch, would soon become an open sewer.[39]

Street improvements were one part of the solution to attaining better sanitation and drainage. The other part was suggested in a plan adopted by the common council at its August meeting, in which it was proposed that the city build underground sewers to empty into the Passaic River.

The plan, which originated in a special committee of the council, had been devised after lengthy consultation with engineers employed in sewer construction in New York City and was based on sewerage advances that had been made in Europe.[40]

In the 1830s and 1840s a new plan of drainage employing water-carriage sewerage had been developed in England by its great sanitary reformer Edwin Chadwick. He had learned from an engineer that the high velocity of water flow that resulted from the passage of even modest amounts of water through small, egg-shaped pipe sewers would loosen all solid sewage and even bricks and rats and sweep them swiftly down to the sewer's outfall. If houses were connected to the sewers, the motive power provided by the waste water from water closets and kitchen sinks could be employed in the continual self-cleaning of the sewers. Chadwick's plans also envisioned a change in the cross-section of the streets from concave to convex. By building gutters, or surface drains, at the sides of the streets instead of in the middle, and connecting them to the city's sewerage, and by sloping the streets so that water drained into the gutters, rainwater and street filth could be washed into the gutters and out of the city.[41] Thus the Newark Common Council argued cogently that underground sewers "would provide permanent, useful and durable public works with little or no upkeep."[42]

In 1852 Newark began paving its streets and highways with round stones. By 1858 there was almost sixteen and a half miles of paved streets, about one-fifth the mileage of the city's thoroughfares. Work on the first sewer was begun in 1852 and completed in 1853. As of 1858, four and a half miles of main and branch sewers were constructed. The expense of these improvements was borne partly by the city (which assumed about one-third the cost of the sewers and none of the expense of paving the streets), but mainly by the owners of the property who benefited from them.[43]

Sewers were among the most expensive public improvements undertaken in Newark; the first three sewers cost property owners and the city government $111,000. The high cost of sewers led a considerable number of property owners to attempt to slow down further construction. The Common Council Committee on Sewerage and Drainage answered its critics in a report published in 1855. It reminded them that the sewers had been built upon petition of large numbers of citizens and property owners and pointed to their numerous benefits. Sewers had drained the subsoil in some areas to a depth of from six to ten feet below the surface, permitting the building of cellars where before it was impossible to excavate. Sewers had improved the public health. Moreover, the committee argued that "by adding to the reputation of our city for salubriousness, beauty, and advantages, [sewers] will bring in many persons to reside here, thus adding to our wealth and prosperity."[44]

The *Newark Daily Mercury* was even more emphatic in its defense of sewerage. In 1857 it declared:

> No local improvements have been made since the organization of the city government which have been more successful or more valuable to the best interests of the community. The general health of the city has been improved by the partial or entire removal of sources of disease. Hundreds of building lots, many of them occupied with valuable improvements, participate in the advantages of a good and sufficient drainage, which a few years since were comparatively worthless for the want of it. . . . Our public streets—which were a floating sea of mud, upon which scows might sail, or a frozen mass of ruts—are now transformed into magnificent avenues paved and graded throughout—beautiful at all times. We are no longer in fear that every heavy rain will fill the cellars of a portion of our city, begetting disease and death, for a system of sewerage has been planned, and successfully carried out, which drains thoroughly the surface water of the city.[45]

The *Mercury* had little patience with persons who complained about the high cost of street improvements. It conceded that sewers were expensive. The city debt had been increased to its legal limit of $250,000 and citizens had been heavily taxed. But pavements and sewerage, it scolded property owners, "have added to the value of your property ten times the amount of the assessments *and you know it*. You would not today return to the former conditions of things if you could have all your assessments and extra taxes paid back."[46] The *Mercury* was undoubtedly correct, and yet it would be many years before the entire community, and especially poor neighborhoods, were served with sewers.

In 1857 the board of health initiated a vigorous campaign to cleanse Newark of filth. Four years earlier the city had contracted with a scavenger to remove garbage and other organic wastes. The improved state of the city's health in the late 1850s was generally attributed to the actions of the board of health and to the building of sewers and pavements.[47] Nevertheless, because the city had so much catching up to do, and because of population growth and the opening of new areas for settlement, Newark remained badly in need of sewerage. Still a start had been made, and the course of future improvements had been determined. Where all else had failed, fear of pestilence and public humiliation had succeeded in forcing the municipal fathers to find answers to Newark's sanitary needs.

WHILE THE CITY COULD DEAL WITH SOME MATTERS IN a leisurely manner, water supply was a problem that demanded immediate attention. One of the first priorities of every new community was to find a dependable water supply. Newark originally received its water from two streams that came together near the center of town to form a small triangular pond, which the city fathers set aside as a watering place. Here townspeople came to water cattle and to fill pails and buckets.[48] Cisterns were placed beneath the streets to aid in fire fighting, and public pumps were built throughout the community for the convenience of residents. For over a century Newark's aquatic needs were met in this manner, supplemented by water drawn from private wells and springs.[49]

By 1800 rusticity had become a luxury the town could ill afford. To head off a water famine, the state legislature granted permission to a group of residents to form the Newark Aqueduct Company to supply the community with water. Reservoirs were constructed in the western hill area, and water was carried by bored logs to the homes of the company's subscribers. As the settlement grew, the physical plant was modernized and expanded. New reservoirs were built, wooden pipes were replaced with cast-iron conduits, and the water supply was enlarged to include a system of driven wells in the area of what is now Branch Brook Park in the northwestern section of the city.[50]

The water supply of Newark was of mixed quality. The "watering place" was fed by uncontaminated springs and its water therefore was probably excellent. Spring water also made up a sizable part of the aqueduct company's supply. Furthermore, its water underwent natural purification through storage in reservoirs. There were, however, scattered complaints that the water supplied by the company was murky, and occasionally small fish could be detected, prompting some residents to attach filters to their faucets. Well water was suspect because of the strong possibility of contamination from nearby privies. The danger was borne out by a chemical analysis made in 1853 of water samples taken from widely scattered wells, which revealed that Newark's well water was "decidedly bad."[51]

The creation of the Newark Aqueduct Company had been more in the nature of a civic undertaking than a commercial venture. Public welfare rather than private profit had been its dominant motif.[52] But when the company failed to provide needed community services, public sentiment turned against it. As early as 1828, appeals had been made to the company for hydrants. Unwilling to risk the chance of a fire, several businesses installed their own plugs. The wisdom of their foresight was soon demonstrated. On October 27, 1836, Newark experienced its first disastrous fire. The conflagration swept the manufacturing center of the city, destroying all the buildings in a one-square-block area fronting on Broad Street. In combating the blaze, fire fighters were handicapped by a broken water hose and a lack of hydrants. The fire burned out of control for five hours and at one point threatened the city's entire southeastern quarter.[53]

Agitation for municipal ownership of the water supply now began in earnest. As Newark's charter did not empower the city to provide its inhabitants with water, recourse had to be made once again to the state legislature, where the aqueduct company was influential. In 1838 a bill was passed authorizing the city to raise money for a water plant, but with the proviso that the municipality purchase the entire stock, works, and property of the company. In dire want of a larger water supply, but unwilling to meet the company's price, in 1845 Newark entered into a contract with the company for a water supply for fire-fighting purposes. The company further agreed to furnish a limited supply of water for household use.[54]

Halfway measures failed to stem the wave of discontent engulfing the city. Because the aqueduct company had failed to keep its plant abreast of population growth, more than 85 percent of Newark's 55,000 residents in 1855 were forced to rely on wells, cisterns, and rain barrels. The elevated western hillside was without water, as were the upper stories of buildings on Broad Street. The water obtained from wells was highly alkaline and thus unsuitable for boilers.[55] Dissatisfaction was rampant, as attested to by a resolution adopted by the common council on April 6, 1855:

> Whereas, owing to the want of an adequate supply of water in every part of our city, for domestic, mechanical and other purposes, and the destitution of the outer section of the city of such supply, and the evident incompetency of the present supply, therefore,
>
> Resolved, That a special committee of five be appointed to examine into the subject and report upon the best means of obtaining such supply of water as shall be entirely adequate to the wants of every portion of the city, and as will be sufficient for every emergency.[56]

Not one, but two special committees laboring for nearly one and a half years were needed to complete the study. Determined to adopt a plan that would be "permanent in its character, and as expansive in its means of water supply as the city itself," the committees conducted an exhaustive inquiry into the water resources of the Newark area. The kinds of water sources that could be tapped had been greatly broadened in the early nineteenth century by the invention of the steam engine, which put out a constant supply of power for operating water pumps. It also greatly enhanced the ability of engineers to raise water from low-lying rivers and lakes. Some years earlier Jersey City had begun pumping water from the Passaic River. The water parcels of the Morris Canal Company also held out promise. After narrowing their choice to purchasing water from the Morris Canal Company or building a municipally owned pumping station on the Passaic River below Paterson, the committee called in the state geologist and a group of consulting engineers to make the final decision. Basing their decision in part on Jersey City's success and in part on the city's desire to have its own water supply, the engineers selected the Passaic River.[57]

Shortly after the engineers made their recommendation the depression of 1857 occurred, dashing any hope that the water crisis would be quickly resolved. The depression caused Newarkers to adopt a more conservative attitude toward public improvements. Hence when prosperity returned in 1858, the cost of the new water supply, estimated at $725,000, aroused great opposition. In the 1850s Newark property owners had been hit with special assessments and higher taxes for lighting, pavements, sewers, public schools, and police and fire protection. A new water supply, they pleaded, would impose a crushing debt on both them and the city.[58]

In the face of strong opposition from property owners, it fell to Mayor Moses Bigelow to press the issue before the common council. In his annual reports for 1859 and 1860, Bigelow stressed the importance of an ample water supply to the city and asked for permission to obtain the necessary approval from the state legislature. Calling the existing facilities "notoriously insufficient," he noted that aqueduct water was only available in a few wards and there in inadequate amounts. Moreover, with the growth of population the wells in the outlying Fifth and Sixth Wards had become contaminated with seepage from nearby privies and cesspools, placing residents of these areas in grave danger. "In my opinion," he declared, "a liberal, reliable and permanent supply of this important element is secondary to no other public agency in preserving the health, protecting the property and facilitating the individual enterprises of our people, and attracting within our borders, not only capital and skill, but those desiring a pleasant, safe and comfortable residence."[59] A year earlier, Major Bigelow had said, "An element so indispensable to the protection of property, and to the health, comfort, and cleanliness of the city, and so intimately connected with its growth and prosperity, ought not, in its supply, to depend upon the pecuniary interest of an incorporated company."[60]

The *Newark Daily Mercury* supported the mayor by emphasizing the need for better fire protection. The *Mercury* warned that a fire in the congested central business district would be disastrous. The "great fire" of 1835 in New York City had caused $13 million in damages. The threat of fire and the need for a more adequate supply of water in general had led New York City to build the enormously expensive Croton Reservoir waterworks to bring in water from the mountains forty miles away. Newark was more fortunate, since it could tap the nearby Passaic River for a small fraction of the cost New York had incurred. The new water supply would benefit private and public interests alike. It would afford the city better fire protection and facilitate the cleansing of the streets, gutters, and sewers; it would serve industrialists by providing pure, copious water for their plants; and it would be used by homeowners for bathing, laundering, and cooking.[61]

In its deliberations about the source of the city's new water supply, the *Newark Daily Mercury* was undoubtedly influenced by the Passaic River's purity up until that time. Before it became hopelessly polluted after the Civil War, the Passaic River was widely used for fishing, swimming, and boating. Crabs and shrimps abounded in the river's inlets, while in deeper waters fishermen angled for perch, pickerel, shad, smelt, and bass. The Passaic River was especially known for its shad, which was featured in the area's better restaurants.[62]

Swimmers dived into the crystal-clear water from the piers that lined the river. Many of Newark's most prominent families built their homes a little upstream from the piers, where there was no commercial development to mar the river's beauty and tranquility. Much of the city's social life revolved around the waterway. Exclusive boat clubs held regattas, and the river was used extensively for canoeing and picnicking.[63]

In March 1860 the legislature authorized the creation of the Newark Aqueduct Board and directed it to take over the property and rights of the Newark Aqueduct Company at a cost of $150,000.[64] By then some Newarkers were beginning to have doubts about the wisdom of tapping the Passaic River should the city decide to go there for its water supply. In the summer of 1860 a correspondent from the Hill area inquired in one of the local newspapers whether the city was to be

> supplied with water from the Passaic after it has taken to its friendly bosom the wash of Paterson, Belleville, and the various manufactories, slaughterhouses, etc., that line its banks on either side. The time is not far distant when the waters of the river will be a counterpart to the celebrated Thames [London] water, so thoroughly alive with animalcula that those who imbibe have food and drink at the same cost. . . . The fact cannot be ignored that the

waters of the river must become more impure in the proportion that the country becomes more densely populated.[65]

He suggested that the lake above the summit of the Morris Canal be used instead. He was reluctant to press the matter for fear it would delay the development of a new water supply. The residents of the Hill area were becoming desperate. Most of the public wells had been closed and "the few remaining ones are besieged daily by thirsty throngs until long before night fall they are as dry as the thirsty multitudes." He implored the common council to be cautious, but to go ahead, "for the great demand of the day is Water, Water, Water."[66]

In June 1861 George H. Bailey of Jersey City was appointed chief engineer of the Newark Aqueduct Board and instructed to prepare a report on a new water supply. Bailey settled on the same two choices that had previously been considered: the Passaic River and the Morris Canal. Once again the Passaic River was chosen and once again there was a postponement. The Civil War forced the aqueduct board to delay construction of the waterworks, and for the remainder of the war the operation of the aqueduct board had to be limited to enlarging and improving old sources and equipment. On July 1, 1865, two months after the war had ended, a five-year contract was signed with the Morris Canal Company for a daily supply of three hundred thousand gallons at a cost of $128 per million gallons, which it was hoped would meet the city's needs until the municipal waterworks was completed.[67]

3 CHOLERA

BY 1832 SMALLPOX AND YELLOW FEVER, THE TWO great scourges of the colonial and early national periods, were in retreat. The discovery of vaccination in 1796 provided almost certain protection against smallpox. Henceforth smallpox would threaten only the most downtrodden and unenlightened. Yellow fever remained active in the South but, for reasons unknown, disappeared north of the Mason-Dixon line. A new pestilence, however, was to take their place. Cholera epidemics occurred in American communities from 1832 to 1866 with so profound an impact that one historian has called this period "the Cholera Years."[1]

Cholera is an acute specific infection of the gastrointestinal tract transmitted primarily through polluted water supplies. The incubation period of the pestilence is about seventy-two hours, and usually there is a crisis within a few days after the appearance of the first symptoms. The onset of the disease is marked by violent diarrhea, spasmodic vomiting, and painful cramps. Soon, the bodily evacuations turn watery, the stool taking on a "rice-water" appearance. Subsequent dehydration and chemical imbalance lead to disquieting changes in the appearance of the victim, frequently culminating in bodily collapse and death.[2] A nineteenth-century New Jersey physician provides this harrowing description of the course of the disease:

> The cramps, which first were confined to the fingers and toes, attack the extremities themselves, and the patient cries out with agony. The features of the face assume that indescribable but never-to-be forgotten appearance, which is so characteristic of the disease. The skin assumes a leaden or brownish colour. The countenance becomes sharpened and elongated. . . . The extremities also now begin to feel cold, and that coldness approaches the trunk. By degrees, the pulse becomes weaker and quicker, till it is no longer perceptible; the voice becomes fainter and fainter, and finally dies

away into a scarcely audible whisper; the thirst increases to an intolerable
degree. Purging and vomiting may or may not continue, the secretion of
urine ceases, the countenance assumes a more lurid hue, the features continue to sharpen, the eyes turn upward . . . the nervous derangement seems
to increase, a cold, clammy sweat breaks out over the whole body, and the
patient sinks into a state of almost irrevocable collapse.[3]

Drugs are not effective in combating the cholera vibrio and without
intravenous or oral replacement of lost body fluids and minerals the disease runs a rapid and often fatal course. During the nineteenth century,
before effective therapy became available, cholera had a case fatality
rate of nearly 50 percent. Some protection is provided by previous exposure, as persons who survive an attack of cholera are usually immune
to the disease for several years.[4]

Cholera is spread through the fecal-oral route and thus may be transmitted by any medium that provides a circuit between the excreta of an
infected individual and the intestinal tract of a healthy person. In cool,
moist environments the cholera vibrio can survive in fecally contaminated clothing for from one to three days, and on the surfaces of fresh
fruits and vegetables for four to seven days. Nevertheless, the disease
is not highly contagious. The cholera vibrio is a frail organism that dies
upon exposure to light or when deprived of moisture. Person-to-person
transmission takes place only where the most wretched living conditions
prevail and little or no attention is paid to personal hygiene. Principally
the disease is spread through fecalized water supplies.[5]

Cholera is endemic in the Indian subcontinent.[6] Before 1820 the relative isolation of the area and the short incubation period of the disease
confined cholera to its homeland. In the early nineteenth century the invention of the steamboat greatly reduced the travel time between Europe and the Orient. Free of the chains that had previously bound it, the
pestilence now embarked on a fifty-year odyssey, wreaking havoc in
nearly every section of the globe.

Cholera made its first appearance in the United States in 1832.
Though never endemic in the United States, cholera was epidemic in
1832, 1849, and 1866 and was also present in 1854 and 1873. The disease came to the United States from aboard crowded immigrant ships

bound from Bremen and Liverpool to New York, Boston, and New Orleans. From these great commercial marts the disease worked its way inland and along the coast.

The appearance of cholera in an urban community was a terrifying experience. The disease caused great morbidity and mortality. The traditional defenses employed by cities against epidemic diseases—isolation of the victims and emergency sanitary measures to rid the community of organic wastes—seldom had much effect on the course of a cholera epidemic. The pestilence spread with appalling speed, its mode of transmission a mystery. Within a matter of days an entire community could be infected. Individuals far removed from the disease and seemingly safe would be felled. Not knowing where the disease would strike next or how to combat it, cities stood defenseless before the onslaught of the pestilence.

Many of the "better" class of citizens comforted themselves with the belief that high moral standards and an exemplary life afforded protection against the disease. They saw it as a sign of God's justice that the intemperate and the downtrodden, especially the Irish and the blacks, suffered the most. It was claimed that in European cities prostitutes and drunkards had died in great numbers. Cholera, of course, was prevalent among the urban poor for the same reasons it could be found aboard immigrant ships: unsanitary living conditions, overcrowding, and the inability to flee.

Though cholera was classified as an atmospheric malaise, it was widely maintained that intemperance, erratic behavior, and immorality conspired to render a person susceptible to the disease. "When individuals of comfortable, regular mode of life and temperate habits became victims, some exciting cause, such as excessive fatigue, imprudent diet, or more than usual dread of the malady was [found to have been] almost always present."[7] Victims of the disease were castigated for living in squalor. Sickness, it was argued, could be avoided by repentance. Unfortunately, social leaders were insensitive to the living conditions of the poor, which made appeals for moral uplift quixotic. The only "sin" of urban slum dwellers was poverty.

Most physicians believed that cholera was not communicable. Physicians seldom caught it from their patients and frequently cases oc-

curred simultaneously in widely separated areas. Nevertheless, the
frightened citizenry invariably insisted upon the isolation of the infected. Those who were fortunate were treated at home. Those without
family, friends, or money were sent to "municipal slaughterhouses,"
euphemistically known as cholera hospitals.

Treatment of cholera ran the gamut of the materia medica. Most
remedies were harmless, a few were dangerous. Though no hope was
offered for collapsed patients, it was generally believed that the disease
could be cured if the premonitory symptoms were quickly treated.
Since cholera was considered an exaggerated case of "cholera mor-
bus," a flexible term used to describe a variety of ailments characterized by a loose stool, it is apparent that those who were cured either (1)
had not had cholera, or (2) had had a mild case and, in all probability,
would have recovered regardless of the treatment.

As cholera approached Newark in 1832, the inhabitants of the town
became engrossed in the nature of this latest "divine judgment." On
June 19 the advance of the disease in North America was reported by
the *Newark Daily Advertiser* and the *Sentinel of Freedom*, Newark's
two leading newspapers.[8] During the next few days, editorials and let-
ters on the pestilence, along with advertisements for its prevention and
cure, appeared in the newspapers. A lecture on the subject was delivered before the Newark Mechanics' Association.[9] The *Sentinel of
Freedom* warned that "drunkards are generally the first victims."[10]

At a specially convened meeting of the physicians of Newark held
on June 21 a series of resolutions were adopted calling upon the public
authorities to (1) remove all organic matter and other filth from the
town; (2) drain or purify stagnant pools; and (3) establish a cholera hospital. Homeowners were told to clean their cellars, sinks, drains, and
cisterns with a solution of lime or chloride of lime. Individuals were
advised to stay calm and to avoid unnecessary exposure to inclement
weather. Stern admonishments were issued against intemperance and
the consumption of raw fruits and vegetables.[11]

From June 23 through June 28 town meetings were held at which it
was agreed to have the Township Committee, Newark's executive
branch of government, constituted as a board of health and to invest it
with the power to appropriate funds to combat the epidemic and aid the

stricken. In addition, citizens' committees were appointed in the road districts to help the overseers of the highways clean the streets.[12]

The first victim of the disease, the wife of a steamboat captain, was taken ill on July 6, after having just returned from New York, where she had resided in an area in which several persons had died of cholera. But her illness did not trigger the long-awaited epidemic, for she died within twelve hours, and a second case did not develop in Newark until nearly a week later.[13]

The first case of local origin occurred on July 11 in "a small filthy house" situated on the edge of a marsh near the Centre Street wharf.[14] The board of health described the house as a "place of rendezvous for carousel." In residence were "about 20 degraded inmates of the most unclean habits."[15] The *Newark Daily Advertiser* wrote: "Among such a community, guilty of all kinds of excesses, it would not at all be surprising that disease should be engendered without the assistance of a cause."[16] Nine cases developed, all fatal.[17] The other inhabitants were forcibly removed to a barracks, where they were "crowded in together to live or die, as chance should direct."[18] The barracks, which served as a cholera hospital for the duration of the epidemic, was located "a considerable distance from town."[19] Soon cholera was raging in the areas near the Centre Street wharf, the hospital, and the poorhouse (which was located about a quarter of a mile from the hospital).[20]

As the disease gained a foothold, some persons fled Newark and business declined.[21] Beginning July 19 cases were reported daily in the newspapers—Irish nationality or black race and intemperate or good habits noted.[22] The *Newark Daily Advertiser* reassured its readers that 90 percent of the fatalities were among those whose constitutions had been "previously injured by, and who . . . [had been] at the time [of their death] in the practice of intemperate habits."[23]

The epidemic showed no signs of abating, leading the governor to set aside July 26 as a day of fasting and prayer.[24] That same day the disease appeared in an area far removed from the focal points of the epidemic. The first two cases occurred in the same house. Within a few hours a husband and wife in an adjoining building and a prisoner in the county jail, about two hundred yards away, were stricken. Thereafter, cases occurred in this neighborhood almost continually. The disease was then introduced into yet another neighborhood by a person attempting to flee contamination,[25] and "while the disease was thus endemically prevailing in these several distinct localities, solitary cases were almost daily appearing in various sections of the town, in persons who had not, as well as those who had been exposed to emanations from diseased persons."[26]

On July 28 at a meeting of the physicians and citizens of Newark a resolution was adopted asking the town committee to prevail upon retailers to curtail the sale of intoxicating beverages.[27] The popularity of preachments and tracts inveighing against the consumption of alcohol was indicative of the piety that colored the thinking of medical and nonmedical persons alike. Wrote one Passaic County physician: "The man of regular habits was cut down, and the sot that wallowed in the mire of intoxication escaped." Notwithstanding this he continued: "I must beg, sir, not to be understood, in the bare mention of an anomalous fact of the immunity of the drunkards of our vicinity from diarrhoea and cholera, as denying the truth that intemperance predisposes to these diseases. If it not be so in fact, still, for the sake of temperance and good order, let it stand recorded that the drunkard is peculiarly the victim of cholera. Let us all live and die sober men."[28]

The epidemic raged out of control until late August. By a quirk of fate the last case occurred in early September in the same house in which the disease had first appeared some two months earlier. In all, 127 persons had contracted cholera and 65 had died.[29]

Statistics on cholera deaths only provide a rough estimate of the number of persons killed by the disease. It is likely that public reports underestimated the toll from cholera, since overworked physicians sometimes did not report deaths in the midst of an epidemic and families of the afflicted sought to keep the authorities from learning about the presence of the disease in their households. To die from cholera was to die under suspicious circumstances. Since cholera was linked to dissolute habits and immoral behavior such as was believed to be characteristic of Irish immigrants, blacks, and poor whites, many deaths among "respectable" members of the community were falsely attributed to dysentery, diarrhea, and cholera infantum.[30]

THE APPROACH OF CHOLERA IN 1849 WAS HERALDED by an avalanche of advertisements for its cure and prevention. A dismayed editor complained, "One would think, to read the manifold advertisements of specifics for the Cholera, that there ought to be no apprehension of danger from the disease."[31] Though antithetic in their effects, advertisements for astringents and cathartics carrying the testimonials of distinguished persons appeared side by side in the newspapers. Sarsaparilla, sulphur, charcoal, camphor, narcotics, salts, chlorides, "and indeed the whole contents of the Materia Medica" were sold to a bewildered, frightened, and gullible public. Lacking faith in the ability of physicians to treat the disease or governmental authorities to halt its deadly march, individuals grasped at any and all treatments that promised relief. Pharmacists and physicians who peddled specifics for cholera were not the only ones to profit from the disease. Perfume and soap makers stressed the importance of cleanliness; liquor dealers promoted the medicinal powers of brandy and port; rural innkeepers were eloquent on the subject of the tonic provided by a long rest in the bracing country air; steamboat and railroad companies advocated the health-restoring properties of short and frequent excursions; haberdashers emphasized the need for protection against the elements. "In the midst of all this diversity of interests and opinions," lamented the editor, "what are the poor uninitiated to do—but stand aloof and wait?"[32]

The first case occurred on May 31. A number of cases were reported in June, but the disease remained under control until about the middle of July.[33] On July 18 a man with an advanced case of cholera, found on the road between Newark and New York, was taken to the city almshouse, precipitating thirty-eight deaths, including that of the superintendent.[34]

In light of the conditions that existed at the almshouse, it is not surprising that cholera raged; many had died there during the epidemic of 1832.[35] The almshouse was adjacent to the salt meadows at the extreme southern end of the city, about one and a half miles from downtown Newark. The occupants were those whom society had cast aside, principally the indigent poor. The inmates nursed their own sick. A privy vault was located under the building near the almshouse well into which it drained. A more favorable set of conditions for the spread of cholera can scarcely be imagined.[36]

The *Newark Daily Advertiser* reported that the epidemic's victims were mainly "foreigners in a low condition of life, who lived without due prudence,"[37] but another observer stated that by August the disease was "reaching even to the better classes and the best positions."[38] The epidemic did not abate until September. In all, 149 persons died, the casualties falling about equally between foreign born and native, male and female, young and old.[39] Newark's population was then thirty-two thousand.

Cholera's second visit to the United States, in 1849, was the most calamitous. A little more than five thousand New Yorkers died from the disease, and yet Net York's experience was mild compared to that of other cities. Several western cities lost nearly a tenth or more of their populations. In Saint Louis, where there were from forty-five hundred to six thousand deaths, overworked sextons and undertakers put corpses in the forest or on sandbars in the Mississippi River. The city council fled, later to be replaced by a citizen's Committee of Public Health, which directed cleanup operations. Eighteen percent of Sandusky's population was said to have been carried off by cholera. In Aurora, Indiana, on the Ohio River, 80 percent of the town's two thousand inhabitants fled after cholera appeared downstream in nearby Madison, Indiana, leaving behind only those who were too sick to leave. President Zachary Taylor declared Friday, August 3, 1849, a day of national fasting and prayer, and citizens were asked to implore the help of Providence to stay the destroying hand of the pestilence. In the South an estimated ten thousand slaves died, causing the price of bondsmen to rise.[40]

Newark had gotten off lightly in its first two encounters with cholera. Sixty-five persons had died in 1832 and 149 in 1849, or about 0.5 percent of the city's population in both epidemics. In 1832 Quebec and New Orleans lost nearly 10 percent of their populations. Washington, D.C., with twice the population of Newark, had nearly six times as many deaths. Cholera passed over Lexington, Kentucky, in 1832 but returned with savage fury the following year. Nearly one-third of the city's six thousand residents fled and among the less than four thousand who remained there were 502 deaths. Only two of America's larger cities, Boston and Charleston, were relatively untouched. New Orleans, which lost five thousand persons to the pestilence in 1832, was hit the hardest. Not only did Newark have far fewer cholera deaths than other cities, there were no reports of dead bodies lying unburied in the streets, of deserted neighborhoods, or of a city in near chaos, such as filtered out of New York City, where there were thirty-five hundred deaths.[41]

Throughout the period when cholera was epidemic in the United States, physicians clung to the belief that the disease could be treated if it was caught early enough, though, as one physician admitted, it was likely that "if the patient recovered, the merit belonged to the strength of the constitution of the patient rather than to the skill of the physician."[42] External applications were applied to the extremities in an effort to maintain body temperature and to relieve cramps. The heat was applied with warm bricks, hot water bottles, mustard plasters, spice plasters, and heated bags of sand or salt.

Internal remedies, of which "a great variety was [sic] used, and often of a very opposite kind," constituted the principal method of treatment. Calomel, "the Sampson of the materia medica," was used extensively as a purgative. Opium and later chloroform were added to the calomel to relieve pains and spasms and to regulate stool movements. Soda water, ice, cold water, and spots of camphor were administered to quiet the stomach. Faltering constitutions were restored with brandy and other stimulants. Both stimulants and sedatives were used to excess. When fever was present the patient was bled, though the practice was losing favor.[43] A few physicians reported good results, but the effect of medical treatment is probably best summed up in the candid statement of a Newark physician who observed that "patients uniformly died either yielding to the disease in spite of my remedies or . . . no doubt [as] the result of my treatment (in many cases at least)."[44]

On the basis of their experiences in 1832 and 1849, the medical profession's view of cholera slowly underwent a change. While continuing to stress personal habits, physicians began to acknowledge the association of cholera with squalor. Gradually the specificity of the disease was recognized. The question of communicability, however, continued to perplex physicians. On the one hand, the disease often remained confined to certain localities and did not seem to affect physicians, friends, and others who had been exposed. Yet, there were many instances where entire families had been stricken and where the introduction of just a single case into a hospital or a crowded tenement had led to a severe outbreak. Confronted with this enigma, most physicians adopted the view that cholera was contingently contagious; that it was contagious when certain predisposing factors were present.[45] "An atmosphere is generated in the apartment of the sick which will be communicated to those who are in any way rendered susceptible of attack," wrote one physician.[46] Another stated: "I believe the disease to be caused by an atmospheric posion, exposure to which, together with predisposition of the system, are necessary to its production."[47]

Opinion differed on the method by which the atmosphere became poisoned. Some held that microorganisms emanating from marshes or cholera patients were responsible. Most physicians adhered to the theory that the atmosphere was poisoned by "fermentation" or decomposition of organic matter.[48] "Although the remote causes of the disease are enveloped in impenetrable mystery," wrote Dr. J. Henry Clark, "among the facts that we do know are these: that its favorite place of development is where *filth* abounds; where *many are crowded into too small a place; and where noxious exhalations arise*."[49]

EVERY SUMMER FROM 1850 TO 1853 SPORADIC CASES of cholera occurred in Newark, but were hidden from the public "to avoid exciting any unnecessary apprehensions."[50] Isolated cases were reported in June 1854, and by the first week of July the disease had again reached epidemic proportions.[51] On July 6 lime was distributed to the citizens of the city,[52] and on July 7 a special Health Committee, consisting of the mayor, two aldermen, and a physician, was organized to deal with the emergency. The committee, which was empowered to investigate and abate nuisances,[53] began a vigorous drive to improve sanitary conditions. Scavengers were hired to cart away garbage; privies were cleaned; stagnant pools were covered with lime; gutters and alleys were swept clean; excretus was removed from animal pens; and an ordinance was passed regulating the keeping of swine and the butchering of animals. The board of health received numerous complaints about unsanitary conditions, and one newspaper advocated the establishment of a permanent health officer.[54]

Special attention was paid to tenements, where the laboring poor were crowded into poorly lighted and badly ventilated apartments and damp basements. When cholera appeared in a tenement in the slum-ridden Down Neck area of Newark, a special committee (apparently a subcommittee of the Health Committee) was appointed to investigate. As a result of its inquiry, forty of the sixty families in residence were required to move, and the landlord was ordered to make needed sanitary repairs. Similar actions were taken in other cholera-infested tenements.[55] In some instances, tenants living in adjacent buildings were also evicted.[56]

The human instinct to succor the sick was strained during the crisis by the residents' fear of contracting the disease. Because the long trip to the distant pesthouse endangered the patient, the Health Committee sought to establish a more centrally located hospital. The committee, however, failed to find a replacement for the pesthouse, for no neighborhood was willing to run the risk of having the disease in its midst.[57]

The experiences of health officers and physicians in other cities were studied and postmortem examinations were made, all to no avail.[58] "The progress of the epidemic, and at times its extraordinary virulence, excited great alarm in the community."[59] On July 22 the Health Committee was excused from reporting because of fear of exciting an already aroused populace.[60] The members of the Health Committee later confessed that they had often been "oppressed with apprehension that their labors, though incessant and fatiguing," would not be adequate to stem the scourge.[61]

It is apparent that by late August the disease was afflicting the "better classes." The *Sentinel of Freedom* reported that the miasmatic and intemperance theories of cholera appeared to be invalid. Indeed, the disease had proved fatal to many "who were not particularly subject to any deleterious influence, and who were temperate and regular in personal habits."[62] Aghast at such blasphemy, the *Newark Daily Adver-*

tiser replied that "exceptions do not invalidate a general rule, and indiscretions that may be unobserved or forgotten, probably often prove the cause of attack."[63]

At the same time, it was reported in several out-of-town journals that Newark's suffering was proportionately greater than that of any other community that year,[64] a contention both the *Advertiser* and the *Sentinel* vigorously denied. Nearly six hundred persons, or more than 1 percent of the population, perished from the pestilence. On one street the disease claimed twenty-four of the twenty-eight residents. Because it was feared business interests would be harmed by a full disclosure of the tragedy, the severity of the epidemic was not revealed until the following year.[65]

The Sixth Ward, or Hill section of the city, the home of some ten to fifteen thousand recently arrived German immigrants, was hit hardest.[66] In a letter to the *Newark Daily Advertiser*, a "Committee of Germans" laid the blame for their community's plight on the existence of stagnant pools of water resulting from faulty street construction, which the Germans attributed to discrimination. "We complained often, but we are mostly foreigners; and even yesterday, one of our Street Commissioners answered, 'I don't care if all Dutchmen die in one heap.' It seems Dutchmen are only good to vote and pay taxes. Election day they are dear friends, but afterwards d——d Dutch."[67]

The *Advertiser*, which had been conducting its own examination, suggested that use of contaminated water was responsible for the outbreak. The Hill section was entirely dependent on well water, whereas the downtown area was supplied by the Newark Aqueduct Company with springwater.[68] The substratum in the Hill section is composed of clay, shale, and rock and is therefore impervious. Consequently, instead of being absorbed, wastewater was running into the wells. The *Advertiser* recommended that the water be chemically analyzed and advised the Germans to use hydrant or rainwater in the interim.[69] In a statement pregnant in its implications for the future, the *Advertiser* astutely noted that it was "somewhat singular that during the recent ravages of the cholera in our city, the disease occurred principally in sections where well-water is used by families. . . . It is a matter worthy of investigation, to ascertain if wells in the city do not become infected by the percolations of the water into them through the filth of the streets, cesspools, etc."[70] Similar observations made in London that very year led to an investigation, that revealed the mechanism by which cholera spread and provided sanitarians with the knowledge needed to wage an effective campaign against this dread disease.

Dr. John Snow, a distinguished London anaesthetist, had written a pamphlet in 1849 in which he argued that cholera was a contagious disease caused by an organic poison that attacked the intestines and was excreted in the feces of the patient. Epidemics occurred when the poisoned feces found its way into the water supply. In 1854 Snow had an opportunity to test his hypothesis when cholera flared up near Broad Street, London, killing five hundred persons within a radius of 250 yards. Snow traced the origin of the epidemic to a polluted well. By simply breaking the handle to the pump Snow was able to end the outbreak.

That year cholera was prevalent in London. The city was supplied with water by two companies: the Southwark and Vauxhall Company and the Lambeth Company. The Southwark and Vauxhall Company pumped water from the polluted lower section of the Thames River. The Lambeth Company obtained its supply far enough upstream so that the tide did not carry sewage past its intake. A statistical analysis of the water consumed by cholera victims revealed that the disease had occurred in far greater numbers among subscribers of the Southwark and Vauxhall Company than subscribers of the Lambeth Comany. Since many areas of the city were served by both companies, Snow was able to conclude that, except for a small number of secondary cases, the sewage-contaminated water of the Southwark and Vauxhall Company was responsible for the epidemic.[71]

THROUGH IMMIGRANT PHYSICIANS AND MEDICAL journals the theories of Snow were brought to the United States. In the spring of 1866 cholera invaded New York City for the third time, only this time the city was prepared. As a result of energetic action on the part of the newly created New York Metropolitan Board of Health, the disease was quickly brought under control with far fewer deaths than in 1849. For the first time an American city had turned back an invasion of cholera.[72]

In mid-June two cases of cholera were reported in Newark. Taking heart from New York's success, the city immediately erected sanitary cordons around the stricken.[73] "Some cases will doubtless occur," reported the *Newark Daily Advertiser*, "but it is only necessary that our health authorities should act promptly, at any expense, in destroying every vestige of the contagion which lurks in the discharge."[74] Cholera-infected homes were vacated and the bedding, personal effects, and excreta of the occupants disinfected or destroyed. Only twenty cases developed, and the board of health (which had been organized in 1857) was credited with having prevented an epidemic.[75]

The pestilence had made its last appearance in Newark, but the specter of cholera, reinforced by its presence in the Mississippi Valley in 1873, and by reports of occasional outbreaks aboard immigrant ships docked in New York harbor, would continue to cast a long shadow upon the lives of Newark citizens. Fear of cholera would influence events in Newark—in particular, questions concerning water supply, plumbing, night soil removal, wells, and the powers of the board of health—for many years to come.

4 AN AGE OF GIANTS

WITH THE APPROACH OF THE 1860 PRESIDENTIAL election Newarkers began to pay less attention to local issues as they became absorbed in the national drama concerning slavery. The threat of secession hung heavily over the city's workshops, for the South was their best customer. Southern plantations consumed nearly 65 percent of Newark's industrial output, no small consideration to a community that made its living from manufacturing. Democratic newspapers warned that Lincoln's election would bring ruin. Hence Lincoln ran poorly in Newark and did not receive the support of its citizens until southern secessionists attacked Fort Sumter.[1]

The mass unemployment that had been predicted materialized during the first months of the Civil War, but disappeared with the first influx of war contracts. Newark's large population of skilled artisans made it an ideal center for the manufacture of war goods. Quickly and skillfully, local businessmen shifted their production from carriages and leather goods to outfitting the Union army.[2]

Despite its successful conversion to a war economy, Newark's place in the national urban hierarchy began to fall after 1860. The southern market had been lost to Atlanta, Memphis, Houston, and the other new cities of the South and West that achieved prominence after the Civil War. Moreover, the head start Newark had gotten in industrialization was erased as both new communities and old commercial centers turned to manufacturing for their prosperity. Newark businessmen had little control over these events. However, in situations where local initiative could have made a difference, Newark's leaders were unequal to the task. As of 1888, Newark still had not overcome any of the major local obstacles threatening its future growth and prosperity, namely: (1) adoption of a safe municipal water supply; (2) cleansing of the Passaic River; (3) reclamation of the meadows for industrial sites; and (4) building a deep-water port facility. Recently established cities such as

Detroit and Cleveland, began to surpass Newark in size and importance. In the years 1860 to 1910, Newark's place among the nation's
largest cities dropped from eleventh to seventeenth.[3]

NEWARK'S DECLINE WAS ONLY COMPARATIVE, NOT
absolute. The city continued to experience vigorous growth,
and in the years 1860 to 1900 its population increased from 72,000 to
246,000. Newark emerged from the Civil War an industrial giant.
More than half of its wage earners in 1880 were employed in industry.
Several new industries achieved prominence, including chemicals,
electrical machinery, and smelting and refining, revealing a shift from
workshop to factory and from consumer wares to capital goods.[4] Financial institutions followed industry, helping to balance the economy.[5] In the words of Newark's official biographer, it was "an age of
giants," an age of daring entrepreneurs who established great businesses, and of inventors like Edward Wetson (the "normal cell") and
John Wesley Hyatt (celluloid), whose discoveries changed the lives of
all Americans.[6]

In 1868 local businessmen established the Newark Board of Trade.
Membership on the board initially was heavily weighted with manufacturing interests, but gradually became representative of the economy's
growing diversification. The financial, industrial, and commercial
leaders of Newark generally adopted the enlightened attitude that what
was beneficial for Newark was good for business. Through political
influence and public appeals, the board mobilized support for a variety
of municipal improvements that would increase Newark's economic attractiveness. The board was especially eager to improve and extend the
city's sanitary infrastructure and to this end inquired into methods of
garbage disposal used in other cities and paid for a study of Newark's
sewer needs.

Foreign-born immigrants continued to provide the manpower for
Newark's businesses. Nearness to New York City, the nation's largest
port of entry, and the opportunities afforded unskilled labor in industry
and municipal construction attracted large numbers of immigrants to
Newark. In the three decades following the Civil War the foreign born

constituted between 29 and 34 percent of the population. Along with their American-born children, the foreign element made up more than half of the city's population.[7]

The Irish and the Germans remained the largest minority groups, but encountered far less hostility than before. Though they still clashed with native-born Americans over moral and religious issues such as Prohibition and Sabbath day observance, the strife and intolerance that had marked earlier relations between the two groups gradually gave way to a process of accommodation and assimilation. The disproportionately high number of immigrants who had died fighting for the Union erased the doubts of most Anglo-Saxons about their patriotism. As a result of years of association in community activities, fears that the Catholic Church would subvert obedience to lawfully constituted authority were replaced by the realization that the church was a stabilizing force within the immigrant community. Besides, the immigrants were becoming too numerous and powerful to ignore. Irish and German faces became more prominent at city hall, and by 1900 each group had had one of its own elected mayor—the Irish in the 1870s and the Germans in the 1890s. Starting about 1890, Italians, Slavs, and Russian Jews began supplanting the older ethnic stock from northern and western Europe. Desperately poor and unfamiliar with American ways, these new immigrants became the object of a revitalized nativism, often on the part of second- and third-generation Irish and Germans who had forgotten their own mistreatment.[8]

Many of these newcomers settled in Down Neck, or Ironbound, as it was now called (because of the iron foundries and the Pennsylvania Railroad tracks that girded the area). Ironbound also attracted industrialists eager to take advantage of the region's superb rail and water transportation facilities. Soon the combination of heavy industry and tenements made Ironbound Newark's worst slum. The inner wards situated between Ironbound and the Hill contained the best residential areas. Large, stately homes were built in downtown Newark, commanding views overlooking Washington and Military parks. Other wealthy residents built houses on South Broad Street and on the ends of the ridge running along High Street. To insulate themselves against the sordid commercialism of the outside world, the inhabitants of these areas established proper Victorian households in which formality, taste, and manners were emphasized.[9]

The city's rapid development posed many problems for which there was virtually no planning. Though population increase put great pressure on municipal services, the city continued to provide them in a largely ad hoc manner. Moreover, while the perplexities of an urban-industrial society required the state to assume additional responsibilities, the tenets of laissez faire capitalism narrowly restricted the role of government to protecting property and maintaining order. Governmental concern did not extend to dilapidated housing or to hazardous employment, for these were areas in which individuals were expected to fend for themselves. Public leaders contended that living conditions would gradually improve as the free enterprise system increased the wealth of society. Similarly, any imbalance in the community, as, for example, between population density and public transportation, or between suburban growth and inner-city decay, was left to the outcome of the private money-making ventures that molded Newark's development.[10]

The commercial bias that infused government was evident in the city's failure to provide parks for its citizens. In 1867 a commission was appointed to plan a park in the northwestern sector of Newark. The commission recommended the acquisition of about seven hundred acres, starting at what is now the corner of Belleville Avenue and Clay Street and running to and including the present Branch Brook Park. But the state legislature would not authorize the one million dollars it was estimated was needed to purchase and improve the land and nothing came of the idea. By the time the newly created Essex County Park Commission revived it in 1895, only about one-third of the original site was still available, commercial development having claimed the remainder, at a cost of more than double the original estimate.[11] As of 1885, there were only eleven parks in Newark containing 18.36 acres, "not a very generous supply for a city of 150,000 inhabitants." Buffalo and Washington, with nearly equal populations, contained 620 and 1,000 acres, respectively.[12]

The Old Burying Ground, which for many years had been fighting a losing battle against public abuse and commercial encroachment, finally succumbed in 1886 to the city's desire to build a modern marketplace. When a group of citizens initiated legal action to save the cemetery, the city responded that the cemetery's location in the heart of the business district made it impossible to protect it against desecration. Subsequently the bodies were dug up and moved to Fairmount Cemetery. To mollify the descendents of the persons interred in the Old Burying Ground, the city consented to put a monument on the site perpetuating the memories of the Puritan founders.[13]

Street improvements were another area where the government's unwillingness to finance needed public services led to neglect. As of 1870 Newark had only 27.1 miles of paved streets, mainly of cobblestone. The poor condition of the streets made it treacherous for both pedestrians and teamsters to get around Newark. The *Sentinel of Freedom* commented: "There is hardly an acre of natural road-bed soil within the bounds of Newark, and the only alternative is between [poor] pavements and the worst kind of mud. It cuts up in the fall rains only to freeze into horrible hubs with the winter, to be worn down at heavy cost of wear and tear of vehicles, breaks up and freezes again at intervals through the cold season, furnishes another epoch of mud in the spring and closes out with clouds of dust in the summer."[14]

Under Newark law property owners since 1854 had been required to pay for the entire cost of street improvements. Disgruntled property owners protested that street improvements were a municipal responsibility and in the mid-1870s they got the courts to agree with them. The courts ruled that property owners could only be assessed for the benefits conferred by pavements and all expenses above that amount would have to be absorbed by the city. But if property owners thought that requiring the city to assume part of the financial burden of street improvements would accelerate the work, they were mistaken. Between 1870 and 1880 nineteen miles of city streets were paved. In the following decade less than four miles were added. All together by 1890 less than one-third of Newark's 186 miles of streets were paved.[15]

Streetcars radically altered Newark's residential patterns. The appearance of first the horse-drawn and later the electric trolley prompted an exodus of affluent workers from the inner wards. The cheap land opened up for settlement by the trolley made it possible for commuters to live in spacious, modern houses in rural surroundings without having to sacrifice the economic opportunities that existed in the city. With the arrival of the first wave of southern and eastern European immigrants in the 1890s, the movement to the suburbs accelerated. Fearful of being submerged in an alien sea, native-born Americans deserted the city in droves. Residential sections that lost their middle-class inhabitants either were rezoned for business or were taken over by the newcomers.[16]

Not all native residents fled the arrival of the new immigrants: many could not afford to live in the suburbs, and some had business interests that kept them downtown with the newcomers. The old, the sick, the unsuccessful, and others trapped in the city were forced to live in tenements and lodging houses. Young families stayed in town until they had accumulated enough money for a down payment on a suburban house. Wealthy industrialists who wanted to be near their businesses and were able to isolate themselves and their families from the discomforts and pathologies of city life also stayed behind. The view of downtown Newark presented a discordant juxtaposition of fine homes and ugly tenements and factories, though increasingly work and residence were becoming separated (see Maps 1 and 2).[17]

Newark in this period began to take on the appearance and characteristics of a bustling industrial center. Overhead, telephone and power lines crisscrossed, hiding the city in a cobweb of wires, while below trolleys speeded commuters to and from the suburbs. Department stores opened for business and two outstanding newspapers, the *Sunday Call* and the *Newark Evening News*, were founded. Casting aside the conservative tradition of the Newark press, the new journals offered sprightly, independent news reporting attuned to the variety of tastes of urban readers. By 1900 the *Sunday Call* was publishing editions of sixty pages with feature articles, theater columns, and sports and fashion pages, and it was acknowledged to be one of New Jersey's most influential newspapers. The *News*, by relying less on lengthy, often dated foreign dispatches and by placing more emphasis on investigative journalism of local events, quickly became Newark's largest circulating daily.[18]

Yet amidst all these signs of progress, life in Newark had soured. Sickness and premature death were depriving Newarkers of the rewards of their labors. Growth, urbanization, and industrialization had been recklessly pushed forward without a corresponding expansion of health and welfare services, and the city was now having to pay the price. A newspaper editor in 1857 summed up the city's lopsided development by noting that there were forty churches but not one hospital; by then Newark's population was approaching sixty thousand. A dispensary was established the following year in the offices of the city's newly organized board of health. The dispensary furnished drugs to the poor and provided free vaccinations. Persons too sick to travel were treated in their homes by district physicians attached to the dispensary. Though these instruments of community medicine served a large clientele, they did not take the place of a hospital.[19]

The absence of a hospital in Newark resulted in many hardships for its citizens, especially the laboring classes. Most important, there was no medical center equipped to handle the daily accidents that occurred in the railroad yards and workshops. Frequently, injured workers had to be taken from one doctor's office to another in a frantic search for emergency treatment. In 1856 the *Newark Daily Advertiser* related an incident in which a young man with a mutilated arm was seen being

> rushed in and out of almost every physician's office about Market Street, without finding a single member of the profession [most of whom were out making house calls] to dress the wound of the suffering patient. From the last unsuccessful visit they turned to another part of the city in headlong haste, but with no better grounds of hope than before; if they succeeded it was only a providential circumstance, and we know not how long or how far the unfortunate man was obliged to travel to obtain assistance, which in a dense community like this he ought to have been able to receive with much less trouble and suffering. . . . There are . . . in a populous and busy manufacturing city . . . very dangerous accidents constantly occurring, which need instantaneous relief . . . and human life often depending on prompt action, is lost for the want of it.[20]

Persons requiring emergency medical aid were not the only ones in need of a hospital. Individuals convalescing from serious illnesses seldom were able to obtain proper nursing care. Out-of-town businessmen and other visitors who took ill in Newark were forced to seek care in

Map 1

Areas of Newark Opened Up for Settlement by Trolley Lines, 1911

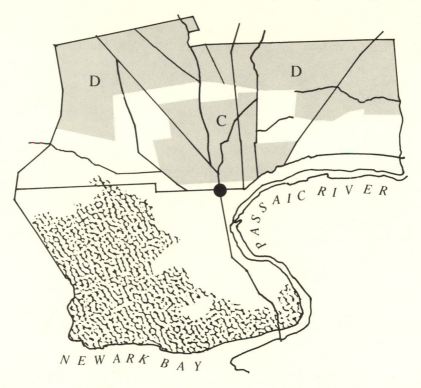

C indicates congested area close to the business and traffic center (the black spot).

D D is the large region to the northwest, west, and southwest, lying partly in and partly outside the city limits, available for homes of moderate cost. It is nearly all high and well drained, and traversed, as shown by trolley lines. Only a very small part of this large suburban area is as yet built up.

SOURCE: George B. Ford and E. P. Goodrich, *Housing Report*, [Reports of] *The City Plan Commission, Newark, N.J.* (Newark: Matthias Plum, 1913).

Map 2
Residential Areas of Newark, 1911

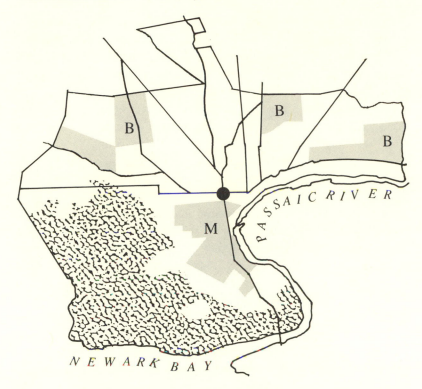

M marks Newark's region of homes of people of
moderate incomes, and B B B mark regions of expensive and high-grade residences.

SOURCE: George B. Ford and E. P. Goodrich, *Housing Report*,
[Report of] *The City Plan Commission, Newark, N.J.* (Newark:
Matthias Plum, 1913).

hotels and boardinghouses and to rely on the altruism of chance ac-
quaintances. Finally, residents needing anything but the simplest surgery were compelled to go to New York City for their operations.[21]

For nearly two hundred years following its founding in 1666, Newark sponged off the medical resources of its neighbor across the Hudson
River. In 1853 a movement for a public hospital in Newark began when
it was revealed that an anonymous benefactor was willing to donate ten
thousand dollars toward such a facility if the community would raise an
additional thirty thousand dollars and if the city would agree to build
the hospital in the center of the Old Burying Ground. The cemetery was
considered a desirable hospital site because of its central location and
because the lack of any adjacent buildings would enable patients to receive the benefits of fresh air and sunshine. The site, however, was opposed by many who looked upon the proposed buildings as trespassing
upon the remains of the dead. Others feared the hospital would spread
communicable diseases throughout the community, and in a nine-to-
seven vote the common council rejected the site.[22]

The hospital movement was revived in 1857, and as a first step a
charter for "Newark Hospital" was secured from the state legislature.
At a public meeting called in March by 114 of Newark's leading citizens the city was divided into districts and persons were appointed to
solicit subscriptions. The project seemed to be progressing fairly well
when the depression of 1857 halted charitable giving. The economy
soon recovered, but the fright thrown into Newark businessmen by the
depression caused them to tighten their purse strings, and no further action was taken on the hospital.[23] The failure of the plan prompted the
city health officer to remark that the want of a hospital "has been a re-
proach to our people, an injustice to those who might properly demand
attention at our hands, and a burden to the charities of our neighbors."[24]

The devastation of the Civil War led to the founding of Newark's
first hospital. Medical care centers were desperately needed for returning injured soldiers. When trains began bringing back the first
wounded to Newark on May 10, 1862, Marcus L. Ward, the Republican political leader of New Jersey (popularly known as the "Soldiers'
Friend" for his efforts in obtaining pensions and other relief for

wounded soldiers and the families of killed soldiers), assumed the responsibility for organizing a hospital. With money borrowed from the
New Jersey state government, Ward leased a four-story brick ware-
house on Centre Street, between the New Jersey Railroad and the
Passaic River. In just two days the building was scrubbed, fumigated,
outfitted with hospital equipment and readied for occupancy. At its
peak of operation the hospital contained 17 pavilions housing 1,020
beds. The hospital was closed in the summer of 1865 and the facility
converted into a state soldiers' home.[25]

The advantages of a hospital, however, were not lost on the people
of Newark, and within five years of the closing of Ward Hospital, three
private hospitals were established. Saint Barnabas, which was affiliated
with the Episcopal Church, was opened in 1865 but was not incorporated until 1867. Its founders were so anxious to have a permanent general hospital in the city that rather than wait until they had the means to
erect a large, modern facility, they rented a small suite of rooms in the
upper story of a building on McWhorter Street, which they converted
into a makeshift hospital. In its first partial year of operation the hospital cared for only twenty-one patients. In 1867 the hospital was moved
to a new location, which, while it accommodated a few more patients,
was still unsuitable, since the building was cold and drafty and without
water closets.[26]

For several years thereafter, St. Barnabas was confronted with a
chronic shortage of money. Lacking an endowment, the hospital had to
survive on the meager funds raised by subscriptions, charity collections, gifts from local businesses, and the annual Saint Barnabas Charity Ball. To keep operating costs low, women volunteers did all of the
housekeeping and nursing until 1875, as well as much of the fund
raising.[27]

Saint Barnabas sought to improve its financial position by selling
hospital insurance. The plan, which was offered to manufacturers, railroad corporations, workers' associations, and benefit societies, made
available to subscribers the use of one bed for an annual payment
of three hundred dollars. "Hospital clubs," it advised, "may thus be
formed and the members will be relieved from all anxiety in case of accident or sickness."[28] But the response was not encouraging and the

hospital's financial difficulties continued. In the year June 1869–June 1870, it incurred $3,825 in expenses in treating seventy-four patients, of which $1,520 was collected from patients and the rest from contributors. Determined to press ahead with plans for improving the hospital despite its monetary problems, the trustees in 1870 announced that an eye and ear infirmary and a clinic for diseases of women and children would soon be opened two days a week to provide medical care for outpatients.[29]

In 1870, with the help of a substantial gift, a much larger building with room for thirty-five beds was built at Montgomery and High streets close to the center of town. In its first twelve months of operation in its new home, the hospital treated twice as many patients as in the previous year.[30] According to the chaplain, the Reverend Joseph H. Smith, most of the patients were "destitute and friendless strangers in the city."[31] In addition, there were a large number of accident victims. The general usefulness of the hospital to the community was enhanced in 1871 by the opening of a lying-in ward. In the year June 1873–June 1874, Saint Barnabas admitted 262 patients, of whom 155 were of American or British nativity.[32] The depression of the mid-1870s brought to a halt further enlargements and it was not until 1883 that there was enough money available for a much-needed new building. The new facility contained an administrative wing and a three-story hospital wing. The hospital building contained wards, clinics, operating rooms, and a dispensary, as well as a kitchen, a laundry, and a dining room.[33] The facilities were continually upgraded and by 1889 included steam heat and an elevator for stretcher patients.[34] The vision and faith of the Episcopalian clergy and laity had been vindicated. Starting with a seven-bed hospital in a cramped, rented apartment, they had managed through perseverance and hard work to give Newark a hospital of which it could be proud.

In 1867 the Sisters of the Poor of Saint Francis, a Catholic order, opened a medical facility that in 1871 became incorporated as Saint Michael's Hospital. As in the case of Saint Barnabas, the sisters started their hospital in rented quarters at 69 Bleecker Street with thirteen beds and a staff of two physicians and five nursing sisters. In 1869 a site was acquired at Central Avenue and High Street for a 100-bed hospital. Initially the sisters attempted to raise the money at a public meeting held on April 26. But the meeting was poorly attended and only ten thousand dollars of the needed fifty thousand dollars was secured. A week later it was announced in all the Catholic churches of the city that an immediate effort would be made to raise the needed money. The plan called for a fair, a general subscription, and a monthly subscription taken up through the sale of books in the sums of five dollars, two dollars, one dollar, fifty and twenty-five cents. Priests urged their parishioners to give the matter their prompt attention, for the laying of the cornerstone was planned for September 29. The Catholic community more than met the challenge, and in 1871 a 150-bed hospital, the largest one in the city until the establishment of Newark City Hospital a little more than a decade later, was opened to the public.[35]

Many Catholics in Newark could not wait until 1871. The demand for hospital treatment among Catholics was so great it was decided to establish enlarged temporary hospital quarters while work on the new building proceeded. In the spring of 1869, the hospital was moved into a house and stable located on the new site. The house was furnished with forty beds and the hay loft of the stable was converted into housing for the sisters. While at this site, the hospital added three outpatient clinics, one for eye and ear diseases, one for treatment of diseases of the throat and chest, and one for skin diseases. Both the hospital and the clinics were overwhelmed by patients and had to turn people away daily. As it had done before with regard to parochial education, the Roman Catholic Church asked the common council to appropriate ten thousand dollars for Saint Michael's. The measure was opposed by the *Newark Daily Advertiser* on the grounds that the Constitution forbade public aid to any religion. The *Advertiser* contended that unavoidably a church-run hospital, even one like Saint Michael's, which accepted persons without regard to religion, nationality, or race, would propagate the faith of that particular church. The common council agreed and the measure was defeated.[36]

In its first year of operation in its new building Saint Michael's treated a thousand patients, of whom half were born in Ireland. An almost equal number of persons visited the hospital clinics: eye and ear, 748; throat and chest, 156; and skin, 63.[37] The largely working-class population served by Saint Michael's led it to specialize in the treatment of traumatic injuries.

> Many emergency cases were brought to St. Michael's, results of both accidents and acts of violence, reflecting the industrial and population expansion of the city of Newark. Bullets were removed, concussions treated, and victims of burns and explosions salvaged. One man's knee was reset after he had injured it in falling from an elevator; another man had his life saved by the amputation of a foot after a freight train had run over him. Lives were saved and injuries healed in most cases; there were of course cases in which lives could not be saved.[38]

With the development of antiseptic surgery, improvements in anesthesia, and the growth of medical specialties that relied on sophisticated instruments for peering into organs and measuring bodily functions, medicine was becoming hospital centered. Thus, in addition to its emergency medical care, Saint Michael's was best known for its eye and ear department. In 1879, 5,729 patients were treated in Saint Michael's, of which 2,388 were eye and ear cases. By 1888 the medical staff of Saint Michael's had grown to ten persons, including two house physicians, two house surgeons, and the first hospital-employed microscopist in Newark.[39]

The opening of Saint Barnabas and Saint Michael's, hospitals that served principally the Anglo-Saxon and Irish communities, respectively, aroused the German population to establish a hospital of its own. Newark's Germans were still smarting from their exclusion from the drive to establish a public hospital in the 1850s. There had not been a single German name among the 114 persons who had issued the first call for a municipal hospital.[40]

There were other voices, however, seeking to establish a public hospital that would serve the entire city. Immigrant participation in the Civil War had led to a decline in anti-German feeling, and when a German hospital association was formed in June 1866 the dormant Newark Hospital Association sought its cooperation in a joint hospital venture.[41]

Unsure as to the sincerity of this new spirit of brotherly cooperation,

German leaders decided to give the plan its support but to keep their fund raising separate. By March 1867 the German solicitors had received more than five thousand dollars in pledges. The Newark Hospital Association, on the other hand, was only able to raise sixteen hundred dollars, in addition to about another forty-five hundred that had been previously pledged. Dismayed by the lack of progress of their associates, the Germans decided to revert back to their original plan for a community-based hospital. At a meeting held on January 19, 1868, attended by representatives of sixty-two lodges, singing societies, and turnvereins, Newark German Hospital was officially launched.[42]

As was true of Saint Barnabas and Saint Michael's, securing adequate financial support was a pressing problem; moreover, not being church affiliated, German Hospital could not rely on the collection plate or church volunteers to raise money. When German benevolent societies refused to deplete their treasuries to finance the hospital, it was decided to stage "a monster fair" the following spring. Despite competition from the New Jersey State Agricultural Society's annual fair and a local billiards match, the event, which ran from May 18 to 26, raised $7,575.[43]

The next step was to pick a site for the hospital. A proposed site near the corner of Brome and Montgomery streets in the heart of the Hill district was rejected when residents of the area protested that the hospital would lower property values and might prove to be a nuisance and a health hazard. Instead a location on West Bank Street between Wallace and Newton streets in the northwest end of the district was chosen. The hospital work was contracted out for a little less than nineteen thousand dollars, about five thousand dollars more than the trustees had in their treasury. To make up the difference, the hospital association resorted to other money-raising projects, including the use of "Hospital Fund" boxes, which were placed in businesses and professional offices around the city. The cornerstone of the hospital was laid on September 14, 1869, and the hospital was officially opened during the 1870 Christmas holiday season. The Reverend Frederick August Lehlbach proudly announced at the dedication that German Hospital would admit the afflicted of every class on a nonsectarian basis.[44]

But though its doors remained open to everyone, it was principally a

hospital run for and by Germans. Of the 2,167 sick and injured patients
cared for during its first eight years of operation, 1,527 were born in
Germany. The funds for running the hospital came almost entirely from
German sources. All of the physicians on the staff when the hospital
opened were German, and the first nurses were recruited from the
famed Institute for Protestant Deaconesses in Kaiserwerth, Germany.[45]

The quality of medical care provided at the hospital ranked with the
best to be found anywhere. Many of the staff members had been trained
in Berlin and Vienna, where they studied under the world's leading
medical scientists. At a time when the relationship between disease and
microorganisms was only beginning to be recognized, German doctors
were among the first to apply the teachings of the British surgeon
Joseph Lister on the occurrence and prevention of postoperative infection. German Hospital was the first hospital in Newark to insist on antiseptic measures in surgery. Its physicians also pioneered a number of
difficult operations, including the first cesarean section in Newark and
the first successful operation in the United States for resection of the
bowels.[46]

Most of the patients treated at the hospital were either accident victims or persons suffering from acute communicable diseases. Unlike
Saint Barnabas and Saint Michael's, which doubled as sanatoriums,
German Hospital was intended to be strictly a therapeutic facility.
Chronically ill patients or terminal cases were discouraged from ap-
plying but might be admitted if "exceptional necessity or humanity
demanded it." While statistics on the kinds of illnesses treated at the
hospital during its early years are sketchy, the age and sex composision
of the patients indicates that most of them were there because of work
injuries. Of the first 100 patients admitted, 78 were men and nearly
two-thirds were in their twenties and thirties. In 1884, 560 patients
were treated, about one-fifth the number admitted to the hospital department of Saint Michael's, but more than were treated in Saint
Barnabas.[47]

The hospital continually flirted with financial insolvency, "only to
be saved by the heroics of the singing societies, the German lodge
members, and the Frauen Verein."[48] To meet expenses, the hospital

endeavored to get nonindigent patients to pay their own way. In its first year nearly two-thirds of the patients paid their bills in full, enabling the hospital to show a small surplus. But because of its restricted financial base and the hard times ushered in by the depression of 1873, the hospital was unable to significantly expand its operations for over a decade.[49]

The prosperity of the 1880s brought about an improvement in the hospital's finances. The city government for some time had been paying for municipal charity patients treated in the hospital, and voluntary giving became more generous. A legacy of five thousand dollars left to the hospital by a wealthy donor in 1884 provided it with a windfall, which the medical staff wanted to use to enlarge the hospital. The additions ended up costing twenty-four thousand dollars, sixteen thousand more than the cost of the original hospital. Still, few persons complained about the cost. The new facilities afforded patients the use of private rooms, "such as can be found in New York," with which to lure paying patients, on whom private hospitals were becoming increasingly dependent. Of greater importance to the community, a children's ward for contagious diseases, the first facility of its kind in Newark, was opened, and in 1893 a nursing school was established.[50]

Medical treatment and nursing care in Newark were also provided in a few other institutions. To begin with, there was the Home for Incurables and Convalescents, a private forty-eight-bed facility for women. Saint James Hospital was opened in the late 1880s but was not incorporated until 1891. Finally there were the almshouse and the isolation hospital located on the meadows. In 1887 the almshouse housed nearly two hundred inmates, whereas the isolation hospital was used only during smallpox epidemics.[51]

THROUGH GREAT EFFORT, AND WITH VIRTUALLY no government support, private individuals motivated by religious faith, humanitarianism, and ethnic and civic pride had succeeded in establishing three private hospitals in Newark. The energy and resourcefulness displayed by these citizens is in direct contrast to the lethargy of public officials. While private hospitals sought to enlarge and modernize their facilities despite having to scrape and beg just to meet their operating expenses, the municipal government used lack of money as an excuse for not doing anything. For nearly two decades following the Civil War, the government of Newark did not undertake any new medical services for its rapidly growing industrial population. The government's unwillingness to establish a hospital during this period of critical need is testimony to its indifference to the suffering of the sick poor.

The establishment of private hospitals did lead indirectly to the development of a municipally supported clinic for treating eye and ear diseases. In 1880 a dispute at Saint Michael's Hospital led to the resignation of thirteen members of the medical board, including both oculists. At the time Saint Michael's was the only hospital in Newark that treated eye and ear disorders, and it was feared that without proper medical treatment many persons would become blind or deaf or else have their hearing or vision impaired to the point that they would be unemployable. To prevent this from happening, a group of prominent businessmen under the leadership of Dr. Charles J. Kipp organized the Newark Charitable Eye and Ear Infirmary.[52]

In its first eleven months of operation $2,395 was raised by voluntary subscription, with the city providing $278 to make up the deficit. Private support for the infirmary slackened during the following year and the city had to start providing about half of its support. In 1884 the infirmary treated 3,476 cases, including 472 operations, of which 25 were for cataracts. The clinic claimed to be one of the largest of its kind in the nation.[53]

Throughout the 1860s, 1870s, and early 1880s the majority of Newark's indigent sick remained dependent on the city dispensary for their medical care. In 1870, to accommodate the growing number of persons seeking medical assistance, the dispensary was moved from the basement in city hall to more spacious offices at Centre Market. The new facility was not much of an improvement, and in 1876 a newspaperman reported that the dispensary was constantly filled with from twenty to fifty persons, mainly women, patiently waiting in line to have their prescriptions filled.[54]

Public use of the dispensary grew rapidly in the late 1870, reaching a peak in 1878 when over 70,500 persons were cared for in a city of less than 140,000. Of this number, 54,999 had prescriptions filled, 1,616 had teeth extracted, and 186 were vaccinated. To meet the increased demand for medical service, the dispensary's hours were extended on weekdays to from 7:00 A.M. to 5:00 P.M., and for the first time the dispensary was opened on Saturday from 8:00 A.M. to 2:00 P.M. In addition there were daily clinics in the morning run by two physicians who donated their time gratis.[55]

Municipal leaders did not view the increased use of the dispensary as an indication of the need for more and better medical facilities. To the contrary, they regarded it as evidence of abuse of the city's medical charities. To hold down expenses and to prevent conflict with private physicians, stringent "reforms" were undertaken. The new rules stipulated that persons seeking free medical treatment first present themselves to the dispensary pharmacist, who would certify their financial eligibility. The maximum anyone could earn and still qualify for aid was ten dollars per week. Despite these precautions, it was widely believed that many individuals were receiving aid unjustly. The *Newark Daily Advertiser* reported that one favorite ruse used by "these people" was to get the district physicians to treat them in their homes on the pretext that they were too sick to travel, since doctors in responding to an emergency call would be less likely to check for eligibility than the staff at the dispensary.[56]

From the government's standpoint, the crackdown proved very effective. In 1879 there were twenty-three thousand fewer prescriptions filled than in the previous year, and in 1882 still thirty-four thousand less than that. The annual report of the dispensary for 1882 noted with satisfaction that the entire cost of the dispensary was "but about $2,200 per year, and although applications for relief have increased 75 per cent, the sum is much less than it was a few years ago."[57]

THE CITY'S PRIMARY HEALTH CARE NEED IN THE years after the Civil War was a large public hospital. In 1870 the city acquired a hospital site on Fairmount Avenue and it appeared that a hospital would soon be built. Shortly thereafter, however, Essex

County was notified by the state that its quota of lunatics in the Trenton asylum was oversubscribed and no new patients would be admitted. Since immediate action was required, the city agreed to turn over its hospital site to the county for use as an insane asylum. In the summer of 1872 the building was opened with about thirty patients in residence sent there from the Newark almshouse and more on the way expected from Trenton.[58]

At about this time, Newark's three private hospitals were moving into new buildings, temporarily alleviating the shortage of hospital beds, and for the next decade the city was content to rely on private charities to provide this basic service. Beginning in the early 1870s the city gave each hospital a yearly appropriation to reserve a fixed number of beds for the use of patients chosen by the overseer of the poor. In 1882 the city rented thirty beds for nine thousand dollars, which were used to care for 489 patients.[59]

The *Newark Daily Advertiser* believed that public aid to church-affiliated institutions violated the separation of church and state provision of the Constitution and therefore sought the establishment of a municipal hospital. Finally in 1882 the Common Council Committee on Poor and Alms converted a wing of the almshouse into a hospital. Thus thirty-eight years after the subject of a public hospital was first considered, Newark City Hospital came into being. The first annual report of the board of directors stated that the hospital was to be "devoted exclusively to the treatment and relief of the indigent sick and disabled." The charity stigma attached to the hospital was further apparent in its location in an institution designed to hide society's castoffs.[60]

The parsimony that characterized all public services for the poor hobbled Newark City Hospital from its inception. The hospital was put into service at a cost of less than two thousand dollars. Hence, although it had the room to accommodate seventy-five patients, it only had the money to maintain twenty-four beds. The city received a substantial gift in 1884 when the county decided to erect a new insane asylum on South Orange Avenue to replace the one it had been using on Fairmount Avenue. In the twelve years the asylum had been open it had grown to 250 beds. The county, which had been renting the land on which the asylum stood for a nominal fee, now paid back to the city the money it had saved by giving it the vacated building for its new hospital. The gift came at a fortuitous time, for in the next thirty years Newark would be swamped with thousands of impoverished Italian, Jewish, and Slavic immigrants who would pack Newark City Hospital to the rafters.[61]

Lack of adequate facilities for treating the sick poor was only one indicator of the city's business orientation. The material progress of Newark during the late nineteenth century had been purchased at the cost of a ravaged environment and an increase in morbidity and mortality. In 1883, alarm over the city's worsening sanitary condition led one Newark newspaper to declare: "Our weekly mortality reports show the outbreaks from time to time of preventable diseases in certain quarters, easily traceable to direct violations of the rules of health, and the ratio of death is generally above the average of our sister cities. If further evidence were needed we have only to use our eyes and noses to discover abounding causes."[62]

Any concern for the hazards of rapid, unplanned growth was sacrified in the pursuit of profits and growth. With growth had come discomfort and disease. The water supply was drawn from the polluted Passaic River, and sewers emptied into sluggish tidal creeks not far from major centers of population. The smell of excreta decomposing in the sun, and of the Passaic River when the water level was low, forced residents to keep their windows closed on even the most uncomfortable summer nights. From spring through fall hordes of mosquitoes took flight from the meadows, making life in the city at night unbearable. The death rate hovered at about 25 per 1,000 population, and at no time before 1895 was it less than 20 per 1,000 population. Three times during the 1870s the mortality rate reached 30 per 1,000 population as a result of epidemics of smallpox and diphtheria.[63]

Tuberculosis was preeminently the disease of the Industrial Revolution. In the dingy sweatshops, the dusty factories, the sunless and ill-ventilated tenements, and wherever else the working poor were found, the disease flourished. Few among the poor had the physical strength to withstand an attack of the white plague. The physical and spiritual exhaustion brought on by malnutrition and oppressive living conditions rendered the poor easy prey. In 1881 tuberculosis accounted for about 16 percent of Newark's fatalities.[64]

The association of tenement housing with tuberculosis was attested to by the census of 1890. The three wards in Newark with tuberculosis death rates of over 400 per 100,000 population were described as follows: "a manufacturing section, with residents in very moderate circumstances"; "principally cheap tenements occupied, for the great part, by Irish"; "principally tenements of a poor class." By way of contrast, the Eighth Ward, which had the lowest death rate, 229.89 per 100,000 population, was said to contain "a mixed population of the middle class plus the finest residential section of the city."[65]

Water supply was a problem that affected equally all segments of society. In need of a vastly enlarged water supply, Newark turned to the Passaic River at the very same time (1870) that communities and factories located along the waterway started using it as a repository for their wastes. A contaminated water supply coupled with faulty sewerage led to an increase in the incidence of waterborne diseases. Gastrointestinal ailments beset citizens, and the typhoid fever mortality rate arched steadily upward until it attained a height municipal leaders could not ignore with impunity.[66]

The innocent suffered the most from Newark's negligence. Diseases of infancy were the city's leading cause of death. Infant deaths in 1881 accounted for 21 percent of all Newark fatalities. Almost two of every ten infants died before their first birthday.[67] The reasons for this unusually high mortality rate were apparent. The water used to wash the infant's bottle was polluted, and the milk on which the infant was weaned came from diseased and emaciated cows and was produced on dairies that, in their sanitary maintenance, resembled pigsties.

Judging from the mortality and morbidity statistics, children must have been continually sick. Measles, chicken pox, mumps, rubella, whooping cough, scarlet fever, and diphtheria were rampant, and it was a rare mother who could not recount the ages at which her children had come down with red spots, pustules, or swollen glands. Scarlet fever and diphtheria caused the greatest anxiety and grief. Acute infectious diseases of childhood, together with malaria, typhoid fever, and smallpox, were responsible in 1881 (a nonepidemic year) for one-seventh of all fatalities. Respiratory illnesses affected all ages and accounted for about 12 percent of Newark's mortality. Other important causes of death included brain and spinal diseases and diseases of the heart and circulatory system. Rabies continued to claim a few victims each year until the mid-1880s, when the first Americans began to undergo the vaccination treatment developed by Louis Pasteur for persons bitten by rabid animals.[68]

PARSIMONY AND PARTISANSHIP AT ONE TIME OR another imperiled every city service. "Police and fire departments were dangerously undermanned and subjected to such petty political control that they verged often on the edge of breakdown."[69] The common council, which until 1891 retained control of most administrative services, lacked the expertise demanded by the increasing complexity of urban government. Though Newark was relatively free of graft and corruption, at least when compared to its neighbors, city services failed to keep pace with municipal growth. There were simply too many improvements to be made at a time when the paramount concern of the city fathers was to keep taxes low so as to attract new business. Those services that were provided were unplanned.[70]

Newark's patchwork administrative services and niggardly attitude toward public improvements caused it to become one of the nation's more unsanitary cities. Only 49 miles of sewers existed in Newark in 1883, as contrasted with 131 miles of improved streets. About two-thirds of the city's residents, including a great number of those living in the central downtown area, were dependent on privies and cesspools. A sanitary investigation made that year disclosed the widespread existence of broken drains, garbage-strewn streets, and gutters made repulsive by kitchen slops and washwater.[71]

The filth that befouled Newark was not only unsightly, it was dangerous. Many of the privies were made of wood or had open bottoms and sides, permitting their contents to contaminate the surrounding soil. As a result, persons who drank from wells were stricken with dysentery and typhoid fever. Newark's poor sanitary state is particularly revealing of the low regard in which life was held by municipal leaders, since it was believed then that decomposing filth was responsible for high mortality rates.[72]

Newark lacked the imagination and boldness displayed by other cities in meeting urban problems. The temper of the community was too conservative for its own welfare. Aside from business matters, moral and religious issues dominated the public forum. Thus, when German residents attempted to visit beer gardens and stage festivals on the Sabbath, they incurred the wrath of Protestant ministers. A bitter controversy ensued, and for a number of years the issue was the focal point of the mayoral elections.[73] While Newarkers wrestled with their consciences, they lived in filth; blue laws, Prohibition,[74] and other such moral dilemmas weighed more heavily on their minds than the thousand persons who perished yearly from preventable diseases.

5 BOARD OF HEALTH

STRUGGLE FOR SURVIVAL AND STATUS

FOR OVER TWO DECADES FOLLOWING ITS CREATION IN
1857, the Newark Board of Health, which had the responsibility of
overseeing sanitary conditions, was moribund. The average annual ex-
penditure of the board during the years 1870–1880 was nine thousand
dollars, or barely seven cents per capita. A corporal's guard of one
meat inspector and four sanitary inspectors made up the field force of
the department. Inspections were made only upon complaint; the board
made no independent investigations of its own. Even when nuisances
were uncovered, prosecution of malefactors was haphazard.[1] The secretary of the American Public Health Association in 1875 reported that
Newark's sanitary governance was "a fiction."[2]

Politics partly accounted for the board of health's ineffectiveness.
Political retainers were put to work as nuisance abaters and street clean-
ers. Men without the intelligence or agility to be schoolteachers, policemen, or firemen were given jobs pushing brooms and loading carts.
Appointment to the department was made on the basis of whom, rather
than what, one knew. Because every change in political administration
witnessed a large turnover in personnel, the department was saddled
with a succession of incompetent inspectors.[3] In 1883 Newark's health
officer was quoted as saying that the men employed in his department
were "totally unfit to perform the duties . . . assigned to them."[4]

The board of health was also hamstrung by legal restrictions on its
nuisance-abating powers, for though the board was authorized to abate
nuisances, it could not define their existence. To remove a nuisance not
expressly covered in the statutes, the board had to secure a special legislative enactment or was constrained to prove in court that the alleged
nuisance endangered the public health. In court "the defendants in the
case would appeal and appeal until all the good that might have been

done, and evil avoided by quick decisive action would be abrogated, and perhaps an epidemic or pestilence fostered by the want of action."[5] Without summary powers to define and abate nuisances, the board could do little to improve the sanitary conditions of the city.

The circumscribed powers of the Newark Board of Health are indicative of the business orientation of municipal health work in the mid-nineteenth century. Antebellum municipal boards of health, as Alan I. Marcus has shown, had a limited purpose: to ward off or blunt the impact of an anticipated epidemic that threatened to disrupt the business life of the community. During the long periods between epidemics boards of health met infrequently or not at all and their powers were largely restricted to investigating violations of nuisance ordinances reported by private citizens. Boards of health only became active when pestilential diseases such as cholera, yellow fever, and, to a lesser extent, smallpox caused persons to curtail their normal business activities. At such times boards of health were given emergency powers to cleanse the city, to quarantine ships in the harbor, and to isolate the stricken. Once the epidemic subsided, these powers lapsed and the boards of health ceased to function.[6] Marcus comments that "unlike the health agencies of the twentieth century, those of the early 1800s sought not to prevent disease or to promote health, but only to restore cities to their customary state,"[7] so that citizens would be able to pursue their fortunes once again.

Southern municipal leaders were confronted with a menace that did not exist in the North after 1830: yellow fever. A New Orleans physician estimated that the disease cost the city over forty-five million dollars from 1846 to 1850. Yellow fever killed twenty thousand New Orleaneans during the 1850s and, more damaging to the city's future, induced western merchants to take their business to Saint Louis and Chicago, whose railroads gained control of much of New Orleans' river-based commerce. It took Norfolk five years to recover the population and business loss sustained in the yellow fever epidemic of 1855. The psychological damage done to residents' confidence in the future of their city was more long-lasting.[8]

Southern boards of health sought to control yellow fever through quarantine and cleanup campaigns, but evidence of their effectiveness was not compelling. Savannah's experience with yellow fever provided a case in point. Savannah was one of the few American cities that sought to protect itself against acute, communicable diseases through long-range health planning. Between 1817 and 1820 the marshes surrounding the city were drained and rice-growing areas were placed in dry culture. Nevertheless, in the following decades yellow fever continued to ravage the city without letup; however, the death rate from "autumnal diseases" declined sharply.[9]

The inability of southern boards of health to prevent yellow fever epidemics led political officials to take a practical view of the business of health. City officials undertook health improvements on a simple cost-benefit basis. They were reluctant to spend large sums of money on sanitation even though this course of action was recommended by medical authorities, since it did not appear to be effective against yellow fever, the disease that most threatened their cities' economic welfare. They only did so in the midst of a severe epidemic when their businesses and lives were imperiled and when citizens' entreaties compelled them to do something.[10]

Since one city's health disaster might work to another city's economic advantage, municipal leaders sought to contain the damage done by epidemic diseases by resorting to public relations campaigns to protect their city's reputation for salubrity. News of cholera and yellow fever outbreaks were suppressed for as long as possible and when the disease's presence was acknowledged its victims were said to be mainly northerners and immigrants who were unacclimated to the region's debilitating climate.[11]

The rapid growth of cities in the nineteenth century caused serious health problems that local authorities were ill prepared to handle. During the 1800s British and American cities became congested and dirty as municipal services failed to keep pace with population growth. Animal carcasses and household wastes littered the streets and the poor were compelled to live in dark, crowded quarters without running water or other basic sanitary amenities. Decaying organic filth and the miserable living conditions of the poor provided a nursery for acute, communicable diseases. During the nineteenth century, English-speaking cities on both sides of the Atlantic Ocean were savaged by epidemic diseases. Municipal death rates rose steeply and when cholera or yellow fever was present the number of deaths was often extraordinarily high.[12]

High urban mortality rates were a matter of great concern to British reformers, especially Edwin Chadwick. A lawyer who had become interested in the causes and management of poverty, Chadwick in 1832 was appointed to a royal commission to revise the English poor law. The new poor law was harsh, its underlying principle deterrence. Outdoor relief was done away with, and the lot of an able-bodied pauper was to be made worse than that of the poorest self-supporting laborer. The new act also endeavored to secure uniformity and efficiency. A central Poor Law Commission was established to guide local officials in administering the act.[13]

It occurred to Chadwick that poverty—and the taxes needed to support the poor—could be reduced by shielding the poor from the "fevers" and other incapacitating diseases that were prevalent in working-class neighborhoods. In accordance with the miasmatic theory of disease, it was strongly suspected at the time that the high incidence of disease among the poor was related to the environmental degradation of their surroundings. The problem now became one of connecting disease to poor living conditions using statistics. The instrument chosen for this task was the sanitary survey. As secretary of the Poor Law Commission, Chadwick directed extensive surveys of the living conditions of the British working class. The surveys provided the basis for the recommendations of the commission and were contained in a summary document that appeared in 1842: *Report . . . on an Inquiry into the Sanitary Condition of the Labouring Population of Great Britain.*

The third and synoptical volume of this landmark work was written by Chadwick. It furnished incontrovertible evidence that communicable diseases occurred most often where filth and poverty prevailed. Over and over again poor drainage, a polluted water supply, and lack of sanitary means of removing bodily and household wastes were positively correlated with sickness and shortened lives. Moreover, overcrowding, poverty, intemperance, prostitution, crime, and ill health were shown to be linked so that an improvement in the health of the poor would also bring about an improvement in their moral and social behavior. "Chadwick and his collaborators took the survey and employed it to focus attention on the need for sanitary reform and to emphasize the importance of a systematic study of health problems as a basis for administrative action."[14] For the next forty to fifty years the Chadwick report, embracing what became known as the sanitary idea, was used as a model by public health workers in England and America.[15]

For a variety of reasons the public health issue failed to ignite in the United States. The Industrial Revolution came to America later than it did England. American cities were less congested. Other reform movements such as Prohibition, prison reform, women's rights, public education, better treatment of the mentally ill, and, most important of all, abolitionism, held the nation's attention.[16] Moreover, in the United States responsibility for public health rested with state and local governments. Campaigns to educate the public about the need for sanitary reform and legislative battles to overcome the opposition of vested interest groups had to be waged in every jurisdiction, whereas "England with its compact territory and its centralized government could cut the Gordian knot of sanitary reform at one stroke."[17] Then, too, America was a frontier society with weak, limited governments. Hence few antebellum cities established permanent boards of health. When threatened by an epidemic, communities that did not have boards of health appointed temporary health committees and entrusted them with sweeping sanitary powers. Garbage was removed from the city, slaughterhouses were cleaned, and privies and cesspools were disinfected with lime. However, the health committees' authority ended with the passing of the epidemic, at which point sanitary conditions began to slip back to what they had been earlier. Despite the establishment of a far-reaching sanitary reform movement in England in the mid-nineteenth century, there was little improvement in municipal sanitation in the United States until after the Civil War.[18]

The only antebellum city that had a professional health officer was Providence, Rhode Island, which appointed Edwin M. Snow to the job in 1856. A physician who was proficient in the collection and analysis of vital statistics, Snow's annual published reports set a standard for professionalism in public health work for nearly thirty years.[19]

But it was a standard few American public health officers were able to attain because of the intrusion of partisan politics and the spoils system into the work of municipal health departments. Boards of health often had only advisory powers and were subject to political control. Health inspectors were selected from among the party faithful and as a rule were grossly incompetent.[20] Dorman B. Eaton, a lawyer who helped draft the law establishing the New York Metropolitan Board of Health in 1866, later recalled that at mid-century the New York City Department of Health was so riddled with corruption and patronage that "mayors of New York, by no means scrupulous or timid, did not dare for a whole term to even call a meeting of the N.Y. Board of Health; that of 48 health wardens and assistants, more than half were keepers of corner groggeries (the other half were partizan [sic] repeaters and bullies); and that nearly the whole sanitary force of the city was in reality a scandal and a peril to a civilized community."[21]

In the early 1860s a Citizens' Association consisting of one hundred prominent New Yorkers was organized to oppose "boss" William Tweed and his Tammany Hall gang of thieves and spoilsmen. The Citizens' Association organized a Committee on Public Health to lend support to efforts already under way to wrest control of health services from corrupt politicians by establishing a metropolitan board of health for New York City and outlying districts that would be controlled by physicians and other public health professionals.[22]

In order to document the city's poor health conditions the Committee on Public Health undertook a sanitary survey, which was published in full in 1865. The city health inspector, a Tammany appointee, denied that the city was without sanitary protection against disease and either convinced or bribed enough state legislators to prevent any changes from being made in New York City's health governance. The matter aroused considerable public interest, and several legislators who had voted against reform were defeated in the next election. Luckily for the reformers, cholera reappeared in New York City in 1866, stirring up memories of past visitations and the health department's inability to contain the pestilence. Fear of cholera accomplished what the reformers could not. The Citizens' Association bill, which provided for the establishment of a metropolitan board of health, passed the legislature on its third try in 1866. Because of the energetic work of the new board, the death rate from cholera that year was a small fraction of what it had been in previous epidemics. For the first time an American community had turned back an onslaught of cholera. The success of the board had ramifications far beyond New York, for it provided the impetus to the creation of municipal and state health departments throughout the nation.[23]

Ironically, though the establishment of the New York Metropolitan Board of Health in 1866 was a pivotal point in the history of American public health, the board lasted only four years. In 1870 Tammany succeeded in excluding New York City from the Metropolitan Health District, and the politically subservient New York City Board of Health was reestablished. Thereafter the board of health was only effective during the brief periods when reformers were in power in the city or when the "boss" found it politically expedient to support the board.[24]

New York City's experience was paralleled in other cities where the political machine was entrenched, which is to say nearly everywhere. The Cincinnati Board of Health was long composed of one physician and five saloonkeepers. In Philadelphia most of the persons in city government entrusted with responsibility for municipal sanitation and public health were political appointees who had little knowledge of sanitary science and preventive medicine. The Citizens' Association of Philadelphia, in its annual report for 1871, "stated that the Board of Health was not competent to carry out its duties."[25]

The status of municipal health departments did not improve appreciably in the decades that followed. Throughout the late nineteenth century boards of health were dominated by patronage-seeking politicians. Some boards did not have any physician members and almost none operated without political interference. In his 1895 address to the Second Annual Conference of the National Municipal League, John Shaw Billings, one of the country's most distinguished physicians, stated that health officials were appointed and removed from office because of their political affiliations and not because of their knowledge or performance. Billings stressed the importance of assigning responsibility for public health to trained professionals and urged his audience to raise the salaries of health department employees to attract competent people.[26]

Five years later, Dr. Charles V. Chapin, Snow's successor in Providence and the nation's foremost authority on municipal public health, observed that the terms of health officials were short and restricted by politics. He attributed much of the blame for the lack of professionalism in public health to the common belief that public service required no special training: "Unfortunately the idea that fitness is a matter to be at all considered in appointments to office is somewhat rare among the every day citizen as well as among those who are active in political life; . . . The common notion is that one man is as good as another, and that in a democracy everybody ought to have a chance at public honor and emolument."[27] Thus a perversion of the democratic creed led Americans to regard public health employment as simply another one of the spoils of public life.

In many cities the influence of partisan politics extended beyond the board of health to the sewer and water departments. In the early 1870s the District of Columbia squandered a five-million-dollar bond issue when, for political reasons, contractors built the main sewers on a higher grade level than the lateral sewers. Extensive changes had to be made in Cincinnati's sewer system and in Saint Louis's waterworks because both city administrations had rejected engineers' proposals in favor of less costly but politically popular alternatives.[28]

Gradually it was recognized, as Stanley K. Schultz and Clay McShane have written, that sanitary "public works could be built most efficiently by technological and managerial experts who could survey the topography, choose appropriate construction materials, and draw readily upon the experiences of their counterparts in other cities."[29] By the end of the nineteenth century, the details of sewer construction, as Chapin noted, were being "wisely left to the engineers."[30] Moreover, since a reputation for salubrity and modern public works figured prominently in urban economic rivalries, local politicians feared losing the services of skilled sanitary engineers to other cities and permitted them more autonomy than other municipal employees. Prominent waterworks engineers were given de facto tenure before civil service protection became available. "Labeling themselves neutral experts, engineers professed to work above the din of local politics. Usually they tried to isolate themselves from partisan wrangles, and often succeeded."[31]

There was less political interference in New England than in other parts of the country and a greater willingness to entrust sanitary and public health matters to persons with scientific training. Consequently, appointments to the Massachusetts State Board of Health and to the water and sewerage boards that served metropolitan Boston were based on merit. Barbara Rosenkrantz writes that in Massachusetts "the belief that public health was best protected by absolute isolation from the grime of politics became the hallmark of sanitary policy during the three decades following the reconstitution of an independent State Board of Health in 1886."[32] Similarly, in Providence, under the leadership of first Snow and then Chapin, political interference in public health administration was kept to a minimum.[33]

Besides the constraints imposed by politics, public health reform was impeded by the still widely held belief that the poor suffered from bad health mainly because of their intemperance and immorality. Furthermore, the environmental conditions that endangered the lives of city dwellers were regarded as unavoidable. Jacqueline K. Corn, Pittsburgh's public health historian, writes that "both the unsightly smoke and the dangerous factory conditions were accepted by the public as necessary outgrowths of the rapid industrial expansion of Pittsburgh."[34] Thus a combination of factors, including social attitudes toward disease, the belief that pollution was the price society had to pay for progress, political interference, inadequate financing, and lack of scientific knowledge thwarted the efforts of municipal health officials who sought to protect the public health.

The need for sanitary reform in Newark was increasingly commented upon during the 1870s and early 1880s. The mayor, in his annual message for 1870, and again in 1872, pleaded for greater powers for the board of health and a more liberal appropriation. He warned that the existence of stagnant ponds on vacant lots was "poisoning the atmosphere," and until such time as the board was given summary powers to abate nuisances, Newark would continue to suffer from "malarious diseases."[35] Lott Southard, the president of the Essex County Medical Society, estimated that one-third of Newark's mortality for 1876 had been caused by polluted water, foul air, and sewer gas, and hence need not have occurred.[36] In 1880 the powerful Newark Board of Trade revealed its dissatisfaction with the conduct of the board of health.[37]

Newark's mortality experience ran counter to the trend of urban

Table 1

General Death Rate of Northern and Western Cities, and Newark,
1871–1890 (Rate per 1,000 population)

YEAR	NORTHERN AND WESTERN CITIES	NEWARK	PERCENT IN EXCESS (LESS) OF NORTHERN AND WESTERN CITIES
1871	23.7	24.4	3
1872	28.7	34.0	18
1873	25.7	32.9	28
1874	23.7	28.7	2
1875	24.7	27.8	13
1876	24.0	30.0	25
1877	21.1	26.4	25
1878	20.2	24.3	20
1879	20.3	23.4	15
1880	22.0	18.7	(15)
1881	24.9	20.7	(17)
1882	24.6	27.4	11
1883	22.2	23.8	7
1884	21.9	22.5	3
1885	21.6	24.4	13
1886	21.4	23.1	8
1887	22.3	22.8	2
1888	22.0	24.4	11
1889	20.9	24.2	16
1890	21.5	27.2	27

SOURCE: Frederick L. Hoffman, "The General Death Rate of Large American Cities,
1871–1904," *Publications of the American Statistical Association* 10, n.s., no. 73 (March
1906):5, 49.

death rates in the late nineteenth century. In the years 1870–1890, death rates in American cities generally fell from approximately 25 to 30 per 1,000 population to about 20 to 25. Of the large urban centers, only some southern cities and Newark continued to have mortality rates of over 30 per 1,000 population. Newark's death rate exceeded that of comparable northern and western cities in eighteen of twenty years, sometimes by as much as 20 percent. Moreover, Newark's mortality rate was higher than it had been before the Civil War (see Table 1).[38]

The high mortality rates in southern cities was attributable to epidemics of yellow fever and malaria, the presence of a large black population, whose death rate greatly exceeded that of the white population, and the poverty and general backwardness of the South during this period. Newark's high mortality rate is not as easy to explain. Partly it may be accounted for by the city's rapid, unplanned growth after the Civil War. But other cities were also undergoing the trauma of industrialization and had large indigent immigrant populations. Some of Newark's health problems, such as malaria and a fecalized water supply, were rooted in the geography of the Newark area. But here again, Newark's situation was not unique, since many cities had sewage-polluted water supplies, though only a few cities outside of the South were still troubled by malaria.

Perhaps more significant in explaining Newark's unusually high death rate, the reporting of vital statistics in the late nineteenth century in most instances was neither accurate nor honest. There was widespread ignorance of, or indifference to, vital statistics on the part of lawmakers, physicians, and even public health officials. The 1880 U.S. Census death registration area, making up governmental units whose registration of deaths were reasonably accurate and complete (90 percent completeness became the standard), included only two states, Massachusetts and New Jersey, nineteen cities in other states, and the District of Columbia. Communities reluctant to admit to excessive deaths could easily distort their actual mortality experience. Certain cities went so far "as to exclude deaths from violence, suicide, and a number of other causes. . . . Other cities merely report 'officially' the local interments and exclude the deaths of persons whose bodies were shipped for burials elsewhere."[39] In the new cities of the West, civic

boosters commonly tampered with the vital statistics to produce a low
death rate. Finally, crude death rates must be used with care in making
comparisons, since they do not take into account the ethnic origins and
sex and age distribution of the population, though it does not appear
that the composition of Newark's population in these regards was
significantly different from that of other large northern and western
cities.[40]

Edgar Holden, the president of the board of directors of Mutual Benefit Life Insurance Company, laid bare Newark's poor health record in
his treatise *Mortality and Sanitary Record of Newark, New Jersey*
[1859–1879]. Holden attributed Newark's high mortality rate to an
excessive occurrence of preventable diseases. Zymotic[41] diseases
(mainly acute, communicable illnesses), lung ailments, and bowel diseases figured prominently in this category. Stating that for a while he
had considered establishing a citizens' committee to promote sanitary
reform, as had been done to such good effect in New York City,
Holden urged instead that the board of health be reconstituted and its
financial support increased.[42] "A well equipped Sanitary Bureau,"
Holden chided the Newark community, "is a necessity as it is a re-
finement and blessing of modern times, and it is but poorly to the credit
of a large manufacturing city that other and smaller towns have
throughout the United States availed themselves of the modern improvements for cleanliness and hygienic supervision before it."[43]

Meanwhile, the course of public health in Newark was being char-
tered in the state capitol in Trenton. New Jersey was rapidly becoming
urbanized. To meet the health problems attendant upon urbanization, in
the late 1870s and early 1880s New Jersey established a state board of
health and mandated the creation of local health units. In keeping with
the American tradition of city and county responsibility for the face-to-
face aspects of public health work, the local boards organized under
state law were given broad discretionary powers: to define and abate
nuisances, to regulate the keeping and slaughtering of animals, to aid in
enforcing state laws against adulterated food and drink, to regulate garbage disposal, to collect vital statistics, to oversee the connecting of indoor plumbing with sewers and cesspools, to close polluted wells, to
regulate the building and maintenance of privies, to protect water sup-

plies from pollution, and to supervise funerals. Existing boards of
health, upon the consent of the local governing authorities, could avail
themselves of these extensive powers by reorganizing under state
law.[44]

In Newark agitation for public health reform continued to smolder.
J. D. Brumley, the health physician (the chief executive officer) in his
annual report for 1881 complained of the "limited means and powers"
available to the board of health and remarked that the board had been
organized and its powers defined at a time when the city's population,
and consequently its sanitary needs, was much smaller than it was now.
Concerned citizens in 1883 organized the Newark Sanitary Association.[45] By now concern about the salubrity of the city was beginning to
find an outlet in the press. Echoing sentiments expressed by Dr. C. F.
Lehlbach in an address before the Newark Medical Association, the
Newark Daily Advertiser declared that Newark's death rate was generally higher than that of her neighbors and that the causes were evident
to all who could see or smell.[46]

Incensed over the odors from a fat-boiling factory and the unwillingness of the board of health to seek an injunction against the plant, residents of the Sixth Ward in 1883 organized the Sixth Ward Sanitary Association.[47] But proponents of sanitary reform did not acquire a really
effective voice until the Newark Daily Journal took up the cause in August and began featuring articles exposing the city's unsanitary condition and the threat it posed to the public health. The Journal published
the articles partly out of a sense of civic responsibility and partly for
political reasons. The Journal was the city's only Democratic newspaper and 1883 was an election year in Newark. After twenty years of Republican rule, the Democrats were presenting a strong challenge. Here
was an issue that could bring the Democrats back into power.

The articles[48] had their genesis in an accident in which three persons were drowned in a cesspool. The cesspool, which was thirteen
feet deep, was used by several families in two adjoining buildings. On
a hot summer day, when the stench from the cesspool had become intolerable, a resident of one of the buildings attempted to clean the tank
and was overcome by carbonic acid fumes. Two neighbors who attempted to rescue him also succumbed to the fumes. Two of the victims

were married and left behind ten children; the third victim was a boy of nineteen. The bodies were drawn to the surface with grappling irons, "the three ghastly corpses making a picture that never could be forgotten by those who witnessed it."[49] There were ten thousand cesspools in Newark, "each one of them," wrote the *Newark Daily Journal*, "a generator of disease and the cause of much of the sickness and death in the city." In an interview with the paper the health physician remarked that numerous cases of typhoid fever, scarlet fever, dysentery, diarrhea, cholera, and diphtheria could be traced to wells contaminated with seepage from fecal containers. "What profiteth a city though it swells its population and increases its wealth," questioned the *Journal*, "if it increases both the sick list and the death rate?"[50]

Attention was then focused on the method by which night soil was disposed of. Nearly two hundred thousand pounds of excreta were removed daily from Newark, most of it by the dipper and bucket method, an archaic operation that, the health physician asserted, had been abandoned by most cities over fifty years earlier. The excretus was removed by scavengers who sold part of it to farmers for fertilizer and disposed of the remainder as they saw fit. The board of health sought to set aside a dumping ground for night soil but was unsuccessful.[51]

Further sanitary investigations disclosed the existence of broken drains, mosquito-breeding ponds, and streets and yards overrun with mountains of rotting refuse. Newark's death rate, wrote the *Newark Daily Journal*, is "double if not treble what would be the rate if our sanitary condition was anything near perfection, and if our sewerage system and water supply were what they ought to be. . . . Were cholera to cross the Atlantic, [it] would find a rich harvesting ground here."[52]

Public accommodations were the next target of the *Journal*. A public urinal had been built on a section of the Old Burying Ground, "a place," reported the *Journal*, "that reeks with filth and upon whose walls are written the vilest obscenities." Perverts consorted in the area and the basins of the urinals overflowed, covering the floors with ankle-deep water. From a sanitary standpoint, conditions at Centre Market, which straddled the Morris Canal at Broad Street, were even worse. The walls near the butchers' side of the market were encrusted with blood, fat, and brine and emitted a rank odor. Chicken feathers soaked with blood and decaying fruits and vegetables littered the coops and stands. Outside, the sweepings of the market collected in pools among the cobblestones where they were allowed to decompose "for the benefit of the family living across the way."[53] Despite notices from the board of health, the *Journal* reported a month later that the market nuisances had grown worse and had caused some residents of the area to flee from their homes.[54]

The board of health heartily endorsed the work of the *Newark Daily Journal*. Sometimes in August the board, with daily press coverage from the *Journal*, began a house-to-house inspection in the more densely populated wards of the city. The board conducted the investigation in order to establish a correlation between unsanitary conditions and morbidity. In summing up the findings of the inquiry, the *Journal* remarked that "the Health Physician agrees with many other citizens in the belief that Newark should be one of the healthiest cities on the American continent, owing to its proximity to the sea, and otherwise favorable location; yet the average death rate is actually greater than that of New Orleans among the white population except in years when yellow fever or some other epidemic prevails."[55]

On October 10, 1883, the Democrats captured the mayor's office and won control of the common council. Among the reasons offered for the Democratic victory, the *Newark Evening News* suggested a "sanitary condition which [under Republican rule] has brought Newark to the unenviable position of being one of the most unhealthy cities in the Union."[56] Reorganization of the board of health was delayed, however, because the new mayor, Joseph E. Haynes, unexpectedly opposed it. Prior to his election Haynes had maintained a discreet silence on the subject. He now argued that the common council was armed with adequate authority to safeguard the health of the city. Haynes desired the retention of the existing board because he believed that an elective body was more amenable to the public will than an independent board, as provided for under state law. Nevertheless, he stated his willingness to reconstitute the board of health if events proved such a need.[57] Pressure from the city's newspapers, the board of health, and community organizations, coupled with fears of a cholera epidemic and some unfavorable court decisions, forced the mayor's hand, and in

May 1885 the Newark Board of Health was reorganized under state law.[58]

The Newark Board of Health, at long last, was armed to do battle with its eternal enemies, filth and disease. But before the board could effectively employ its new powers, it would have to free itself of political control. Moreover, the board would have to secure guarantees of adequate financial support and would have to assemble an administrative framework capable of supporting its efforts. A time of travail and fierce struggle to survive lay ahead for the board.

A year before its reorganization under state law, the composition of the Newark Board of Health had been changed. The nine-man board established in 1884, and which continued in existence thereafter, was made up of five members chosen by the mayor with the consent of the common council (three of whom were to be physicians in good standing in the Newark medical community), the three members of the Common Council Committee on Public Health, and the mayor. Haynes asserted in his annual messages for 1885 and 1886 that in selecting candidates he had put principle above party in order to create a board of health that would be free of partisan influence and thus better able to serve the public. Upon regaining control of the common council in 1885 the Republicans, Haynes charged, had ignored the example of his statesmanship and had stacked the board with members of their own party. Similarly, the salaried employees of the department—the members of the board of health served without pay—had been selected on the basis of their political affiliations. Of the fourteen inspectors hired, eleven were Republicans. Haynes was deposed as president of the board of health and a Republican, Herman Christopher Henry Herold, was installed in his place. Haynes was not the type of man to look on such machinations with equanimity and in the following years succeeded in recapturing the presidency of the board.[59] The squabbling that characterized the first years of operation of the board set a pattern. For about a decade, the board of health was almost continually embroiled in political intrigue.

The board of health was also beset by financial difficulties. In January 1890 the health officer, Dr. David L. Wallace, asked for a two to threefold increase in appropriations.[60] In making the request Wallace stated that in the previous year inadequate resources had made it "impossible to establish any reforms."[61] Wallace's request apparently went unheeded, for in the years 1890 to 1893, and again in 1896, the board did not publish an annual report. In October 1895 the board resolved to stop work unless more financial support was made available. The resolution was prompted by the suspension, because of lack of funds, of thirteen of the board's sixteen inspectors, and the board's unwillingness to take the blame for any illness that might ensue as a consequence.[62]

To add to its problems, the board of health was opposed by immigrants and laborers, who saw it as their "natural enemy." Property owners disliked having to let board of health inspectors into their homes and, still worse, having to make the expensive sanitary improvements demanded by the board. Given the fact that many diseases attributed to filth, such as diphtheria and scarlet fever, occurred frequently in expensive, spotlessly clean houses as well as in the dilapidated dwellings of the laboring class, the poor rejected the argument of public health officials that the costly renovations they sought were for their own good. Few working-class persons could be persuaded to take money needed for food, coal, and other necessities of life and use it instead for home repairs. Most persons were unwilling to spend money to prevent disease unless the risk to their health was imminent and catastrophic.[63]

The two most unpopular actions of the board of health were the forcible vaccination of persons who had been exposed to smallpox and the removal of persons with the disease to the hated pesthouse.[64] "When I entered the service in 1891," recalled Dr. Edward E. Worl, "the Board of Health had a small office on the second floor of 843 Broad Street. Nobody wanted us in the old City Hall—we were more unpopular than the tax office, and that is saying a great deal."[65]

A more serious indictment of the board of health was its failure to reduce the death rate. The U.S. Census for 1890 reported that Newark was the nation's unhealthiest city. Newark's death rate was 27.4 per 1,000 persons, highest in the nation of any city of over 100,000. The 28 largest American cities had a cumulative death rate of only 21.6 per 1,000 population. Hence Newark, whose population was 182,000, had incurred over 1,000 excessive deaths (27.4 − 21.6 × 182,000/1,000). Newark led the nation in mortality from scarlet fever, deaths of children under five years of age, and infant mortality. It ranked among the top ten in typhoid fever, malaria, tuberculosis, diphtheria, and croup (laryngitis).[66]

The notoriety brought to the board of health by the 1890 census report came on the heels of two incidents in which Newark health officials were accused of incompetence and malfeasance. During the winter of 1889–1890 work had begun on the filling in of the meadows along the line of a proposed railroad route less than a quarter of a mile from a densely populated section of town. Ordinarily, the use of garbage as fill would not have been allowed and was prohibited by city ordinance except under special permit of the board of health. In this instance consent had been given to the project in the belief that the winter frost would act as a disinfectant. As luck would have it, the winter was mild, and with the advent of warm weather the area became a nuisance. Complaints were made about the odors from the exposed garbage, and the area was described as "a perfect banqueting hall for the goats and geese of the neighborhood."[67] Initially the *Newark Evening News* criticized the board of health and the mayor for being apathetic and for failing to act because of fear of offending the railroad. But when a prominent Newark physician attributed two deaths to "sporadic cholera" traceable to gases emanating from the decomposing garbage, the *Newark Evening News* charged the mayor and board officials with criminal negligence and demanded their indictment.

Meanwhile, a deserted stone quarry had become the focal point of still another controversy. The quarry was used as a dumping place by the scavenger hired by the city to remove its wastes and by residents of the neighborhood. Complaints were made to the board of health about odors arising from the excavation, which, the *Sunday Call* reported, the board of health handled "with its accustomed lack of energy."[68] In addition to the health hazard posed by the odors, it was rumored that the remains of every resident of Newark who had mysteriously disappeared from the city during the preceding thirty years could be found in the large pond at the bottom of the pit. The *Call* reported that several members of the board of health had expressed dissatisfaction with its management, and several councilmen hinted at a big shakeup of the board. But in both matters the grand jury that investigated the incidents vindicated the judgment of the board. Moreover, the grand jury took the opportunity to recommend a substantial increase in the board of health's budget. Subsequently the railroad covered the garbage with dirt, and the water from the quarry was pumped out. To the disappointment of many Newarkers, no bodies were found.[69]

City councilmen, who had gleefully anticipated a sharp rebuke of the board of health, refused to accept the grand jury's findings. On a motion of the president of the common council, a committee of aldermen was appointed to confer with the board of health to ascertain if it had been performing its duties in a creditable manner. Understandably, the board of health believed that the common council had acted out of spite, and at a meeting of the two groups accusations and recriminations were exchanged. The board of health asserted that the fifteen thousand dollars appropriated to it for the year did not even cover the salaries of its employees and it would need an appropriation of nearly two and a half times that amount for additional inspectors. The board's request for more inspectors prompted one of the aldermen to complain that the ones they employed at that time did nothing but "loll around the streets."[70] But it had been political intrusion that had forced the board of health to employ the very same laggards and incompetents about whom the aldermen were now complaining.

Public antagonism toward the board of health was further inflamed by the board's conduct during the typhoid fever epidemic of 1891. A total of 876 cases and 196 fatalities from typhoid fever were reported for the year, the great majority occurring in the late summer and fall. Business slumped as outsiders began avoiding entering the city. Residents of Newark prolonged their summer vacations, and druggists were reported doing a thriving business selling mineral waters.[71]

Though it was the worst outbreak of typhoid fever in Newark's history, Dr. William Titus, the health officer, denied that the disease was more active than usual for that time of year and called the epidemic a press fabrication. Titus, however, aroused suspicion by refusing to release daily statistics on new typhoid cases. Furthermore, he stated that well water was safer than the water supplied by the city. The effect of this remark was to undercut five years of work by the board of health in educating the public about the danger of wells, most of which were contaminated. One well that was reopened at this time was blamed for from twelve to fifteen cases of typhoid fever. At a meeting called to discuss methods of combating the epidemic, Titus elicited ill-concealed laughter and smirks by entering into a lengthy discourse on the water supplies of ancient civilizations and by endeavoring to provide what may best be described as a sanitary interpretation of the Bible. The *Sunday Call* wrote that Titus's appointment was a "mistake," and shortly thereafter, either through resignation or failure to secure renomination, Titus's connection with the board of health was severed.[72] Commenting on the criticism that had been leveled against the board of health during the years 1890–1891, Haynes remarked, "A gang of pickpockets would have been treated with more respect and consideration."[73]

More trouble was still to come. In 1892 Tyler Parmly failed to secure reelection as president of the board of health following his unsuccessful bid for the Democratic mayoral nomination.[74] In 1893 the *Newark Evening News* criticized the board of health, calling it "a Board of Excuses." The *News* charged that the board's neglect of the public health had left the city defenseless before an expected invasion of cholera. Some members of the board of health were said to be "disgusted" with the situation and ready to resign.[75] The very existence of the board of health was threatened in 1895 when Mayor Julius A. Lebkuecher introduced a bill into the state legislature to turn over the functions of the board of health to the board of police commissioners. This had been done in 1871 in Jersey City, where, stated Lebkuecher, the public health was being protected at a much lower cost and with much greater effectiveness than in Newark.[76]

OBJECTIVES AND WORK

Until about 1895, the work of the Newark Board of Health was devoted almost exclusively to improving sanitary conditions, safeguarding the food supply, and controlling epidemics of smallpox.

Since dirt, contaminated water, noxious odors, "sewer gas," and decaying vegetable matter were believed to be the principal etiological
agents of disease, the board concentrated its efforts on cleansing the environment. To gather information on the salubrity of the city, a sanitary
survey was made in 1885 of all homes except those of "the better
classes." Houses containing nuisances, private wells, defective plumbing, and unvaccinated persons were noted in a file card index kept in
the offices of the board. A comprehensive sanitary code was promulgated in 1888, and in 1890 a plumbing code was enacted.[77]

The job of policing the city's health fell primarily to the sanitary inspectors of the department. As the health department assumed additional responsibilities, some of the inspectors were assigned to new
divisions created within the department. Food inspection was taken over
by the food and drug division, and enforcement of the plumbing code
was entrusted to the plumbing division. Still, the sanitation division remained the largest and most important unit. Besides abating nuisances
found in homes and public places, the sanitation division, through its
power to issue licenses and permits, also exercised control over the
maintenance of stables, the keeping of chicken coops, the operation of
slaughterhouses, the removal of night soil, the disposal of garbage, and
the overseeing of sanitary conditions in saloons, restaurants, and lodging houses.[78]

While the sanitation division's performance in overseeing citywide
health conditions was rather lackadaisical, it was even less effective
in tenement districts, where its services were most needed. The great
influx of immigrants from southern and eastern Europe during the years
1890–1910 severely taxed the resources of the division. In 1911 there
were eighteen inspectors who, along with their other responsibilities,
had to inspect over forty thousand dwelling units. Since few immigrants had either the temerity or the sophistication to report violations
of health laws, and since the inspectors had little time to make original
investigations of their own, the "plague spots" of the city continued to
fester.[79]

The immigrants' indifference to and ignorance of sanitary practices
aggravated the problem. The immigrants brought to America their national and religious customs, some of which, particularly those relating

to the handling, preparation, and sale of food, violated canons of accepted sanitary and hygienic practices. Polish and Russian Jews, for example, because of their religion's requirements concerning ritualistic slaughter of animals used for food, kept and butchered fowl in and around their dwellings. The birds' incessant clucking and cackling and the odors arising from the dung and blood-soaked feathers in the slaughtering room created an egregious nuisance, which health officials labored in vain to abate. Having suffered from the oppressive policies of authoritarian governments in their native countries, the immigrants tended to be suspicious of public authority. Moreover, immigrants were reluctant to appear before unfamiliar government bureaucrats, whose contempt for "ignorant, unwashed foreigners" was all too apparent. Critics of the health department charged that inspectors did not enforce the sanitary and plumbing codes in tenement houses because they were owned by the rich and powerful. The problem of commercial and political bias in regulating housing conditions would grow as more and more of Newark's working-class population were shunted into tenement houses.[80]

There were also less damning reasons for the failure of the sanitation division to improve living conditions in tenement districts. For one thing, a language barrier often impeded communication with immigrants. Then, too, the operating procedures of the division left much to be desired. It was the policy of the division to give first priority to citizens' complaints, many of which (for example, reports of choked catch basins and decayed and dangerous trees) the board of health might have better routed to other departments. Whether by design or poor planning, the sanitation division failed to provide much assistance to the immigrants in adjusting to their new and unhealthy surroundings. It is difficult to escape the conclusion that the sanitation division acted more as a self-serving institution than as a servant and friend of the immigrant.[81]

Privies and night soil removal early called themselves to the attention of the board of health. The house-to-house survey undertaken by the board in 1885 revealed that many privies in Newark were made of wood or had open bottoms and sides, permitting their contents to contaminate the surrounding soil.[82] Fecal containers were not cleaned until the smell became intolerable or the night soil threatened to spill over the sides, and were the source of numerous complaints. Even worse, many homeowners had wells situated near cesspools and outhouses. The hazards posed by privies were somewhat exaggerated by the *Sunday Call*, which reported that the typhoid germs contained in them "may be carried by the rains into streams from which drinking water is to be taken from the city. They may be conveyed into the human stomach through the milk of cows which pasture upon the polluted ground and drink the tainted water. The germs, dried by the summer sun, may be driven over the city by the winds, or they may come to us in the ice cut from shallow ponds which drain the land upon which night soil has been deposited."[83]

A scavenger was employed by the city to remove night soil. To make his work easier, the city authorized the daytime cleaning of privies, provided that the work was done under cover, away from the sun's destructive rays. Other than this restriction, the scavenger was a free agent.[84]

The scavenger did not reciprocate the favors bestowed upon him by the city. To the contrary, night soil was removed in a careless manner that offended the aesthetic sensibilities of citizens. Excreta oozed from the wagons of the scavenger, and its smell filled the air. A succinct analysis of the situation was made by the *Sunday Call*, when it asserted that the city could not

> hope for a remedy from a body of men [the common council] who are afraid of putting a few of their night soil scavenger constituents to an inconvenience. . . .
>
> . . . we need an ordinance to compel the use of some odorless system in cleansing out-houses. The present systems are merely travesties of the original plan, and an awning made of several old gunnybags gives the scavengers a license to perform their disgusting work by daylight.[85]

The *Call* evidently had in mind the odorless excavating machine that was adopted by several cities during the mid- and late 1870s. The apparatus consisted of a pump, a hose, a tank, and a charcoal furnace for destroying odors, and was both sanitary and economical to operate.[86]

The answer to the night soil problem was contained in the sanitary code of 1888. Homeowners were prohibited from building privies or cesspools without a permit from the board of health and were required to abandon their vaults whenever sewer connections became available. In addition, the board was given the power to regulate the location, usage, cleaning, and maintenance of privies. The aesthetic sensibilities of Newark residents were not forgotten. Scavengers were compelled to use an odorless apparatus and were forbidden to spend "an unreasonable length of time" in loading or unloading.[87] Finally, a permit was issued to the Newark Sanitary and Manufacturing Company in 1881 to turn night soil into poudrette (fertilizer made from deodorized night soil).[88] In a report made to the City Plan Commission in 1911, Newark's handling of the disposal of night soil was said to be better than that of most large cities and vastly superior to that of her neighbors, Elizabeth, Jersey City, and Philadelphia.[89] The board of health in 1915 reported that there were relatively few privy vaults or cesspools in Newark.[90]

Closely related to the privy question was the subject of wells. Well water constituted an important element in the city's water supply. At no time prior to 1880 was either the Newark Aqueduct Company or the Newark Aqueduct Board able to supply Newark with more than 75 percent of its water needs.[91] Most of the wells in use were badly polluted. The ordinary municipal lot was twenty-five by one hundred feet. The front sixty-foot section back from the street was occupied by buildings and walkways, leaving a small yard twenty-five by forty feet in which to dig a well and a privy. The sides and bottoms of the privies were usually porous. The water in the wells was drawn from near the surface of the earth and thus was easily polluted (as opposed to water drawn from deep subterranean streams or mountain springs). Compounding the danger, the wells were sunk farther into the ground than the privies. The average well was about twelve feet deep; cesspools and privies, ground permitting, only had to be dug to a depth of eight feet.[92]

The hazard presented by the city's dependence on wells had been noted several times. In 1854 an epidemic of cholera that swept the Hill section of Newark was tentatively traced to the use of polluted well water.[93] A chemical analysis in 1873 of three of Newark's most popu-

lar wells showed that two of them were grossly polluted.[94] And an examination made by the board of health in 1883 of thirty-four samples of
well water drawn from different sections of Newark disclosed that there
were no areas of the city where it was safe to use well water.[95]

In 1884 the board of health began to move against polluted wells.
The chemical test for fecal contamination was not entirely reliable, and
wells the board considered dangerous on the basis of the environmental
surveys it made in conjunction with the tests often passed inspection.
Wells situated in the drainage path of privies passed examination after
examination, only to be implicated later in outbreaks of typhoid fever.
Frustrated in its desire to close suspicious wells, the board launched a
publicity campaign to alert homeowners to the dangers lurking in their
drinking water. In newspaper articles and public talks health officials
pleaded with homeowners to abandon their wells before they were
stricken.[96]

Though health department actions against private wells usually went
unnoticed, the closing of a public pump generated considerable opposition. To begin with, the city's regular source of water supply, the
Passaic River, was, with good reason, considered dangerous. Newark's public pumps had attained the status of neighborhood fixtures.
The pumps were a convenience and a source of pride to the persons
who used them. Several of the pumps had been built at the expense of
the persons living in the neighborhood and had been carefully maintained over the years. Newarkers had favorite wells and would drink
from no others. One pump was used by over a thousand persons a
week. During the summer, the more popular wells were visited by a
continuous stream of persons bearing pitchers and pails.[97] There were
Newarkers who believed the board's antiwell campaign was part of an
aldermanic scheme to induce them to purchase water from the Newark
Aqueduct Board and these people "were no more inclined to pay for
water than they were for the air they breathed."[98] Many individuals
scoffed at the suggestion that communicable diseases could be transmitted through water and resented the health department's intrusion. Inquired one resident: "What does the Board of Health know about this
water? We know what we want. We drink the water. If it does kill us,
what business is that of the Board of Health?"[99]

Nevertheless, the rapid extension of water mains throughout the city after 1880, combined with the work of the board of health, led most homeowners to abandon their wells. In the years 1884–1890 over one thousand of Newark's more than fifteen hundred wells were closed. A temporary setback occurred during the typhoid fever epidemic of 1891, when persons who feared to drink from the polluted Passaic River again resorted to well water. In an attempt to avoid pollution, wells were dug deeper and as far away from privies and cesspools as possible. Some persons relied on their "infallible" sense of smell or taste to detect contamination, for water that was clear, odorless, and free from discoloration was believed to be safe. In its annual report for 1894 the board of health reported that, despite these precautions, fully 57 percent of the municipality's remaining 425 wells were contaminated and an additional 27 percent were regarded with suspicion. In sixty-three instances, typhoid fever had occurred in the immediate vicinity of the wells.[100] "The wells of our city are contaminated to such an extent," commented the board, "that their continuance is a standing menace to the public health. With one of the best water supplies in the world [the new Pequannock River system], and a water department which can and is willing to extend the mains to any necessary point, it seems almost criminal to allow the existence of surface wells."[101]

Plumbing, because of the belief in the danger from "sewer gas," was given a high priority by the board of health. "An escape of sewer gas," wrote the board, "spreads its deadly poison insidiously day and night, and it may destroy the lives or sap the health of whole households, and so far from being uncommon it is of daily occurrence."[102] The great demand for indoor sanitary appliances that developed during the last three decades of the nineteenth century came at a time when there were few recognized standards of sanitary engineering and few qualified plumbers. Hence the work done by plumbers was frequently slipshod. The board of health had the power to rectify defective plumbing, and often the repairs required by the board amounted to new installations. In 1886 New Jersey municipalities were authorized "to compel, prescribe, regulate, and control the plumbing, ventilation, and drainage of all buildings," and in 1890 a plumbing supplement to the Newark Sanitary Code was enacted.[103] Plumbers were required to register with the board of health and to submit all work plans to the board for approval. Other provisions of the supplement specified the standards of design, material, and workmanship to be met. Enforcement of the code became the responsibility of the plumbing division and remained a function of the health department until sometime after 1918, when it was taken over by the buildings department.[104]

Meat inspection and supervision of slaughterhouses were among the more important items on the board of health's agenda. Meat coming into Newark was checked to protect the public against fraud and to prevent the sale of diseased meat. Slaughterhouses were considered dangerous because they were associated with "foul air," a broad term used to connote conditions found in damp basement dwellings or in meat-processing establishments. Foul air, when it did not cause illness directly, did so indirectly, it was believed, by weakening innate, bodily resistance to disease.

Inspection of the city's fifteen slaughterhouses during the early 1880s uncovered an almost total disregard of sanitary care. "With but two exceptions," reported the board of health, "there is but little or no attempt made by the owners to properly remove the offal and cleanse the place thoroughly."[105] Entrails and other inedible parts of butchered animals were fed to pigs kept in pens under the slaughterhouses. The wastes, a mixture of blood, bones, and excrement, were disposed of in foul-smelling receiving vats or were dumped on vacant lots. The few drains in use were not connected with sewers or were poorly constructed. Floors were dry-swept instead of washed. Since the slaughterhouses received little ventilation, rancid odors permeated the buildings and clung to the workers' garments. Rectification of the majority of these abuses was a simple and inexpensive matter; all that was needed was a little prodding of the slaughterhouse owners. In 1885 the board of health was given the power to license slaughterhouses, and from that point on, sanitary conditions in the slaughterhouses began to improve appreciably.[106]

In its campaign to improve sanitary conditions in slaughterhouses, rendering firms, fertilizer plants, and other trades that used the meat or remains of butchered animals, the board was greatly aided by technological advances and the appearance of larger, more efficiently managed businesses. In the mid-nineteenth century, the slaughtering and preparation of meat was commonly done on the premises of local butchers. Often, as has been seen, the animals were slaughtered in dilapidated buildings and sheds without watertight floors or sewers for disposing of their wastes. After 1865 the number of slaughterhouses began to decline as large, scientifically managed packing houses, such as Armour and Swift, began to develop a national market for their products. The large packers tended to have more sanitary operations, for they were likely to use the latest mechanical appliances for eliminating offensive odors, which the small firms could not afford. Also, with fewer businesses, it became easier to restrict slaughterhouses to nonresidential areas of the city.

Similar developments were occurring in nuisance-breeding industries, such as fat rendering, soapmaking, bone boiling, and glue making. In these industries the remains of slaughtered animals were heated and chemically treated, producing rank odors and unsightly byproducts. But by 1880 the essentials of good rendering—airtight tanks, the eliminiation of offensive odors, and sanitation—were known, and with the aid of applied chemistry commercial uses were found for the blood, bones, offal, and other refuse materials of the animals.[107]

Diseases that are communicable from animals to man are called zoonoses. Of these, the most serious are undulant fever, bovine tuberculosis, Q-fever, glanders, anthrax, trichinosis, and salmonella.[108] Through the timely intercession of the Newark Board of Health and the New Jersey Board of Health, severe epidemics of glanders that struck the Newark area in the 1880s and 1890s were quickly brought under control without loss of human life.[109]

Meat inspectors and veterinarians were engaged by the board of health to inspect livestock and to examine meat sold in butcher shops and markets. Extant legislation gave the board the power to condemn tainted meat and this power was extended in 1886 by an ordinance authorizing the board to quarantine stalls whose owners were caught slaughtering animals in "an over-heated, feverish or diseased condition." To facilitate the work of its inspectors, the board sought to construct a public abattoir. By building an abattoir and a general cattle yard and locating them near an outlying railroad station, the board also hoped to eliminate the discomforts occasioned by the existence of several slaughterhouses in or near residential districts.[110]

But the public abattoir was never built. Moreover, the meat and livestock inspection work of the board seems to have faltered after 1885, the year Julius Gerth, Jr., one of the two veterinarians employed by the board, resigned to take a position with the New Jersey Board of Health.[111] An analysis made in 1919 of the meat inspection work of the department revealed that about 80 percent of the meat butchered in Newark was not examined by either federal or local officials. Of the different kinds of meat, only beef had to be stamped as fit for human consumption.[112]

A meteorologist was retained by the Newark Board of Health until 1916. Tables of meteorological data were published in the hope of finding a correlation between morbidity and atmospheric conditions. Going back as far as the time of Hippocrates, physicians believed that the collection of data about weather, climate, and other atmospheric phenomena would reveal the causes of infectious diseases. Since the physical environment of every community was unique to some extent, theoretically each community would have a distinct pattern of disease and would require its own meteorological investigation. Hence medical-topographical studies of American communities were frequently undertaken during the early 1800s.[113] With the ascendancy of bacteriology, the atmospheric theory of disease came to be regarded as unscientific, and the board of health abolished the meteorologist's position.

The work of the meteorologist was not the department's only failure. For many years the board of health attempted to have itself made the official repository of vital statistics, as was usual in most cities, in place of the city clerk. The board argued that it needed to have jurisdiction over vital statistics to insure the safe burial of persons who had died from epidemic diseases. But the city clerk was a powerful figure in Newark politics and successfully resisted any diminution of his authority. Consequently the vital statistics of the city remained a shambles.[114]

In recounting the activities of the board of health, it is also important to note what it did not do.[115] The board only concerned itself with diseases that could disrupt the life of the community, especially its business activities. It ignored diseases not believed to be contagious, including some that were responsible for much of the city's morbidity and mortality, most notably tuberculosis. Furthermore, it did not explore the relationship between poverty and sickness, since it was widely believed that economic status and health were matters of choice. If a man did not want to live amidst filth and disease, he simply moved or bettered himself through hard work and thrift. With few exceptions the board also failed to educate the masses in disease prevention, other than to exhort them to be clean and sober. That they did not have bathtubs and had few escapes other than alcohol was seldom taken into account. In restricting its aims this way, the board was conforming to the medical theories and moral precepts of the times.

6 SEWERAGE

THE TOPOGRAPHY OF MUCH OF THE NEWARK AREA provides excellent natural drainage. The city is situated on the eastern side of the Orange Mountains on a gently sloping plain that extends to the Passaic River on the east and the meadows adjoining the river and Newark Bay on the south. Partly because of its advantageous location, Newark was without any sewers until 1854.[1]

Prior to 1854, privy and cesspool wastes not absorbed by the soil drained into the city's waterways and into ditches and other open conduits. Stream currents and storm waters were relied upon to flush the fecal deposits that accumulated on the beds and the banks of the conduits. During times of drought or low tide the effluent decomposed in the sun and gave off a horrible stench. The odors emanating from the conduits were thought to poison the atmosphere and were held responsible for the intermittent fevers that plagued nearby residents.[2] Consequently in 1857 the city was authorized to build sewers upon petition of a majority of the property owners fronting the proposed route.[3]

As the population of the city increased and the older areas of town became congested, real estate promoters began securing title to the western heights. In the years immediately following the Civil War speculative mania swept the region and "improvements ran mad. . . . Streets were laid out in pasture lands where they would not be needed for many years to come. . . . Sewers were built in streets that were not graded, and while all this was going on, the center of the city was neglected."[4]

The curbing and grading of streets and the filling in of watercourses impeded drainage in the suburban uplands. Unable to find an outlet for their wastes, developers converted vacant lots into sewage repositories, endangering health and threatening property values. When residents in the area complained, the common council responded by undertaking an extensive program of sewer construction.[5]

The outlay of large sums of money for public improvements came to an abrupt end during the depression of 1873. Saddled with property they could not sell, promoters lost their zeal for speculation, and the construction of sewers did not fully revive for several years.[6]

With the return of prosperity in the early 1880s, property owners and civic and business leaders began pleading again for the building of additional sewers. In 1884 the president of the board of trade declared:

> Our city has now reached a point where improvement in the system of our sewerage and the proper drainage of our meadows has become one of the vital questions to be met and determined. As to what is or is not done in this matter the growth of our city will be advanced or retarded. . . . Stagnant waters and imperfect sewerage means sickness and disease and an increased death rate and all this besides distress and sorrow means injury to our reputation as a healthful city and inflicts more . . . damage to property interests than many times . . . the cost of applying the remedy.[7]

The board of trade indicated just how seriously it regarded the matter by employing a group of engineers to study Newark's sewer needs.

For many years the sewerage question was entangled in the medical controversy over the origin of disease.[8] Most physicians believed that disease was caused by "miasma," a loose term used to describe the noxious vapors emanating from decaying organic matter. That polluted air caused epidemics seemed apparent to physicians as far back as Hippocrates, because when many persons suddenly became ill, there had to be a single cause—the air they all breathed. And as the experience of the nineteenth century demonstrated, cities with their mounds of decomposing offal, garbage, and night soil were particularly subject to epidemics.[9]

The miasmatic theory of disease was challenged by John Snow in his investigations of cholera and also by William Budd in his studies of typhoid fever. Through the use of field studies and statistical investigation, Budd obtained evidence indicating that typhoid fever was caused by a minute organism transmitted through fecalized water supplies. Nevertheless, the miasmatic theory continued to exert a powerful influence. No one had ever looked under a microscope at the microorganism responsible for typhoid fever, much less identify it as the sole cause of the disease.[10]

The leading advocate of the miasmatic theory of disease after the Civil War was a German scientist, Max von Pettenkofer. One of the most prominent figures in nineteenth-century medicine, he is best known for his pioneering studies in experimental hygiene. As health officer of Munich, Pettenkofer secured a new water supply and improved sanitation, effecting a marked reduction in the city's death rate. He was a convert of Snow but with an important difference: he believed that the excretus of cholera victims was not dangerous unless allowed to ferment or germinate in the watery subsoil or in sewers. While accepting the notion of the specificity of disease, Pettenkofer maintained that epidemics could only occur where groundwater levels favored the nurturing of pathogenic microorganisms. He believed that sewers were dangerous for two reasons: (1) they hindered the drainage of the subsoil, increasing the likelihood of an epidemic; and (2) when not properly collected, they emitted deadly "sewer gas" (gas or gases emitted by the decomposing organic filth in sewers). Pettenkofer believed that sewer gas could induce certain specific diseases, especially the ones commonly found in the crowded urban communities of the nineteenth century, as well as weaken the resistance of its victims to attacks by other diseases.[11]

Gradually the germ theory of disease began to gain ground against the miasmatic theory. During the 1860s Louis Pasteur demonstrated the role of microorganisms in fermentation and Joseph Lister established an antiseptic method of surgery, which saved the lives of countless patients who otherwise would have died of postoperative infection. In the 1880s Robert Koch provided the long-awaited laboratory proof of the germ origin of disease. Soon bacteria were identified as the cause of several of man's most frightful diseases. The discovery in the early twentieth century of the part played by the carrier and by the insect vector in transmitting disease provided the final missing links in the germ theory of disease and completed the rout of the miasmists.[12]

The triumph of the germ theory of disease enabled health officials to convince homeowners and political leaders of the necessity of finding more sanitary means of disposing of human wastes other than was pro-

vided by leaching cesspools and privies. In 1914, Leonard Metcalf and
Harrison P. Eddy, two of the nation's foremost authorities on sewerage, commented that "the strong feeling that good public health is a
valuable municipal asset and depends to a large extent upon good sewerage has been a leading cause of the willingness of taxpayers recently
to embark on expensive sewerage undertakings."[13]

The demand for sewerage was also shaped by increased water consumption. The middle decades of the nineteenth century witnessed an
enormous increase in water usage. Homeowners demanded water for
washing, cooking, bathing, and other domestic needs. Businessmen
who wanted to obtain lower fire insurance premiums and industrialists
in need of copious amounts of water for cooling and condensing lobbied
for the acquisition of municipal water supplies. In the years 1865–
1896 over three thousand waterworks were built. Meanwhile, cities
with existing public water supplies struggled continuously to keep their
waterworks' capacities and distribution systems abreast of population
growth. By 1870 Philadelphia had laid nearly five hundred miles of
water mains. In the years 1843–1895, New York City increased the capacity of its Croton reservoir system from 42 million gallons a day to
425 million gallons.[14]

The enlargement of municipal water supplies was necessitated in
part by population increase but mainly because, as indoor plumbing
fixtures became available, household use of water increased dramati-
cally. In Philadelphia per capita consumption of water surged from 8
gallons a day in 1810 to 55.1 in 1870. Cities located on the Great Lakes
had almost inexhaustible supplies of water, which they liberally made
available for both household and industrial use. In 1882 per capita consumption of water in Chicago and Detroit exceeded 140 gallons per
day.[15]

Most of the increase in domestic water consumption resulted from
the installation of sinks, bathtubs, and especially water closets.
Whereas in the early nineteenth century water-using fixtures were luxu-
ries found in a few expensive homes and hotels in the nation's leading
metropolises, in the late 1860s and 1870s they were widely adopted by
affluent homeowners. By 1880 nearly one of every four urban households had a water closet. In 1847 only 6.5 percent of Philadelphia

homes contained bathtubs; by 1870 almost one-fourth had them. The great number and variety of bathroom amenities found in Philadelphia prompted the *New York Times* to suggest that instead of referring to Philadelphia as "the City of Brotherly Love," owing to its Quaker heritage, it might be more accurate to call it "the City of Bodily Comfort."[16]

The growing market for water-using fixtures attracted the attention of American inventors and manufacturers. By the early 1870s a full line of cast-iron plumbing goods were being manufactured in New York City. The first American-made sanitary earthenware was marketed shortly thereafter, and during the 1880s more than 180 American patents for water closets were issued. Sewer construction lagged behind the adoption of indoor flush toilets. As late as 1890 many communities of less than ten thousand and even a few large cities, including New Orleans and Baltimore, had no sewers at all. Moreover, most of the sewers built before 1890 were designed for surface drainage from streets and became clogged with nauseating filth when homeowners connected their cesspools to them by means of overflow pipes. Several cities enacted ordinaces forbidding their use for the removal of household wastes, but the laws were allowed to lapse, since homeowners had no other means of removing wastewater from their premises.[17]

As urban households began to use ever larger volumes of water, the existing wastewater collection system had to absorb the increased wastewater loads. At the time of the Civil War, most American cities had at best only a few underground sewers and some large open drains for removing storm water. Bodily wastes and kitchen slops were disposed of in privy vaults and leaching cesspools. Consequently, what Jon Peterson calls the "private-lot waste removal" system was overtaxed and began to break down. Privy vaults and cesspools overflowed, polluting the soil around them. Backyards were turned into marshes, and basements were flooded with noxious fluids. Some cities responded to the strains placed on their primitive wastewater collection systems by permitting homeowners to connect their privies and cesspools to street gutters and storm water sewers, though the practice was still opposed by many sanitarians. When this happened, the street gutters became filled with repulsive matter, and it soon became apparent that the only viable solution to the city's wastewater problem was to build underground sewers connected to private homes.[18]

Most of the principles of water-carriage sewage had been developed in England before the Civil War, and in the 1880s American cities initiated extensive programs of sewer construction. At first sewers were poorly built. Many of the older sewers were made of wood, brick, stone, or some other porous material, and oozed their contents into the soil. Few sewers were properly graded, causing them to become clogged with liquid filth. Some sanitarians opposed sewers on the ground they were nothing more than "elongated cesspools." The design problems that resulted in leaky, poorly trapped, and unventilated sewers were largely overcome by 1890. Indoor plumbing fixtures were standardized and became safe and sanitary to use.[19] Sewer construction was turned over to municipal engineers; plumbing standards were established; and well-designed, integrated sewer systems began to appear. Between 1890 and 1909 nearly seventeen thousand miles of sewers were built in the United States, more than double the mileage that had been laid in the previous forty years.[20]

Meanwhile, the cause of sewer construction in Newark received an important boost in 1880, when Edgar Holden, president of the board of directors of Mutual Benefit Life Insurance Company, revealed the city's poor health record in his treatise *Mortality and Sanitary Record of Newark, New Jersey* [1859–1877].[21] At the time it was widely believed that sewer gas was responsible for cholera, diphtheria, scarlet fever, and other epidemic diseases. Thus Newark's mayor, Henry J. Yates, was convinced that much of the municipality's illness was caused by improperly constructed sewers and faulty drainage. In his annual message for 1878, Yates asked if homeowners should be compelled to run sewer ventilation pipes above house roofs, where the gases could be passed off safely. He believed that roof pipes would protect the health of households while bringing about better ventilation of poorly trapped sewers.[22]

Holden also thought that sewers might be detrimental to health. To test this theory, he prepared two maps of Newark for the years 1872 and 1876, on which he plotted the location of every death from "preventable diseases" and the state of sewer development. To his surprise, he found an inverse correlation between sewers and fatalities. Similarly, a third map, "Showing the Made Land and the Different Depths of Filling and also the Old Water Courses," indicated that the death rate was lower in areas drained by sewers than in neighborhoods served by privies.[23] "In summing up the investigation," Holden wrote, "I have been struck by the fact that theories, however plausible on the subject of a city's sanitary surroundings, are valueless against stubborn facts and figures."[24]

In deciding whether to live in town or to move to the suburbs, Newark residents had to weigh the advantages of more spacious houses and semirural surroundings against a loss of city services. Residents of Roseville, located on the western edge of Newark, had chosen trees and bigger houses over sewers, but they began to regret their decision during the 1880s, when malaria and typhoid fever became endemic in the area. Community leaders blamed the increased sickness on the presence of disease-breeding filth. The Roseville Improvement Association, in its annual report for 1883, pleaded with the Newark municipal fathers to extend sewerage to the Roseville border. Addressing itself also to Roseville property owners who opposed increased public expenditures, the association declared that sewerage justified higher taxes, since without health all the amenities of suburban life were a mirage. Sewers, it concluded, would provide a permanent relief from the malarial exhalations of Roseville's foul-smelling cesspools.[25]

In 1886 the *Sunday Call* reported that sewers were gaining support because of their supposed health benefits and attributed this development to the influence of Holden's treatise on mortality and sanitation.[26] At the same time there was a rapid increase in the demand for water closets and other bathroom fixtures. Indoor plumbing was becoming a standard feature in the construction of new homes and a necessity for the middle-class market. With the consequent increase in per capita consumption of water, it seems unlikely that the introduction of sewers could have been long delayed despite lingering fears about their safety.[27]

Newark was badly in need of sewerage. In 1883 there were ninety miles of improved streets in Newark that were not connected to sewers. Lack of sewerage was not limited to the municipality's outlying sections. Nearly two-thirds of the core area, containing the greatest concentration of homes and businesses in Newark, was without sewers.[28] "Certain sections of our city are in such need of sewers," reported the board of health four years later, "as to constitute a constant source of danger and of high mortality to those in the immediate vicinity."[29]

At Newark's request, a state law was enacted in 1882 making it easier for cities and property owners to secure sewers. The statute stipulated the construction of sewers upon the petition of any number of property owners along the route of the proposed sewer, provided not more than 50 percent of the affected parties objected. Municipalities were authorized to pay the cost of new sewers by the sale of three-year Temporary Improvement Certificates, or bonds. The financing provision of the law was amended in 1886 to enable local governing councils to refinance the certificates by issuing new bonds, thereby removing virtually all financial restraints on sewer building.[30]

The city's sewerage was augmented by private sewers. Newark authorities encouraged the installation of private sewers when the delays and expenses attendant upon the construction of public sewers threatened to preclude their undertaking.[31] Building a public sewer was a cumbersome affair. First, the common council's resolution of intention to construct a sewer had to be published in at least two newspapers for ten consecutive days to provide time for property owners to object. Upon completion of the sewer, commissioners were appointed by the circuit court to assess the benefits conferred by the sewer. Property owners were then given three months in which to present objections to the commissioners, whose decision could be appealed to the circuit court for final adjudication.[32] The cost of advertisements, commission fees, and other miscellaneous expenses was between $350 and $400, which in some instances was more than the cost of the sewer. The city government in 1885 acknowledged the importance of private sewers by placing their construction under the supervision of the city surveyor. For the most part, private sewers were of two types: (1) very short sewers, from fifty to two hundred feet in length; and (2) sewers built by land companies through large tracts of land being developed for sale.[33] As of 1910, private sewers accounted for about 12 percent of the mileage of Newark's sewerage.[34]

Sewer construction was not unopposed and for a time was successfully impeded. Sewers were resisted for several reasons. Though a
sewer connection increased the value of a house, many property owners opposed them because the gain could not be realized until the house
was sold, whereas the sewer had to be paid for annually in hard cash.
As a result of the poor construction of many houses, homeowners also
objected that the indoor plumbing to which sewers were connected often froze during cold weather. Moreover, sewers were expensive. The
replacement value of Newark sewers in 1908 was several million
dollars. Because of the opposition of Mayor Joseph E. Haynes and
William T. Hunt, editor of the influential *Sunday Call* after 1885, both
of whom displayed an almost morbid fear of incurring debt, relatively
few sewers were built in Newark in the years 1883–1893.[35]

In resisting appeals for more sewers, Mayor Haynes and the editor
of the *Sunday Call* pointed out the inability of the city to pay for existing sewers. Frequently, after waiting several years for payment of
sewer assessments, the city had to settle for from one-quarter to one-
half the bill (which by then included interest on the assessment). Unable to fund the Temporary Issuance Certificates authorized in 1882,
Newark was constrained to issue long-term bonds at the high interest
rate of 6 percent.[36]

The manner in which sewer assessments were determined antago-
nized property owners, making the task of sewerage proponents that
much more difficult. Property owners could only be assessed for the actual benefit derived from a sewer. In the case of laterals, or service
sewers, the assessments were levied on the properties abutting the
sewer. For collection sewers, intercepting sewers, and trunk sewers,
assessments were levied on all property located within the drainage district served by the sewer.[37] But how does one measure the benefits
gained from the installation of a sewer? The *Sunday Call* commented:
"Most cities have adopted a sewerage plan for the whole community,
with a consistent plan of paying the cost. They have fixed the price of
sewer connection at so much a lot, or they have placed the cost of all
sewers on the entire municipality, or they have assessed each lot according to frontage for the cost of the sewer, and charged the city at
large with trunk sewer construction."[38] In Newark no general plan ex-

isted, the method of sewer assessment having "grown upon the city." Since assessors had to treat each case individually, not infrequently the sewer rates assessed were challenged and taken to court.[39]

Sewer construction in Newark proceeded without the benefit of a master plan and was nearly bereft of any planning whatsoever. Sewers were built "only as the needs of separate localities forced themselves upon public attention."[40] Historian Samuel H. Popper comments that "in the development and expansion of Newark's sewage disposal system can be seen, better perhaps than in the development of any other municipal service, the complete lack of city planning and the improvised manner in which municipal services evolved."[41] The city did not even possess an accurate topographical map showing the region's watercourses, valleys, and elevations. Without such a map, engineers had no way of determining the best locations and outlets for sewers. When asked about the status of the city's sewerage program, the mayor's secretary admitted there was no general drainage plan covering the entire city and each locality was being served "according to its special requirements."[42]

Lack of planning delayed construction, complicated maintenance, and increased costs. In the absence of a master plan, sanitary engineers were hard put to determine the size, gradation, and depth of proposed sewers. Moreover, no records existed of private sewers built before 1885.[43] In some instances sewers were laid under unpaved streets where they were easily clogged by street dirt washing into them through the inlets. Because of faulty planning, sewers designed to carry storm water had to be used to carry sewage as well. The older sewers were made of porous materials and were expensive to maintain. Finally, decomposing deposits in poorly graded sewers emitted offensive odors making life unbearable for nearby residents. The only time sewers were adequately flushed was during a heavy rainfall.[44] Mayor J. A. Lebkuecher summarized the reasons for Newark's patchwork sewerage by declaring that "sewers have been constructed in piecemeal, at excessive expense, and in a way that has precluded the idea of permanent utility."[45]

Inadequate sewerage was an especially troublesome problem in the flat, low-lying southeastern quadrant of the city. The sewers in this section had little fall and emptied into sluggish tidal creeks that when swollen by high tide or heavy rains overflowed their banks and backed up on the meadows.[46] "Under these circumstances," wrote one newspaper, "it has been found almost impossible to get rid of the sewage. For the greater part of the twenty-four hours the sewage does not flow out at all, but remains dormant as in cesspools, from which, under the action of the sun, all kinds of foul odors arise and diseases are bred."[47] A newspaperman sent to investigate complaints in the area reported that "the stench arising from the black and sluggish water was so overpowering that only a strict sense of duty prevented a hasty retreat."[48] In one creek the reporter found the bloated carcasses of two large dogs, lying almost motionless upon the water, "upon which a cloud of flies were banquetting," while in an adjacent creek boys swam in the "dark green scum" unmindful or perhaps oblivious to the danger.[49]

The matter became a "cause célèbre" and the object of the most ambitious public improvement undertaken in Newark to date. It was first proposed to rid the area of sewage by harnessing the tide. This had been done successfully on the English coast where the tide reached twenty feet. Despite warnings from experts that the plan was an "absurdity," the city forged ahead at a cost of seventy-five thousand dollars. Two ditches were dug out to Newark Bay, one to hold the sewage, and the other to catch and impound the tide.

As had been predicted, the scheme was an utter fiasco. The common council now engaged the services of two prominent engineers, who recommended the construction of a great intercepting sewer to service the sewers on the meadows. Work on the project was completed in 1887 at a cost of over six hundred thousand dollars. The sewage was brought to a pumping station on the edge of the meadows, where it was lifted and pumped through culverts laid beneath the ground to an outlet some two hundred feet into Newark Bay.[50] The success of the project led to proposals for linking the Great Intercepting Sewer on the meadows to trunk sewers to be built in the city's other natural drainage districts. The pumps on the meadows had a capacity of about thirty million gallons per day, which was more than the combined sewage flow of the city. Through this scheme it was hoped to end Newark's chaotic sewerage and to reduce the pollution of the Passaic River, from which the city drew its drinking water. However, after the city acquired a new water supply in 1889, it lost its incentive for cleansing the Passaic River, and nothing more was heard of the plan.[51]

Throughout the 1880s and early 1890s sewer construction failed to keep pace with the city's expansion. Though the city's sewerage more than doubled, there were more miles of paved streets without sewers at the end of Mayor Haynes's administration than at its beginning.[52] In his inaugural message of 1894, Mayor Lebkuecher observed that Newark's sewers, "built in the main without regard to general utility or future requirements, fall far short of our needs, and the lack of them, in many sections, is a menace to the public health."[53]

But Lebkuecher was unaware of forces that would shortly bring abut a dramatic increase in sewer construction in Newark and throughout the nation. For one thing, the new science of bacteriology proved beyond a shadow of a doubt the perils of allowing excreta to accumulate in or near population centers. Then, too, the elimination of hand labor in the manufacture of plumbing fixtures in the early 1900s reduced their cost to the point that almost all homeowners could afford them. Public health arguments and the growing demand for bathroom amenities soon proved irresistible. In 1890 the board of health was authorized to require sewer connections in houses on streets with sewer lines.[54] Armed with this authority, the board began a vigorous drive to rid the city of outhouses, cesspools, manure pits, and other remnants of an unsanitary age. The period 1894–1910 marks the greatest era of sewer construction in Newark. Approximately two hundred miles of sewers were built, almost double the mileage that had heretofore existed.[55] To rectify the city's crazy-quilt sewer pattern, drainage districts were established and a series of large intercepting sewers were built.[56] By 1919, 95 percnt of the improved area of Newark was provided with sewers (see Table 2).[57]

After overcoming considerable difficulties, sanitary reformers had succeeded in establishing drainage facilities for ridding Newark of its liquid wastes. Yet the progress suggested by the extension of the city's sewerage was partly an illusion, since many citizens in areas served by sewers were still forced to rely on privies and outhouses. Though by 1919 nearly every section of Newark had sewers, the construction of

Table 2
Sewer Building in Newark, 1853–1918

YEAR ENDING	NUMBER OF MILES OF SEWERS
1853	—
1870	12.5
1880	47.0
1883	49.0
1890	87.0
1893	112.0
1910	310.6
1918	314.5

SOURCE: Newark, Board of Education, *Newark Study Leaflets* (1914), no. 27, *Sewerage and Its Disposal*, 3; *Newark Annual Reports, 1870 Mayor's Message*, 11; Joel A. Tarr, James McCurley, and Terry F. Yosie, "The Development and Impact of Urban Wastewater Technology: Changing Concepts of Water Quality Control, 1850–1930," in *Pollution and Reform in American Cities, 1870–1930*, ed. Martin V. Melosi (Austin: University of Texas Press, 1980), 66–67; *Newark Daily Journal*, August 7, 9, 1883; *Annual Report of the Newark Board of Health, 1894*, 20; *Newark Annual Reports, 1910, Board of Health*, 574; Bureau of Municipal Research, New York, "A Survey of the Government, Finances, and Administration of the City of Newark, N.J." (November 1, 1919), 588, Newark Public Library, New Jersey Reference Division.

sewer mains did not insure the use of flush toilets. The city's responsibility for providing sanitary services ended at the street line. A property owner could tap in at the curb, but he did so at his own expense. This division of responsibility worked to the satisfaction of a majority of city dwellers, but left many poor persons without adequate sanitary facilities. Well-to-do homeowners were willing to pay the small costs involved in obtaining the latest sanitary improvements,[58] but this was not true of slumlords, who generally provided the least amount of services the law allowed. The board of health was authorized to require property owners abutting on a sewer to tap in but was unwilling to risk antagonizing politically influential landlords. In a 1912 survey of

Newark's impoverished Ironbound district, Willard D. Price, a social worker in the community, discovered that several old houses that were being rented to workers and their families did not have water and sewer connections, which he attributed to the discretionary powers given the board of health in enforcing the sanitary code. Price observed that "the opportunities afforded by such powers for political and commercial favoritism are obvious, and it is also obvious to anyone living in 'The Ironbound District' that such opportunities are not always lost."[59]

Fear of disease and the comforts afforded by indoor plumbing led Newark during the years 1853–1918 to construct a sewer system of over three hundred miles valued at several million dollars. But even though sewer lines from the house to the street could have been provided at little extra cost, and tax monies had partly paid for the system, the laissez faire attitude that removed private property from the realm of public policy and the unwillingness of affluent citizens to extend to the working class the same housing standards they enjoyed prevented the city from making this humanitarian addition to its sewerage system. Thousands of city dwellers were thus denied the rudimentary essentials of a safe, sanitary environment because they were poor.[60]

7 GARBAGE DISPOSAL

U NTIL THE MID-NINETEENTH CENTURY, THE DISPOSAL
of household wastes was an individual responsibility. As the city
grew and became congested, laissez faire in garbage removal proved
untenable. Pigs were penned up, depriving the city the services of its
best scavengers, and vacant lots that had been used as garbage repositories were put to more productive use. The existence of uncollected refuse and garbage offended the aesthetic sensibilities of citizens and
threatened their health and safety. The common council was petitioned
for relief, and beginning in the 1850s scavengers were placed under
contract to cart away solid wastes.[1]

The contract required the scavenger to make daily collections in the
downtown area of the city and biweekly collections in the outlying districts. At the time, the outer wards were inhabited mainly by first- and
second-generation Irish and German immigrants. During the summer
and fall of 1883, complaints from these immigrant communities were
aired in the *Newark Daily Journal*. As a result, subsequent contracts
stipulated that collections be made every other day in the outlying
wards.[2] The benefits that were derived from this change lasted only a
short time. Within a few years numerous complaints were again being
received about the poor service in the suburban districts.[3]

The contract system worked to the disadvantage of both the scavenger and the city. Either because they consistently underestimated their
expenses or because of the highly competitive nature of their business,
scavengers frequently removed the city's wastes at a loss. About 50
percent of the scavengers engaged by the city appear to have lost
money.[4] The city lost as well, for the only way the scavenger could
show a profit was by cutting back services. To avoid the extra expense
entailed by long hauls, outlying districts were neglected; in some instances the garbage was simply dumped on vacant lots. Collection
schedules were seldom adhered to, with the result that sidewalks were

frequently piled high with garbage and trash containers. Garbage spilled onto the streets from the uncovered wagons that carried away the city's wastes, and blowing ashes smudged the faces and clothing of pedestrians.[5]

If citizens protested about the way their garbage was removed, the board of health was more concerned about its ultimate disposal. The three classes of municipal wastes—garbage, refuse, and ashes—were collected as mixed trash and disposed of by dumping. Some of the mixed trash was used to fill sunken lots to bring them up to street grade, the scavenger contracting with private parties for the work. With regard to these practices, the board of health warned that "all sanitary authorities are satisfied . . . dumping is exceedingly detrimental to the health of the inhabitants living adjacent to these grounds; and as for allowing dwellings or factories to be built over such material, it would be next to criminal."[6]

The city dumps made a mockery of Newark's pretensions to sanitary enlightenment. The dumps were festering sores breeding blight and disease in the neighborhoods in which they were located. In warm weather, rotting garbage emitted a sickening stench. Fires smoldered in the dumps and occasionally burned out of control, filling the sky with acrid smoke. Children used the areas as playgrounds, while adults scrounged for coal, kindling wood, bottles, cans, paper, rags, clothing, bedding, and other salvageable refuse. Finally, the dumps attracted flies, mosquitoes, rats, and other vermin that infested neighboring areas.[7] Because they "are usually in the 'poor section' of a city," wrote the *Newark Evening News,* "may explain, but does not excuse, their existence."[8]

The rapid growth of cities after 1800 was accompanied by environmental degradation and a deterioration in sanitary conditions. Because of the limited transportation facilities of the times, most persons had to live in or near the central business district, with the result that cities became crowded and congested. As urban centers became dense with homes and businesses, the problem of removing the city's solid wastes reached crisis proportions.[9] The waste products of nineteenth-century urban civilization included kitchen slops, household rubbish, cinders, coal dust, stable manure, broken cobblestones, slaughterhouse wastes, and dead animals. The stench in warm weather of rotting vegetables and decomposing animals was often unbearable. Health officials feared that the miasma believed to be emitted by organic filth poisoned the atmosphere and produced epidemics.[10]

Horse manure was one of the most troublesome urban pollutants. The average working horse excreted about a half a gallon of urine and from fifteen to twenty-two pounds of manure daily onto the city's then mostly unpaved thoroughfares. Health officials in Milwaukee calculated that in 1907 the city's 12,500 horses produced 133 tons of offal a day. Livery stables stank from the mingled smell of urine-soaked hay, harness oil, and manure. Worst of all, horse dung attracted swarms of flies, each one of which might carry away any of thirty different diseases, including dysentery and typhoid.[11]

From the earliest times in American cities, pigs and other animals were used as scavengers. Herds of swine roamed the streets in search of edible wastes. Though effective scavengers and an important source of food for urban households, pigs had some unpleasant habits that detracted from their value. When not wallowing in the mud they often could be found rooting up vegetable gardens and occasionally were known to attack small children. In southern cities turkeys and cattle were employed sometimes as scavengers. In Milwaukee the pigs had to compete with "swill children," immigrant youngsters who sorted through the garbage dumped in backyards and alleys looking for kitchen refuse that their families could consume or sell to farmers for pig food or fertilizer.[12]

By the end of the Civil War, most American cities were replacing animals with human scavengers. In communities with a population of less than thirty thousand, householders and merchants often disposed of their own wastes or contracted with private individuals and businesses to do it for them. In the nation's larger urban centers, the municipal government assumed the responsibility for picking up and disposing of refuse or negotiated with scavenger firms for the work.[13]

The methods employed by private scavengers and municipal sanitation departments for disposing of the city's wastes elicited innumerable citizen complaints and warnings from health officials. The simplest and most primitive method of disposal was dumping on land or in water.

Inland cities deposited their wastes on vacant lots in lightly populated
suburban districts or in garbage dumps located in immigrant neighborhoods. The dumps were an eyesore and a health hazard and were bitterly opposed by the neighborhoods in which they were located. Edible
wastes were sold to pig farms, and animal manure was purchased for
fertilizer. Mixed refuse was used to fill in low-lying areas, though
boards of health considered the practice dangerous. Coastal cities were
more fortunate in that they could employ scows to dump their garbage
in the ocean. Not infrequently, however, the garbage washed up on
nearby beaches, making bathing impossible and destroying shoreline
property values.[14]

A study undertaken for the 1880 U.S. Census of the methods of garbage disposal used in 199 cities reveals that nearly half dumped their
garbage on land or in water, and another 22 percent sold it to farmers
for fertilizer and animal feed. Fifteen percent of the cities used a combination of methods. Two cities, or 1 percent, burned their wastes. The
remaining 15 percent did not provide any information.[15]

New methods of garbage disposal were marketed in the United
States in the 1880s. In 1888 the Vienna, or Merz, process for extracting
oils, grease, ammonia, potash, and other commercially valuable by-
products obtained through the heating and compressing of garbage was
introduced in Buffalo. The materials were sold mainly as lubricants,
fertilizer, and a perfume base. The process, known as reduction, was
adopted by several midwestern cities, but a fall in price of the salable
by-products led most cities to abandon it after a few years. By 1915
only half of the forty-five reduction plants in the United States were
still in use.[16]

The first furnace for burning mixed refuse, consisting of garbage,
rubbish, and domestic ashes, was put into operation in Nottingham,
England, in 1874. Eleven years later the first American furnace was put
into service in Allegheny, Pennsylvania, and in the following three
decades crematories and incinerators of all types appeared in cities
throughout the United States. Cremation provided a more sanitary
means of disposing of garbage than reduction but also cost more. In
several European cities steam produced from the burning of mixed refuse was utilized to operate municipal power plants for the generation of

electricity, but the idea never gained acceptance in the United States. The cost of building and operating a steam-producing incinerator was considerably higher than for a simple incinerator, and it was claimed that the allegedly high moisture content of American refuse made it unsuitable for burning. In addition, cheaper and more convenient sources of energy were becoming available, further reducing the attractiveness of recovering heat generated in the burning of refuse. During the years 1902–1915 from one-third to one-half of American cities incinerated their garbage. Thereafter the number of municipal furnaces for burning garbage dropped markedly, especially in the late 1930s, when sanitary-landfill operations were widely adopted.[17]

Partisan politics and the patronage opportunities afforded politicians in street cleaning and garbage disposal severely hampered the efforts of health officials who sought to effect more sanitary and efficient means of collecting and removing the city's wastes. Hence when George E. Waring, Jr., probably the best-known American sanitarian of the nineteenth century, was asked by reform mayor William L. Strong to become street-cleaning commissioner of New York in 1895, he was promised complete freedom from political interference. Waring rid the sanitation department of spoils politicians and improved the training and morale of its employees. As a symbol of the cleanliness he wanted citizens to associate with his administration, the sweepers were issued white uniforms. The more than two thousand men employed in the "white wings" won national accolades for their accomplishments in ridding New York City streets of manure, rotting garbage, and mud accumulations. Waring also opened a reduction plant and began a land reclamation program using trash for landfill. However, he placed primary emphasis on the development of human resources rather than the use of new technology. The gains made by Waring were short-lived, for when Tammany Hall politicians retook control of New York in 1898 Waring was dismissed, and in the following years much of his work was undone.[18]

Garbage collection and disposal was a difficult problem for almost all American cities. For nearly three decades Milwaukee experimented with all known methods of disposing of solid wastes without success. Finally in 1910 a municipal cremation plant was built that would serve the city satisfactorily until 1955. Garbage disposal was turned over to the engineers in the department of public works, where it was removed from politics and patronage.[19]

Other cities were not so fortunate. As late as 1928, sanitary engineers regarded street cleaning and garbage disposal as an "orphan child" of the engineering profession. They attributed this in part to the unwillingness of municipal politicians to surrender the patronage plums the work provided. "As a result," commented one engineer, "there are numerous examples of failures in practically every method of handling the problem, and practically every city official in whose department the refuse collection and disposal is contained feels that he has started his duties with a veritable stone hung around his neck."[20] Moreover, leading American sanitarians were in disagreement over the best method of garbage disposal. Several methods were deemed satisfactory, but not every one was regarded as suitable for all cities. Each city, it was believed, had to decide what was best for itself depending on its size, location, and the composition of its garbage.[21]

During the closing years of the 1880s, the Newark Board of Health resolved to improve the city's methods of garbage disposal. The use of garbage to fill in land, except under special permit from the board, was prohibited in the Sanitary Code of 1888, as was dumping within the city limits of any substances that were "offensive" or if decayed were likely "to become putrid or to render the atmosphere impure or unwholesome."[22] But how were sunken lots to be filled? Section 45 of the Sanitary Code required that all sunken lots be brought up to street level, and mixed trash was the only available fill. Much of Newark, particularly the area bordering the meadows, was below street level. Consequently, the Sanitary Code's prohibitions could not be enforced. In 1897 the board of health estimated that nearly one-twelfth of the lots in the city were being filled with mixed refuse and garbage.[23] As a possible solution to the problem, the board of health proposed that a dual system of collection be adopted whereby city wastes would be separated into organic matter (household garbage) and inorganic matter (ashes and cinders). The organic matter, it was argued, could easily and economically be disposed of through incineration or reduction, while the inorganic matter would provide a safe, sanitary fill.[24]

New technology was brought to bear on the problem in the late nineteenth century as cities searched for more sanitary means of disposing of their wastes. In 1890 a delegation of the board of health was taken on an all-expenses-paid tour of midwestern cities to witness a demonstration of a disposal process in which garbage was incinerated. The company sponsoring the tour had secured the exclusive marketing rights to the process in the United States. Prevented from accompanying the delegation by a previous commitment, Mayor Haynes joined a later tour conducted for the Paterson Board of Health. Though impressed by what they had seen, Haynes and the Newark Board of Health were prevented by a lack of funds from accepting an offer from the company. Newark's inability to obtain the new disposal process ignited verbal fireworks. The *Newark Evening News,* which at the time was calling for the indictment of the mayor and the board of health for having allowed the use of uncovered garbage to fill in a part of the meadows, referred to the board of health as the "Board of Junket." The mayor retorted by alluding to the *Newark Evening News* as "the Evening Nuisance." Mayor Haynes, in his annual message for 1890, hinted that the reason money had not been appropriated to acquire the Vienna process was because the common council was unwilling to surrender the patronage opportunities that came with choosing the city scavenger every five years. In 1901, 445 men were employed in street cleaning and garbage disposal; the majority of them owed their positions to political connections.[25]

Undaunted by this failure, the board of health continued to criticize the modus operandi of the city scavenger and proposed that garbage disposal be made a function of the health department.[26] The *Sunday Call* in 1896 announced that a plan had been adopted to dispose of wastes by cremation. But the announcement turned out to be premature, since the common council believed that $130,000 was too much to spend for a crematory;[27] the common council was not about to voluntarily surrender any of its patronage powers.[28]

In 1902 a number of events dovetailed, giving the board of health the opening it was seeking. The volume of complaints about the scavenger service was reaching a crescendo. The ten-year scavenger contract entered into in 1892 was about to expire, and the common council, as a result of state legislation, was about to lose its power to award contracts for most municipal services to the board of street and water commissioners, an independent administrative body.[29] Sensing that the time for vigorous action had come, the board of health adopted a resolution that the scavenger contract not be renewed unless fundamental revisions were made. Referring to the existing system as "a relic of barbarism," the health officer, David D. Chandler, again warned of the danger from promiscuous dumping.[30]

The new scavenger contract incorporated many of the recommendations of the board of health. In a reform first introduced in New York City by Waring in the late 1890s, municipal wastes were divided into three categories: (1) garbage, comprising animal and vegetable waste matter collected from kitchens, markets, and slaughterhouses; (2) ashes, constituting the residuals from the burning of fuels, plus small accumulations of dirt and floor sweepings; and (3) refuse, comprising dry, combustible trash such as paper, old clothes, and discarded bedding. The contract called for separate collections of garbage, ashes, and rubbish. To effect this change, an ordinance was passed requiring householders to separate their wastes into the three specified classes and to provide suitable receptacles for each. The contract further stipulated that garbage be disposed of in a manner "unodorous and sanitary in every particular."[31]

A plant for the reduction of garbage was put into operation by the city scavenger in 1903. The garbage, which averaged from thirty to seventy tons a day depending on the season, was carted to the city piers, where scows picked it up and took it to the meadows. The garbage was then heated and pressed. The solid remains were used in the manufacture of fertilizer and the grease obtained from pressing, after having been strained and filtered, was sold to soap manufacturers.[32] At the time, reduction plants were highly regarded as a profitable means of disposing of garbage. In the following years, however, as was discussed earlier, the industry lost money and was abandoned by all but a few of the very largest metropolises.[33] Sometime between 1909 and 1912, the meadows plant was closed.[34]

Even while the reduction plant was in operation, the garbage situation deteriorated; this despite the fact that by 1910 Newark was spending two hundred thousand dollars annually for removal of its solid wastes, eight times more than it had paid in 1873.[35] The dumping of mixed trash continued unabated. Householders balked at the purchase of additional garbage cans, and little or no effort was made by the scavenger to keep the different categories of wastes separate.[36] Aroused to action by the poor service and the spiraling cost of waste removal, the board of trade made inquiries into the methods of garbage disposal used in over one hundred cities. On the basis of this inquiry, recommendations were made, a majority of which, the board claimed, were incorporated into the 1908 scavenger contract. But a comparison of the 1908 contract with the one that preceded it reveals few differences.[37]

The board of street and water commissioners was also displeased by the garbage mess, and in 1912 ordered its deputy engineer and its consulting engineer to investigate the disposal plants of ten cities in New York, New England, the Midwest, and Canada. In their report the engineers discussed five methods of solid waste disposal: dumping, reduction, cremation, incineration, and the destructor system (the last three were virtually identical).[38] Having sanitary rather than economic considerations uppermost in mind, though admitting that it was difficult to divorce the two, the engineers recommended that: (1) the municipality assume responsibility for the scavenger service; (2) the separate collection of wastes be eliminated; and (3) the three classes of municipal wastes be disposed of through burning at temperatures that would destroy all microscopic life and inhibit objectionable odors. The engineers further proposed that the heat used to sterilize the wastes be harnessed to generate electrical power.[39] A resolution was passed by the board of street and water commissioners asking for the establishment of an electrical lighting plant supplemental to the building of a garbage destructor system to supply one-third of Newark's power needs. To no one's surprise, the common council ignored the resolution.[40]

During the years 1912–1915 relations between the city and the scavenger reached their lowest ebb. Complaints poured in from all over the city, and for the first time since Mayor Haynes's administration (1883–1893), public officials other than the members of the board of health began to openly criticize the scavenger.[41] In January 1915 the mayor appointed an advisory committee to meet with the board of street and water commissioners to reconsider the report made by the board's engineers, which since 1912 had been reposing "peacefully somewhere in that mystic region known as the city archives."[42] Later that year, the city scavenger, the Newark Paving Company, asked to be released from the five-year contract it had entered into with the city. The company asserted that because of an office mistake its bid on the contract was five hundred thousand dollars less than what it had intended. The bid submitted by the scavenger ($893,200) was nearly three hundred thousand dollars lower than the next best offer made to the city, which is the amount the company would have had to forfeit if it attempted to break the contract.[43] In December 1915 the city began withholding money from the scavenger because of nonfulfillment of the provisions of the contract.[44] The *Sunday Call,* however, was skeptical that the city really intended any punitive action. Garbage disposal had been a source of complaint for nearly half a century, prompting the *Call* to state that "the public authorities now declare the garbage collection system intolerable, and propose to fine the contractor an impossible sum, which, of course, they never mean to collect."[45] The *Call* proposed that instead of making empty threats, the city take over the operation of the scavenger service.[46]

In the summer of 1916 an unwelcome visitor appeared in Newark: poliomyelitis. Because there was some reason to believe that the disease was being spread by an insect vector, Newark's backward methods of garbage disposal suddenly became a subject of great concern. Urgent complaints were received by the board of health from residents of the Tenth Ward, one of the focal points of the epidemic, that garbage was going uncollected for two or more days, endangering the children of the area. Though shorthanded because of the epidemic, the board assigned a squad of five inspectors to undertake a limited cleanup of the section.[47] In the early part of August the Vailsburgh Improvement Association made a poignant appeal to the board to close the Vailsburgh dumps: "Vailsburgh is full of flies now. They are breeding by the millions. The dumps are within fifty feet of houses where there are a lot of children and the mothers are in fear of their health with the present epidemic of infantile paralysis."[48] The Forrest Hills Improvement Association went to court to seek an injunction to prevent the scavenger from operating the dumps in its area. As a result of citizens' complaints, both dumps were closed.[49]

Meanwhile, the scavenger had threatened to break the contract unless he received extra compensation to recover his losses. The board of street and water commissioners wanted to grant the relief but lacked the power.[50] Toward the end of August, with the epidemic still raging, the *Newark Evening News* wrote a series of articles exposing the scavenger's neglect.[51] Accompanying the criticism were descriptions of several municipally operated garbage disposal systems that, almost without exception, were said to be "better and cheaper" than Newark's. For good measure, the *News* roasted past and present administrations for having neglected the matter for so many years. The mayor, sensing the political danger posed by the epidemic, was quick to respond. In a communication to the board of street and water commissioners, deliberately leaked to the press, he declared that "the importance of immediate consideration of this matter lies deeper than the mere inconvenience to citizens. The city should not permit any condition which may possibly be remotely responsible for the scourge of infantile paralysis now afflicting our community to continue."[52] Calling the existing system antiquated and the city's experience with private garbage removal "unsatisfactory," he proposed that the city take over the service and replace the dumps with incinerators.

The board of street and water commissioners, which had been forewarned of the mayor's message, then announced an almost identical plan.[53] After failing to come to terms with the scavenger on a purchase price, on August 31 the board declared its intention of serving notice on the scavenger to show cause why the contract should not be abrogated.[54] The company acted first by announcing that it was terminating the contract and filing suit to recover damages for losses incurred because of the city's failure to compel homeowners to separate their wastes as stipulated in the contract.[55] Thus after forty-three years the city's dependence on private enterpise for the removal of household wastes came to an end. What years of patient protest had not accomplished a few months of panic had.

Municipal assumption of responsibility for garbage disposal in and of itself could not and did not solve anything. As the epidemic faded, plans for the construction of incinerators were forgotten and the zeal with which the city had taken up the work waned.[56] One year after the epidemic, the *Newark Evening News* reported that though improvements in garbage disposal had been made, solutions were not much nearer than when the engineers had made their report in 1912.[57] The right to pick the dumps had been leased to a private contractor who reneged on his agreement to maintain good sanitary conditions at the dumps, which, as ever, were abysmal eyesores.[58] Efforts to enforce the separate collection of wastes were a "complete failure," with responsibility about equally divided between the city and its inhabitants.[59] As of 1919, Newark still had not found an adequate solution to the vexing problem of how to dispose of its solid wastes. Neither had many other American cities.

8 SMALLPOX

SMALLPOX, KNOWN MEDICALLY AS VARIOLA, WAS AN acute infectious disease caused by a filter-passing virus. The first symptoms of the disease were a very high temperature, pains in the loins and back, an intense headache, and vomiting. On the third or fourth day after the appearance of the initial symptoms, small red spots emerged on the forehead, face, and wrists. These eruptions spread over the body and developed into the dreaded pustules that identified the disease. Patients then passed through a critical period in which they ran the risk of blindness or death. Smallpox had a case fatality rate of about 25 percent; however, the rate varied depending on the virulence of the invading microorganisms and the resistance of the host. Mortality rates in late nineteenth-century America usually stayed under 30 percent. Blindness in persons who survived an attack of smallpox was much less common than was believed at one time. But even if patients recovered with their eyesight intact, they did not escape unscathed, for their scarred and pockmarked faces bore witness the rest of their lives to smallpox's frightful power.[1]

A highly infectious disease, smallpox was normally transmitted through human contact; indirect transmission through infected articles, though possible, was rare. No individual or group was naturally immune to the disease, and only through a previous attack or vaccination could an individual acquire immunity. There was no cure for smallpox, and the case fatality rate was high. Owing to its heinous and highly contagious nature, smallpox was one of the most feared diseases.

Smallpox first became a serious public health menace in the United States during the second half of the seventeenth century and continued to ravage the colonies throughout the colonial period. "[From] 1675 to 1775 the infection was absent from the colonies for as long as five years on only two occasions."[2] Seaports, because of their congestion and constant exposure to foreigners, were particularly susceptible to outbreaks of the disease. Though never endemic in the United States, smallpox was periodically epidemic. Without warning and with numbing speed smallpox would sweep through a community, leaving in its wake a trail of illness and death. Often the illness did not burn itself out until the nonimmune in the community had been eliminated through affliction and flight. During severe epidemics schools closed and governments adjourned. The economic life of the city ground to a halt. Artisans and merchants closed their shops, and frightened farmers stopped coming to the city to trade their produce. As a means of allaying fears and revitalizing business, municipal governments sometimes published false reports minimizing the danger they knew to be in their midst.[3]

Smallpox was finally brought under control in the United States toward the end of the colonial period through the use of quarantine, isolation, and, most important, inoculation; the adage an ounce of prevention is worth a pound of cure was never more true than when applied to smallpox. Quarantine was effected by requiring incoming ships to sit at anchor while colonial officials inspected their hulls for decaying cargoes and examined their crews for symptoms of infectious diseases. But sanitary cordons were seldom effective in keeping smallpox at bay. Sailors who broke quarantine and travelers arriving by land easily pierced the city's smallpox defenses. Smallpox victims within the community were isolated by removing them to a pesthouse situated on an island in the harbor or in some remote, outlying area. Quarantine and isolation were borrowed from England. Inoculation, the next great advance in fighting smallpox, was an American innovation. The practice originated in the Middle East but was first used on a large scale in the Western world during an epidemic of smallpox in Boston in 1721.[4]

Inoculation should not be confused with vaccination. Inoculation, or variolation, is a process whereby pus is transplanted from the pustules of a patient recovering from smallpox into a puncture or an incision of a healthy person. By exposing his or her body to weakened smallpox virus, the individual contracts a much milder case of the disease than if it was caught during an epidemic. There are three drawbacks to inoculation: (1) the patient has to be in good enough health to withstand even a weakened bout of smallpox; (2) the strength of the inoculant is hard to control; and (3) the inoculated person has to be isolated to prevent him or her from becoming the focal point of a new smallpox outbreak. Vaccination, the successor to inoculation, eliminated these risks by replacing attenuated smallpox virus with cowpox vaccine, a relatively safe and equally effective inoculant.[5]

The discovery of vaccination by Edward Jenner in 1796 held out the promise not merely of control of the pestilence, but of global extermination. Smallpox was preeminently a communicable disease of humans. Seizing upon the fact that there was no reservoir of the disease other than human beings, Western governments, through programs of rigid quarantine and compulsory vaccination, were able to eradicate smallpox in their lands by the mid-twentieth century. The elimination of smallpox in developing nations was slower. The final assault on smallpox was made by the World Health Organization in Africa. The last case in the world of naturally acquired smallpox occurred in Somalia in October 1977.[6]

But for over a hundred years following Jenner's discovery, the potential benefits of vaccination were not fully realized. Vaccination as first practiced had too many pitfalls to gain universal acceptance. The vaccines used were unreliable and the operation was risky. Smallpox was to linger on in the United States until medical science and government action rendered vaccination a completely safe and dependable procedure.

The principal limitation of vaccination was that immunity diminished with the passage of time. The first, or primary, vaccination provided protection for from two to ten years; revaccination conferred immunity for an indefinite though usually longer period of time. Persons whose immunities elapsed frequently acquired only a mild case of smallpox but were carriers of the more virulent form of the disease.[7]

Vaccination was not so simple a procedure that it could be entrusted to druggists, clergymen, midwives, and "old women," as was fairly common throughout much of the nineteenth century.[8] The vaccine had to be guarded against heat and moisture. Often several vaccinations were required before a successful "take" was obtained, and the determination of a "take" called for a degree of medical sophistication.[9] "We find varioloid [smallpox in vaccinated persons] occurring so much more frequently of late years than heretofore," reported one Newark physician in 1849, that should it "continue to spread as it has here for several years past, the confidence of the community in vaccination as a preventive measure will be lost to such a degree as to lead to its desertion, for few will be willing to submit to it unless they feel that it is an effectual and a perpetual protection."[10]

Great difficulty was encountered in finding a reliable vaccine. Initially, humanized cowpox pulp or lymph, consisting of the crust or serous fluid contained in the vesicles of vaccinated persons, was used. This "arm to arm" technique of vaccination carried with it the danger of erysipelas, syphilis, and other diseases that travel through the bloodstream.[11] The actual risk was far less than what the public imagined. A case in point is provided by an editorial in the *Newark Evening News* that made the startling assertion that "in not a few cases" vaccinated individuals had contracted "diphtheria, typhoid fever [both of which could not be transmitted in this way], and other diseases."[12] Another disadvantage of "arm to arm" vaccination was that an adequate supply of humanized cowpox vaccine could not be insured unless several recently vaccinated persons were on hand.

The dangers attendant upon the use of human vaccine were eliminated by the introduction of bovine vaccine. In 1843 Negri of Naples began using cowpox vaccine that had been obtained by passing the virus from cow to cow, and by the 1870s bovine vaccine was being marketed in the United States.[13] Still, public health officials had a long way to go in eliminating smallpox, for the new vaccine had almost as many liabilities as the old one. Farmers sometimes diagnosed engorged udders as cowpox and the lymph taken from these cows was worthless. In 1871 in the midst of a severe smallpox epidemic, the board of health of Lowell, Massachusetts, declared that since vaccination had not provided the protection claimed for it and several well-vaccinated persons had died, it was relying mainly on isolation control measures to stop the spread of the disease.[14]

As bovine vaccine came into general use, physicians became dependent on commercial suppliers for their vaccine stock. Safety standards for the production of vaccines did not exist and, in the absence of any regulatory controls, fraud became commonplace. Fly-by-night drug firms and unscrupulous druggists flooded the market with cheap, inferior vaccine. There is reason to believe, reported the New Jersey Board of Health in its annual report for 1880, "that much is sold for bovine virus which is not such . . . because of age and imperfect keeping."[15] During the smallpox epidemic that swept the United States in 1902, forty-five definite cases and eighteen likely cases of tetanus were traced to vaccine containing tetanus spores.[16]

Antiseptic conditions for performing vaccination were rarely present. Frequently, persons with dirty arms were vaccinated, resulting in streptococcal and staphylococcal infections. Even when stringent precautions were taken, persons undergoing vaccination sometimes developed incapacitating arm sores requiring from four to eight weeks to heal. The sores were caused principally by the use of vaccine contaminated by bacteria entering from the skin of the calf or the dust of the stable. Infection also resulted from failure to sterilize the instrument or the site selected for vaccination, lack of proper care of the wound, and faulty methods of vaccination.[17]

To a great extent, smallpox continued to afflict American communities after the introduction of vaccination because Americans had lost their fear of the disease. The smallpox epidemic of 1871–1874 killed more Newarkers than the great cholera epidemic of 1854 and yet it was almost totally ignored by the local newspapers and by public officials. Smallpox had become a class disease, an affliction of the lower socioeconomic strata of society.

Peter Razzell argues persuasively that in England as a result of the adoption of inoculation, "smallpox had virtually disappeared as a disease amongst the wealthy classes by about 1770."[18] Donald Hopkins, in his study of smallpox in history, says that in nineteenth-century Europe smallpox was an affliction of the poor.[19] Cyril W. Dixon, in his authoritative medical treatise, in part attributes nineteenth-century England's failure to make vaccination compulsory to the fact that smallpox had become "primarily a disease of the lower classes."[20] Similarly, in one of the best-known nineteenth-century American textbooks of public health, smallpox was described as a disease that struck the poorer areas of the community.[21]

In the United States the educated and the affluent bought protection against the pestilence. If the poor did not avail themselves of the opportunity to be vaccinated gratuitously at charitable clinics, then it only confirmed the widely purported truism that sickness and poverty were signs of basic character flaws. "Some people have the idea," remarked one Newark health official, "that it is only the 'nasty, dirty people' who get smallpox."[22] Smallpox did not arouse panic among the clergymen, newspaper editors, businessmen, and other civic leaders who, as John Duffy observes, "usually determine the pattern of a society's reaction to the menace of epidemic diseases."[23] What concerned community leaders was not that persons were dying from an easily preventable disease, but that conditions in the isolation hospital might reflect poorly on the city's good name and on their own reputations as Christian providers for the indigent poor. There can be little doubt that had community leaders felt as imminently imperiled by smallpox as by cholera and yellow fever, vaccination would have been made compulsory and smallpox eliminated at an earlier date.

Judith W. Leavitt states that in Milwaukee smallpox caused "fear and panic and an immediate governmental response to alleviate conditions."[24] Attempts to forcibly remove smallpox patients to the municipal pesthouse during the epidemic of 1894–1895 sparked widespread rioting in the German and Polish southside wards and led to the dismissal of the health commissioner.[25] But the "fear and panic" induced by smallpox epidemics was of a very different kind and magnitude than that seen in outbreaks of cholera and yellow fever. John Duffy, as Leavitt acknowledges, maintains that smallpox ran a distant third to cholera and yellow fever in providing an impetus to public health reform in the late nineteenth century because a preventive was availiable for it but not for the others.[26] Indeed, Milwaukee's encounter with smallpox in 1894 resulted in a loss of power for the board of health.[27] The terror caused by visitations of smallpox was largely limited to immigrant neighborhoods and resulted from their inhabitants' fear of being sent to the city pesthouse, a contemptible facility that provided neither care nor healing. Local elites were not at risk from smallpox and hence paid it little attention. The affluent did not flee the city, as they did in the epidemics of cholera and yellow fever, and business did not come to a standstill.

The state of social and political development of the nation along with the zeitgeist also militated against strong smallpox measures. Public health reform was only undertaken in the face of an epidemic. Permanent public health bodies possessing the will and the power to act without the spur of community pressure did not exist. Laissez faire doctrine held that governments were to be provided with the very minimum authority necessary to maintain law and order and protect property. Many persons regarded compulsory vaccination as an infringement on their personal freedom. Antivaccination societies in England and the United States strenuously opposed the practice, as did "irregular physicians" (practitioners of sectarian medicine).[28]

Antivaccination sentiment was especially strong in England. In 1880 the Antivaccination Society was established; its supporters included members of Parliament, the playwright George Bernard Shaw, and the statistician Alfred Wallace. While most British physicians and scientists supported vaccination, some thought it harmful. The leading medical antivaccinationist was Dr. Charles Creighton, at one time "demonstrator of anatomy" at Cambridge and author of a well-known history of British epidemics. The Antivaccinationist Society published a monthly journal in which it appealed to the traditional opposition of the British to any state action that limited personal freedom. The society presented its case so effectively that the movement for compulsory vaccination in England collapsed around the turn of the twentieth century. Under the new Vaccination Acts of 1898 and 1907, parents with "conscientious objections" to the practice were permitted to keep their children unvaccinated.[29]

Joan Retsinas has studied the vaccination controversy in Rhode Island. Here the battle centered on the efforts of antivaccinationists to repeal an 1881 statute that required compulsory vaccination of schoolchildren. The adversaries were well matched. The vaccinationists, who had the support of the regular medical profession, were led by the redoubtable Dr. Charles V. Chapin, the health officer of Providence. The antivaccinationist cause was championed by two prominent laymen, Samuel Darling, a retired toolmaker, and Sidney S. Rider, an antiquarian book dealer. They were aided by the state's sectarian physicians, who offered as a substitute for vaccination their own herbal and chemical remedies.[30]

The antivaccinationists opposed vaccination for both medical and

libertarian reasons. Vaccination was an empirically validated procedure. Opponents of vaccination argued that medical science could offer
no good theoretical reason to explain why the pus of a diseased cow injected into a healthy person could protect that person against smallpox.
Inoculating someone with an animal disease might be dangerous. To
support their position, the antivaccinationists presented medical and
lay testimony of that time that linked vaccination to tetanus, lockjaw,
syphilis, erysipelas, and other frightful diseases. They also accused the
medical profession of being mercenary, of supporting vaccination because of the fees and medical practice it brought physicians.[31]

Many Americans claimed they objected not to vaccination, but to
compulsory legislation that interfered with an individual's right to be
the judge of what health protection he and his family required. Representative Joseph McDonald of Pawtucket, in speaking against a bill
providing for compulsory adult vaccination in Rhode Island, voiced the
sentiment of many of his colleagues when he declared: "This matter of
government compulsion is a tremendous exercise of governmental
power. If a man has any rights, they are over his own person, and to
compel a man to take poisonous virus into his system that might dis-
figure him for life is going beyond the rights of Government. I would
leave vaccination to each individual."[32] Even Chapin opposed compulsory vaccination of adults, and the measure did not get very far.
However, the antivaccinationists' campaign to overturn mandatory
vaccination of schoolchildren was defeated by a small majority in the
lower house of the state legislature. Similarly, in other states the antivaccinationists won a few skirmishes but lost the main battle over compulsory school vaccination.[33]

The rapid growth of public education in the nineteenth century presented new health dangers and opportunities. The crowding of children
into ill-ventilated and unsanitary school buildings fostered the spread of
communicable diseases. At the same time, by requiring vaccination of
schoolchildren, the incidence of smallpox could be greatly reduced.
The school vaccination movement began after the Civil War in the
large cities. New England led the way, followed by the Midwest, with
the South the last section of the nation to fall in line.[34]

At the prodding of newly established state and local boards of health, state legislatures and city councils began to require proof of vaccination as a condition of admission to the public schools. Enforcement of compulsory vaccination, however, was another matter. A small but vocal group of antivaccinationists frightened parents with stories of "vaccination tragedies," and compulsory vaccination was hotly debated in local school elections. Many school officials were apathetic or opposed to vaccination and only enforced the law during epidemics. The decentralization of school systems placed authority in local hands. "State education and health officials could plead, cajole, and order local school boards to take action, but unless the township or school district officials believed in school vaccination, the orders, edicts and regulations of the state boards received scant attention."[35] Moreover, education officials were upset by the large number of children who were kept out of school because they were not vaccinated. They also clashed with local health authorities over jurisdiction of vaccination programs. Nevertheless, according to John Duffy, the historian of the movement, by 1900 compulsory school vaccination was firmly established in the United States. In his 1901 textbook on municipal public health, Chapin commented that the nation's school population was well protected by vaccination.[36]

Adults were not as well protected against smallpox as schoolchildren. In 1913 Chapin opined that the United States was the "least vaccinated of any civilized country."[37] Chapin may have been engaging in a bit of hyperbole or perhaps he had in mind only English and German-speaking nations, for in southern and eastern Europe there were thousands and even hundreds of thousands of smallpox deaths during the first decade of the twentieth century.[38] The continual arrival of unvaccinated immigrants from these lands and the large number of parents who did not vaccinate their preschool-age children or have themselves periodically revaccinated left considerable numbers of persons vulnerable to smallpox. Even among the school-age population there were many without immunity. An 1894 loophole in Massachusetts' compulsory vaccination law exempted students who were "unfit for vaccination." Antivaccinationists subsequently announced that they would provide a certificate of unfitness to every person who wanted one. In rural areas free vaccination was often not available to the poor.

As late as 1898 the New Jersey State Board of Health reported that nearly one-fourth of the state's 472,000 schoolchildren had not been vaccinated.[39]

Epidemics of smallpox occurred in Newark about every six to twelve years from 1848 to 1903, and the disease was seldom completely absent in other years. The worse epidemic, claiming 644 lives, began in 1871 and lasted until 1874. Another major epidemic, in which there were 258 deaths and 1,281 cases, occurred in the years 1901–1902.[40]

The first line of defense against smallpox was, of course, vaccination. Vaccination was strongly endorsed by nearly every recognized medical authority in New Jersey: local and county medical societies, the New Jersey Medical Society, and the New Jersey Board of Health.[41] "By the process of vaccination alone," declared Dr. Ezra Mundy Hunt, the state's leading public health authority, "thousands upon thousands have been rescued not only from death, but from disfiguring diseases."[42] Typical of the work performed by physicians in promoting vaccination was the following resolution, adopted by the Essex County Medical Society at a special meeting called on February 16, 1870, which the society had published in the county newspaper:

> Whereas the protective power of Vaccination has, of late, been frequently inpugned and the propriety of it called into question, Resolved:
>
> I. Successful vaccination and re-vaccination are a full and complete protection against Small-Pox.
>
> II. Vaccination with pure and fresh virus is not prejudicial to health nor productive of the ills and maladies often attributed to it.
>
> III. Re-vaccination after a lapse of from five (5) to seven (7) years is always expedient and is recommended as the only means of securing perfect immunity from Small-Pox.[43]

Nineteen years earlier the society had proposed the establishment of a "Vaccine Depot."[44] The need for an adequate supply of reliable vaccine was underscored by events in Newark in 1852. Smallpox flared up that year, and because cowpox vaccine was in short supply, several

Newarkers had themselves inoculated rather than vaccinated.[45] By inoculating themselves, however, they created new foci of smallpox infection, and the disease began to spread. With the outbreak threatening to get out of hand, a law prohibiting inoculation was rushed through the common council. Individuals who had already been inoculated were compelled to leave the city and were not allowed back in until they were free of all symptoms of the disease.[46]

During its first full year of operation (1858) the Newark Board of Health vaccinated 337 persons. The exact number of persons protected against smallpox by the board in subsequent years is unknown. Only 627 individuals received the prophylactic in the years 1876–1878, but this may have been because of the large number of persons who undoubtedly were vaccinated during the 1871–1874 epidemic. At any rate, the board announced in its annual report for 1881 that it was strenuously urging vaccination upon the poor, with good results. As evidence of this, in 1885 the dispensary vaccinated over three thousand persons.[47]

Fear of vaccination and disbelief in its value were pronounced among certain ethnic groups, especially the Germans,[48] though in Newark the greatest opposition came from the Italian community. Many immigrants had come from nations with authoritarian governments and consequently looked with suspicion upon any enlargement of state power that abridged their freedom. In 1882 Buffalo's health officer wrote that the Germans in his city were resisting vaccination. He was puzzled by this, since vaccination had been compulsory in Germany for nearly a decade, Germany and Sweden had the fewest number of smallpox deaths of all Western nations, and few persons born in Germany were unvaccinated.[49] But, he declared, "The moment they land on our free soil, they imbibe the spirit of freedom, especially as regards vaccination."[50]

In Milwaukee the German medical community was divided over the issue of vaccination, because many German doctors doubted its protective value and worried about its risks. Despite opposition from some of its German members, however, the Milwaukee Medical Society endorsed the practice, as did the local and state boards of health.[51] Nationally, opponents of vaccination constituted a small minority within the regular medical profession. In Newark, which had a large German population, no segment of the medical community openly opposed vaccination, but, as will be seen, phony vaccination certificates were easy to obtain, indicating that some physicians sympathized with parents who opposed vaccination of their children.

A potentially significant advance in the fight against smallpox in Newark was made in 1885, when the board of education began asking proof of vaccination as a condition of admission to the public schools. But for many years the rule was not well enforced. Often physicians relied on the word of the parent or the child that the vaccination had "taken." In other instances obliging family physicians simply waived the procedure and fraudulently signed vaccination certificates. An investigation made by the board of health disclosed that one thousand schoolchildren who possessed vaccination certificates had not been vaccinated.[52]

The board of health urged the board of education to make the visible scar of vaccination the proof of the operation in place of the vaccination certificate. Unfortunately, relations between the board of health and the board of education were strained. The school superintendent, William N. Barringer, was personally opposed to vaccination, having lost a son who died of complications from the procedure. When the district physicians employed by the board of health tried to enter the public schools to vaccinate students during an outbreak of smallpox in 1891, they were stopped by Barringer. The superintendent's actions were upheld by the board of education, which insisted that parents be given the prerogative of selecting who would vaccinate their children. (One school official advised Barringer to forcibly evict the next district physician he encountered.) Furthermore, until 1900, the board of education did not employ a medical staff and so lacked the means of implementing the reforms suggested by the board of health. Instead of strengthening its vaccination requirements, the board of education weakened them. Beginning in 1895, students who demonstrated an "insusceptibility to the vaccine virus"[53] were permitted to attend school.[54]

The problem of guarding Newark against visitations of smallpox was compounded by the constant influx of immigrants. Preschool-age children and blacks had the lowest rates of vaccination. The house-to-house inspection undertaken by the board of health in the years 1885–1887 disclosed that there were at least 6,446 persons in Newark who had never been vaccinated. The number of unprotected persons in 1897 was estimated at about five thousand, and it was from among this group that most of the fatalities in the 1901–1902 epidemic occurred.[55]

When an outbreak of smallpox developed, the board of health sought to vaccinate everyone who had been exposed to the disease. Most individuals were only too glad to get the protection afforded by vaccination and presented themselves willingly to the district physicians or to the doctors at the dispensary. Though the service was offered free of charge, a few hesitated. Some were ignorant of the need for vaccination. Many non-English-speaking immigrants were unwilling to place themselves in the hands of a physician with whom they could not communicate. A few feared the pain or were afraid they would develop sore arms that would prevent them from being able to work for a period of time. Individuals who refused to be vaccinated endangered both themselves and the community. To reach these individuals the district physicians conducted house-to-house vaccination campaigns in areas where smallpox was raging.

The forcible vaccination of recalcitrant citizens was a trying experience. Persons who had been warned of the approach of the district physicians fled their homes or locked themselves in their rooms. When taken by surprise, they hid in barrels and closets and physically resisted their would-be "tormentors." During an outbreak of smallpox in an Italian tenement district in 1887 the vaccinating party was attacked with chains and rolling pins, forcing a hasty retreat from one of the buildings they had entered. One physician asked for police protection and said that without such help it would be impossible to vaccinate these "ignorant, hot-blooded and impulsive people." Prejudice and lack of tact probably accounted for some of the rough treatment shown the vaccinators and on other occasions undoubtedly made their task that much more difficult.[56]

Medical authorities disagreed over the wisdom of house-to-house vaccination campaigns, and hence forcible vaccination of persons exposed to smallpox was practiced in some cities but not in others. Allan McLane Hamilton and Bache McE. Emmett claimed it was their experience in New York City in the 1870s that an appeal to reason was sufficient to induce the poor to submit to vaccination and force "worse than useless." But Chapin in 1901 argued that house-to-house inspection was the only method during an epidemic by which concealed or unrecognized cases could be discovered. In a few cities house-to-house vaccination campaigns, instead of being undertaken after the disease appeared, were a planned annual event. By combating the disease when it was not present, public health officials could act with less haste and more tact in seeking to persuade individuals to submit voluntarily to vaccination, whereas when they had to contain a smallpox epidemic they were compelled to enter people's homes without their permission and to forcibly vaccinate, which, as Hamilton and McE. Emmett declared, was frequently counterproductive.[57]

Cases of smallpox had to be isolated to prevent the disease from spreading. Powers to this end were contained in the ordinance establishing a board of health in Newark. Physicians were compelled to report cases of infectious diseases, and the board of health was authorized to send infected persons to an isolation hospital. The board of health was also given the power to disinfect or destroy infected goods and to placard buildings infected with smallpox.[58] Despite these provisions, quarantine was difficult to enforce. In 1860 the health physician reported:

> There appears to be an inclination on the part of some to avoid, if possible, reporting cases of smallpox or varioloid, fearing that it might act to their prejudice, or make the house in which the disease occurs notorious, and thereby avoided. The occupants object, frequently, to have the notice attached to the building as the ordinance requires, and will tear the same down after it has been affixed by the Health Inspector.[59]

The "Report of Interments" for 1868 listed only four deaths from smallpox. "Probably others occurred, but were attributed to other causes, from the natural desire of friends to suppress the fact of the existence of the terrible disease in their midst."[60]

In most cities smallpox hospitals were described as disgraceful, and therefore some individuals, and occasionally whole communities, violently resisted the efforts of health officials to forcibly move their loved ones there.[61] In Provincetown, Massachusetts, physicians frequently did not report the disease to the board of health to avoid having their patients sent to the smallpox hospital, which "at an 1872 town meeting . . . was said to be 'totally unfit for the purpose of receiving patients.' At times, 'nurses could not be found who were willing to take up abode in the pest house' because of its sorry condition."[62] In the Milwaukee epidemic of 1894–1895, as was already related, the forcible separation of ill children from their parents and the belief that the sick would be in greater danger in the decrepit pesthouse than if allowed to stay in their homes occasioned a general uprising in the affected neighborhoods.

Many persons did not report cases of smallpox because of the stigma attached to the disease. In Provincetown, smallpox deaths occurring in prominent families were attributed to other causes and the names of affluent victims were kept secret while those of the poor were published in the newspapers.[63] Then, too, smallpox was frequently misdiagnosed. It was often confused with chicken pox and sometimes mistaken for measles, eczema, acne, and other eruptive diseases.[64]

Local quarantines designed to bottle up the disease and keep it from spreading proved ineffective. The hardships caused by quarantine made it unpopular, and ingenious citizens could usually find openings in the quarantine picket lines thrown up around stricken communities. To insure the effectiveness of quarantine, the authorities had to strike swiftly and in force. Brutal police actions were conducted in which tenants were ejected from their apartments. Sometimes entire neighborhoods were isolated by armed guards.

The imposition of quarantine was also an expensive task. Guards had to be stationed around the buildings and the inhabitants supplied with provisions. During the smallpox epidemic of 1894, nine hundred persons were quarantined at a cost of slightly under $10,750. At the height of the epidemic, thirty houses containing over three hundred individuals were under guard. The total expenses incurred by the board of health in 1894 in fighting smallpox amounted to over $24,500, or 70 percent of the board's tax appropriation for the year.[65]

Many citizens who contracted smallpox were isolated in their attics or some other little-used part of their homes. Victims of the disease who lived in tenements or in private homes where complete isolation or proper care could not be guaranteed were removed to the despicable smallpox hospital on the edge of the Newark salt meadows. Though a new, improved facility was built in 1871, the hospital remained a horror. The building was completely lacking in modern conveniences, was located in an unhealthy area, and was so poorly maintained that in 1894 it was considered beyond repair. A "Pest House . . . of the type of bygone centuries" was the way the health officer described it. The hospital had still other shortcomings. It could only accommodate thirty patients, necessitating the use of tents during epidemics to house the overflow. Operation of the hospital was uneconomical, since it was used about every four or five years, and then usually for only a month.[66]

Aside from two scares, one occurring in 1882 and the other in 1894, in which there were 120 cases and fourteen fatalities and 131 cases and eighteen fatalities, respectively, Newark was spared a major epidemic of smallpox for about twenty-seven years following the epidemic of 1871–1874.[67] But the city was not out of danger. Every year scores of unvaccinated immigrants settled in Newark, and babies were born, fresh fodder for a new slaughter. Lulled into a false sense of security by the long absence of the disease, residents became careless about revaccination. In the years 1901–1902 the citizens of Newark would once again be subjected to the ravages of smallpox.

The first case of smallpox was contracted on March 16, by an itinerant peddler in a lodging house. Unlicensed, unregulated, and unsanitary, lodging houses were nurseries of communicable diseases. Moreover, their 50 percent daily turnover of boarders insured the widest possible dissemination of germs nurtured there. On March 30, inspectors of the board of health were instructed to canvas the cheap lodging houses of the city and to vaccinate anyone who had been exposed to the disease. Hearing the approach of the inspectors, a number of boarders escaped by climbing down fire escapes or by shimmying down hastily rigged sheet ropes, some of which were several stories high. Two days later the inspectors came again, only this time they arrived at midnight with policemen in tow. But the board's efforts were futile: new cases kept occurring, and the disease could not be confined.

By April 19 the dispensary was being deluged with persons seeking to be vaccinated. Employers began insisting on the vaccination of their workers, and the inspectors were instructed to vaccinate in stores and factories upon request of the proprietors.[68]

As the epidemic grew in severity, public attention turned to conditions at the pesthouse. The isolation hospital was in its usually sorry state. The building was mosquito-ridden and lacked even rudimentary plumbing; there were neither toilet facilities nor hot water. Kerosene lamps provided the only light, and the stoves had to be lit to obtain heat. Aside from some cots, the rooms that housed the patients were bare. In these cheerless wards the patients awaited death practically unattended.[69]

The board of health had been endeavoring for years to get a new isolation hospital. The *Newark Evening News* editorialized that "the time to erect an isolation hospital is now and the place is within the city boundaries. Too much tenderness has been shown individuals. The public safety is paramount to the interests of private property owners."[70] A grand jury presentment made on June 15 contained a scathing indictment of the hospital and asked that top priority be given to the construction of a new facility.[71]

There was a lull in the epidemic during the summer, but it was expected that when the weather turned cold and persons were forced indoors, the epidemic would pick up again. Portable hospital quarters were planned, and twenty thousand dollars was made available to the board of health for the building of an isolation hospital. On September 16 the board announced that it had taken an option on a piece of land in the Eighth Ward on the banks of the Second River to be used as the site for a new isolation hospital.[72]

The owners, however, refused to hand over the deed to the property when they learned the purpose for which it was to be used. In addition, three prominent city officials threatened court action to prevent the city from using the land for a pesthouse. Almost immediately, the mayor and the board of health began to back down. On September 26 the mayor issued a statement to the effect that had he forseen the furor the site acquisition would arouse, he would not have supported it. About the same time, the board of health announced that, if necessary, makeshift hospital facilities could be improvised. A petition protesting the location of the isolation hospital and bearing the signatures of over 130 businessmen in the area was presented to the board of health on October 1. Two days later the owners of the site were given an indemnity bond for $17,500, the purchase price agreed upon for the property, to cover any losses that might result from failure to convey the deed to the city. To acquire the land the city would either have to seek it through condemnation or file suit for execution of the option.[73]

Cowed by the opposition of property owners and by the equivocation of government officials, the board of health abandoned its attempts to secure a site in Newark. The board still had one option left. The city of Newark owned some property in the nearby town of Irvington, New Jersey. An offer was made to the town to treat residents afflicted with acute, infectious diseases without cost in return for permission to build an isolation hospital. At a mass meeting held in Irvington on November 2, during which speakers were frequently interrupted by cheers, hissing, and cries of "pesthouse," opponents of the plan warned of mischief and of depressed property values if it was accepted. By a near unanimous vote a resolution was adopted instructing the town council to reject the offer. On November 8 the Newark city counsel advised the common council he did not believe the city could condemn property for an isolation hospital site, and the Second River site was abandoned. On the same day, the common council voted money for the erection and outfitting of two portable hospital buildings.[74]

The epidemic raged out of control through the winter of 1901–1902. To eliminate every focal point of the disease in the city, the board of health was empowered to remove all ambulatory smallpox victims to the isolation hospital. On February 6 the board of education ordered its medical examiners to vaccinate public school students, but when the medical examiners objected that the order would bring them into conflict with private practitioners "by taking away probable patients from them" the order was rescinded.[75]

The records of the board of health for 1901–1902 do not contain expenses for employment of guards, indicating no attempt was made to enforce quarantine once the epidemic had gotten out of control. Rather, the board fought the pestilence by removing smallpox victims from the community and by urging citizens to get themselves vaccinated or re-vaccinated. In these efforts the board was quite successful. Of the 187 fatalities from smallpox in 1901, 180 occurred in the pesthouse, and upwards of one hundred thousand persons were vaccinated.[76] In the summer of 1902 the epidemic ended, but no one could be sure that this dread, though easily preventable disease, would not return and cause still more needless suffering and death.

During the 1890s, better methods were devised of insuring the reliability of the cowpox vaccine and of reducing the incidence and severity of inflammatory reactions. It was discovered that furnishing the vaccine in a glycerine solution in capillary tubes would sterilize the virus and eliminate most vaccination infections. In the early 1900s the state and federal governments began to exercise control over the production and distribution of serums and vaccines. Reforms in medical education improved the skills of vaccinators, and as a result of all these changes there were fewer "vaccination tragedies."[77]

There was also a major change in the disease itself that influenced public attitudes toward vaccination. A mild strain of smallpox, subsequently named *Variola minor,* was recognized in the late nineteenth century and spread to the United States in 1896. The disease had a case fatality rate of 1 percent or less but otherwise was indistinguishable from the more familiar and virulent *Variola major.* In the first decades of the twentieth century *Variola minor* replaced the more severe form of the disease in North America. Thereafter, though smallpox outbreaks continued to occur, they caused little loss of life and consequently induced less intensive control efforts. As late as 1930 only ten states had compulsory vaccination laws.[78]

Therefore, though a majority of the American population was immunized as a result of having attended public schools, and communities could vaccinate large numbers of persons during an epidemic, smallpox persisted. During the decade 1901–1910 there were 283,000 cases reported throughout the United States, with *Variola minor* greatly predominating. In the following two decades there were hundreds of thousands of cases of smallpox, nearly all of them mild. Occasionally, however, smallpox could still sting. There were sixteen thousand cases of severe smallpox reported in the nationwide epidemic of 1902–1903, and in the years 1912–1914 *Variola major* caused ninety-nine deaths in Pittsburgh, Los Angeles, and El Paso.[79]

Throughout the nineteenth century the high points in Newark's death-rate curve were occasioned by epidemics of smallpox and cholera. More Newarkers died from smallpox than cholera, but it was cholera that frightened public leaders and galvanized the community to act. For cholera menaced the rich and the poor alike and caused business to slump, while smallpox, once artificial immunity became available, was no longer viewed with alarm by the city's policy makers. Hence cholera was eradicated in Newark within a few years after its method of transmission was revealed, whereas smallpox, despite the existence of an inexpensive and easily obtainable preventive, continued to afflict the city's ignorant and poor until well into the twentieth century.

9 WATER SUPPLY

U NTIL THE MIDDLE OF THE NINETEENTH CENTURY, the water supply question in Newark arose mainly as an adjunct to the problem of fire control. Following publication of Snow's study on cholera, attention shifted to the relationship between polluted water supplies and epidemics.[1] Thus when cholera struck Newark for the fourth time, in 1866, the apprehensions of residents about the quality of their drinking water burst into the open. The heaviest salvo was fired by the Newark Board of Health:

> "Whereas investigations have demonstrated to the satisfaction of the Board of Health that the water furnished by the Newark Aqueduct Board and supplied to the inhabitants of the city is not only inadequate in quantity, but of such an impure and inferior quality as to seriously affect and injure the health of persons using the same, and
>
> "Whereas the public health being thus endangered, this board demands immediate and prompt action in the premises: it is, therefore,
>
> "Resolved, that the water now furnished by the Newark Aqueduct Board is hereby declared to be a nuisance."[2]

The outcry of an aroused citizenry hastened a resumption of work on the Passaic River waterworks, which the Civil War had interrupted. Construction began that summer and was completed in 1870.[3]

Newark's decision to end its dependence on private vendors and local sources of water and to build a municipal waterworks that could meet the city's greatly enlarged needs reflected a national trend. By the mid-nineteenth century, American cities had outgrown the cisterns, wells, and springs that furnished most of the nation's drinking water. Even before then, disastrous fires and epidemics had led New York, Boston, and to a lesser extent Baltimore to look far beyond their corporate boundaries for abundant supplies of pure water. After the Civil War, a copious supply of water for household use, fire fighting, and business purposes came to be regarded as so essential to the public welfare that cities strapped themselves financially in order to secure it. In 1850 there were fewer than one hundred cities with planned water supply systems. By the end of the century there were over three thousand waterworks in operation, of which a little more than half, including nearly all of the largest ones, were municipally owned.[4]

As domestic water sources dried up or became polluted, cities were compelled to develop public water supplies by bringing in water by gravity from mountain streams or, more common, by pumping it from nearby rivers and lakes. As more water was used in the city, it became necessary to construct sewers to remove used water from private residences. Since the large waterways that bordered American cities were the natural outfalls for the sewers, communities that obtained their water from nearby lakes and rivers drank their own sewerage or that of their neighbors upstream. Industries located along the banks of the waterways added their effluents, causing a further deterioration in water quality. The water consumed by urban residents in the late nineteenth century was both unappetizing and dangerous.[5]

Some cities attempted to stop the pollution of their water supplies at the source by taking legal action against factory owners and river bank inhabitants who ran drains into waterways from which the cities obtained their drinking water. A number of cities early on had enacted ordinances to prevent persons from dumping their garbage and refuse into nearby streams. But the common law provided little support for health officials who sought to prevent the defilement of potable water supplies. The law was more concerned with preventing the owner of a river bank from diminishing the quantity of water available to a downstream user than it was with protecting its quality. In the absence of any specific legislative injunction, "the upstream owner could dump sewage, ashes or other kinds of refuse into the stream and be legally liable only if the downstream owner could prove that the polluter had rendered the water unfit for his use."[6] It was not until the second decade of the twentieth century that the courts began to accept the argument of state health officials that governmental action designed to protect the public against the transmission of waterborne diseases was a valid exercise of the police powers of the state.[7]

The problems encountered by cities that sought to use the judicial system to protect the purity of their water supplies can be seen in Philadelphia's experience. Alarmed by the growing pollution of the Schuylkill River, from which it obtained its water, the city in the late 1870s and 1880s brought suit against polluters. Several riparian homeowners who had run privy drains directly into the river were successfully prosecuted and indictments were made against some major industrial polluters. One of the first suits was brought against the owners of a huge wool and cloth mill by the commissioner of the Fairmount Park, acting under the authority granted him by municipal and state legislation to act as guardian of the purity of the Schuylkill River. The suit was dropped, however, upon the request of the city of Philadelphia when the mill owners treatened to close the plant and take its one-million-dollar payroll, twenty-six hundred jobs, and ten thousand dollars paid in annual taxes to a city that was more understanding of its needs.[8]

The master in equity, William Wilkins Carr, in his analysis of these cases, explained why the city was unable to prevent industrialists from using the Schuylkill River as a sink for their wastes. He found that the law itself with regard to pollution of municipal water supplies was weak. Since attempts to enforce antipollution statutes adversely affected the interests of large manufacturers, they had become "dead laws." Carr said that the laws to prevent the pollution of the Schuylkill River needed strengthening, but that in all likelihood this would not happen because of the opposition of factory owners located along the waterway. He castigated city officials for their halfhearted efforts to prevent the pollution of the city's water supply and said that Philadelphia could hardly expect to win the sympathy of the courts or the legislature so long as the drainage of its own sewers, streets, and property was befouling the river.[9]

Before the Civil War, a few cities had experimented with filtering their water supplies in order to make the water more palatable. Typically the water was percolated through a bed of sand and gravel to remove discoloration and suspended matter. But though antebellum methods of filtration improved the physical quality of the water, they were not intended as a program of disease prevention.[10]

On the basis of the statistical investigations and field studies of John Snow, William Budd, and other European investigators, it was strongly suspected that feces-contaminated water was responsible for the transmission of cholera, typhoid fever, and other waterborne diseases, but irrefutable evidence was lacking until the advent of bacteriology and the germ theory of disease. No one had ever seen the bacteria responsible for these diseases, much less demonstrated that living organisms invisible to the naked eye caused them. Many cholera investigators believed that the disease was caused by a chemical poison discharged in the bowel movements of its victims. However, chemical tests of waterways into which sewage was discharged often failed to detect any fecal contamination of the water a few miles downstream of the sewer outlet, leading some chemists to claim that dilution and oxidation of sewage rendered it harmless. The danger of tapping rivers and lakes that received the drainage of urban communities was not conclusively demonstrated until the 1880s, when Robert Koch and other medical scientists provided laboratory proof of the existence of pathogenic microorganisms that could be transmitted through fecalized water supplies.[11]

The cholera vibrio and the typhoid bacillus were soon identified and scientists began to conduct experiments to determine if filtration could keep these microorganisms from entering a city's water supply. The Lawrence, Massachusetts, State Board of Health Experiment Station emerged as the leading research center in water purification and sewage treatment. Many important discoveries were made, including the realization that improved slow sand filters could remove the typhoid bacillus in municipal water supplies. In 1893 the Lawrence Experiment Station built a slow sand filtration plant for the city, which in the past had suffered grievously from typhoid. Within a decade, Lawrence's typhoid fever mortality rate plumeted from an average of about 120 per 100,000 population to between 20 and 30.[12]

Other advances in water purification rapidly followed,[13] but for many municipal officials who had hoped to avoid the expense involved in abandoning an existing water supply the breakthroughs in sanitary engineering that occurred in the 1890s and early 1900s came too late. Frightened by the rising incidence of typhoid fever, several cities had already decided to obtain new water supplies,[14] though in some instances their existing waterworks had only been in service for a few years and had not been paid for yet. Most cities, however, were unwilling to incur the cost of a new supply and thus continued to experience a high incidence of typhoid fever and other waterborne diseases until water purification methods became available.

IN PLANNING A NEW WATER SUPPLY FOR THE CITY OF Newark, the Newark Aqueduct Board conscientiously assessed the factors that might affect its safety. Dr. Chilton, a chemist engaged by the board for this purpose, assured his employer the water of the Passaic River was "equal to that of most rivers, and excelling many in good repute," including the famed Croton River, and was "all that could be desired for drinking and other domestic purposes." Confidence was expressed in the "law of purification," which stated that a stream had the inherent power to purify itself by oxidation after a few miles of flow. Aqueduct officials were also comforted by the belief that the Passaic River was so large it could easily absorb any and all pollutants.[15]

Nevertheless, to be on the safe side, a second line of defense was prepared in case nature's protection against pollution proved fallible. To insure the water's purity, the pumping station was located just north of the bar where the Second River, the boundary between Belleville and Newark, emptied its industrial wastes into the Passaic River. As an additional safety measure, the water was pumped through infiltration basins located on the alluvial sand and gravel on the west bank of the river.[16]

The precautions taken by the Newark Aqueduct Board were unavailing. As cities and industries developed along the Passaic River and its tributaries, the river became hopelessly polluted. In 1872 complaints about the quality of the water supply led to an investigation by the *Newark Daily Advertiser,* which disclosed that the river was being befouled with sewage, animal carcasses, dead bodies, and industrial wastes. "It has been ascertained beyond any doubt," warned the *Advertiser*, "that impure water is sometimes the cause of frightful epidemics."[17] Professor Albert R. Leeds of the Stevens Institute, in a report to the Board of Public Works of Jersey City, stated that chemical tests had revealed "a shocking degree of contamination by organic matter."[18] A state commission in 1873 inquiring into methods of obtaining a water supply for Hoboken and other northern Hudson County communities selected the Hackensack River over the Passaic River because of the latter's growing pollution.[19]

Therefore, almost no sooner was the waterworks completed than demands were made that it be abandoned. The Newark Board of Trade, in its annual report for 1872, recommended that the city prepare for all contingencies by securing control of strategic watersheds and water rights while they were still affordable.[20] In 1873 the New Jersey Legislature authorized the Newark Aqueduct Board and the Board of Public Works of Jersey City to establish a joint commission with the power to issue two million dollars in bonds to procure a new water supply. The commission, however, was shackled in its search for new sources of water by its inability to appropriate the area's better water properties. The property of the Society for Establishing Useful Manufactures, which included rights to the waters of the Passaic River above Paterson, and the holdings of the Morris Canal and Banking Company, which controlled rich water parcels in the northern part of the state, were specifically exempted from the condemnation powers granted to the commission.[21]

A chemist, Professor Henry Wurtz, was hired to analyze water samples of the Passaic River. Wurtz concluded the situation was critical. He pointed to the growing evidence that cholera, typhoid fever, and dysentery were caused by sewage-contaminated water and warned that the excretus from a single cholera victim that found its way into the river would be sufficient to imperil the entire valley.[22]

In an accompanying report, engineer George Bailey recommended the construction of a dam across the Passaic River to prevent the sewage of Newark from being swept upstream by the tide past the Newark and Jersey City intakes. He also suggested that the commission study the possibility of obtaining water from the Morris Canal Company.

Wurtz supported the Morris Canal proposal and admonished the commission to act upon it "immediately, without any dangerous delays."[23]

The commission's study was released at an unfortuitous time. The depression of 1873 struck Newark hard, darkening factories and leaving many destitute. Consequently, as the board of trade regretfully noted, plans for the solution of this "much-vexed question" were either shelved or dismissed as impractical.[24]

But the board of trade was not content to let the matter rest. In its annual report for 1875 it declared:

> The health of our city, on which depends every other interest, is so intimately connected with the subject, that there can be but one mind as to our duty in keeping the subject before you.[25]

> The light that science has recently shed upon the intimate connection of this subject with the health of cities, and upon the origin and cause of dangerous forms of disease, now so prevalent and fatal in our cities, has given it an especial and general interest. The popular mind is being instructed in these matters, and should any calamity overtake our city through a neglect of this subject, will hold to a rigorous responsibility the authorities who have it in charge.[26]

In the years 1874 to 1876 further evidence of the contamination of the Passaic River was supplied by the state geologist and the Geological Survey Laboratory at New Brunswick. By 1876 the sixteen-mile stretch of waterway between Paterson and Newark was receiving the sewage of a rapidly expanding population of nearly two hundred thousand.[27] Anxiety over the growing defilement of the Passaic River led to a meeting in 1876 of the mayors of Newark, Jersey City, Hoboken, Orange, Bayonne, and Bloomfield; however, nothing came of it.[28]

At this juncture, schemes for utilizing the Morris Canal were once again brought up for consideration. The Morris Canal was fed by mountain streams and lakes in the northern part of the state, principally Lake Hopatcong, the state's largest lake, and Greenwood Lake. With the coming of the railroad, the canal had fallen upon hard times and its owner, the Morris Canal Company, a wholly owned subsidiary of the Lehigh Valley Railroad Company, was anxious to sell it. The purity of its waters had been attested to by Newark officials in 1851 and 1861, and as recently as 1873. In response to public pressure, the Newark Aqueduct Board appointed a commission to report on an offer of the company to sell its rights and franchises to the canal. Though the canal was considered ideal in the quantity and quality of its water, the offer was rejected because of the lingering impact of the depression of 1873 on the city's economy.[29]

In 1878 the engineering firm of Croes and Howell was employed by the Newark Aqueduct Board to investigate various schemes of water supply. In an exhaustive report, Croes and Howell considered three proposed solutions: (1) retention of the existing system; (2) removal of the waterworks to Little Falls above Paterson; and (3) abandonment of the pumping station for a gravity system to be obtained from the head-waters of the Passaic River.[30]

There were strong financial incentives for maintaining the existing waterworks. The Passaic River plant had been built at a cost of upward of a million dollars, which was more than Newark's total tax appropriations for 1880. The cost of a new water supply was estimated to be somewhere between two and four million dollars.[31]

Many schemes had been put forth to purify the Passaic River. One plan proposed the construction of filtration beds. In dismissing this and similar proposals, Croes and Howell remarked that "among the numerous processes for the cleansing of polluted water with which we have been acquainted, there is not one which is sufficiently effective to warrant the use for drinking water of water which has once been contaminated with sewage or similar noxious criminal matter."[32] Another solution called for the construction of a dam below the waterworks to prevent the tide from carrying Newark's sewage into its reservoirs. The dam was to be coupled with a great intercepting sewer along the river to carry sewage from the communities located above the pumping station to a point below the dam.[33]

The second proposal, to remove the pumping station to a point above the falls at Paterson, was considered too expensive because of the damages that would have to be paid to the Society for Establishing Useful Manufactures. At the time of its incorporation in 1791, the society had been invested by the legislature with riparian rights in the water of the Passaic River above the falls. The society thus claimed the right to an undiminished flow of Passaic River water to supply motive power for its tenants, the manufacturing establishments of Paterson.[34] On the basis of the relative operating costs of the different plans, Croes and Howell gave their endorsement to the third alternative: the procurement of a water supply by gravity from the mountainous watershed of the Passaic River above Paterson.[35] Casting aside the Morris Canal because of its exposure to contamination and the high costs necessary to repair and maintain it, Croes and Howell selected the Pequannock River as the source of the new supply.[36]

Because of the great vogue of driven wells at the time of its publication, the Croes and Howell report did not receive the attention it merited. About forty driven wells were sunk into the alluvial sand and gravel on the west bank of the Passaic River in the hope of finding an underground stream or a bountiful aquifer. If successful, Newark would have obtained a reliable supply of water at relatively little cost. But the yield was only about one hundred thousand gallons per day, and most of this, it was suspected, was Passaic River water that had filtered into the wells. The project was given little chance of success by either Croes and Howell or the state geologist, and when in the summer of 1881 the holders of the patents to the wells demanded compensation, the project was dropped.[37]

Meanwhile, concern was being expressed about the effect drinking Passaic River water was having on the health of the city's inhabitants. Lott Southard, the president of the Essex County Medical Society, in an 1877 address, "On the Water Supply of the City of Newark and Its Relation to Disease," argued that contaminated water was the major cause of the numerous deaths in Newark from "zymotic diseases." Following a second address on this subject in 1879, the society adopted a resolution calling upon the state to prevent the pollution of its potable water supplies.[38] Edgar Holden believed the water supply was responsible for the high incidence of diarrheal illnesses in Newark.[39] In his annual report for 1880 Dr. Charles M. Zeh, the acting health physician of the Newark Board of Health, warned that contaminated water "unquestionably added to the mortality of a city."[40] The *Sunday Call* voiced the anguish of many Newarkers when it declared:

We are told by physicians that the water we drink contains properties poisonous to the system, and we know that this must be true, because we know that
our drinking water washes the front of two cities and carries off their sewage
and refuse. We are told that much of the mortality of Newark is due to the
use of Passaic water and we cannot doubt the statement for it comes from unquestionable authority and is based upon undisputed fact. . . . Viewed in the
light of the public health, the water question becomes a problem that over-
shadows all other matters relative to the weal of our city. It is the one vital
question that demands a solution immediately, that cannot be put off to a future day.[41]

Having abandoned hopes of obtaining water from driven wells, a
group in Newark seeking to retain the existing supply, led by Bailey
and the Newark Aqueduct Board, revived the plan to build a dam
across the Passaic River. In 1882 a bill for that purpose was introduced
in the state legislature. It was opposed by municipalities and corporations located above the proposed dam site, who feared the dam would
impede navigation on the river, and was defeated.[42]

The pollution problem of the Passaic River was now starting to interest other communities and state officials. Hoboken, which had earlier ignored the advice of a state commission, reversed itself and in
1881 abandoned the Passaic River for the Hackensack River. Consequently, Hoboken's death rate began to decline. The state geologist
strongly urged communities to foresake the Passaic River in favor of
water from nearby mountain streams whose purity was above suspicion.[43] In his first inaugural address Governor George E. Ludlow
counseled the legislature that the health and prosperity of the state's
most highly developed and densely populated section was at stake.
Echoing the sentiments of the state geologist, the governor proposed
that the state help develop the water resources that lay just six miles
west of Newark. The governor coupled his plea with a warning that if
state action was not soon forthcoming, the streams might be utilized for
mill sites or monopolized by a single municipality, "or possibly bought
to satisfy the pressing want of the neighboring metropolis [New
York]."[44] The thought of New York City poaching on the water resources of New Jersey was a prospect that could be counted on to
arouse even the most lethargic legislator.

As a result of the governor's message, a state water commission was established in 1882 to develop plans to impound the waters of the Passaic River for the purpose of creating a joint municipal water supply. The principal sheds of the upper Passaic River valley were examined, and information was obtained on the existing requirements, estimated future needs, and financial resources of the valley communities. The commission's report, which was released in 1884, recommended that water for the project be taken from the Pequannock River and reservoirs be built to provide the cities of the Passaic River valley with an average daily supply of eighty million gallons, which the commission believed would suffice until 1906. The maximum cost of the project was estimated at slightly over $3.25 million.[45]

The Newark Aqueduct Board reacted negatively to the proposal. Unwilling to write off the investment in the pumping station and admit its mistake, the board insisted upon maintaining the Belleville plant. Albert Leeds, who was now the board's chemist, refused to consider the question of a new supply, stating that the objections raised to the idea at previous board meetings appeared "insurmountable," and further discussion "would be futile."[46]

In spite of the mounting evidence, many Newarkers still had doubts about the danger of the water supply. For one thing, the worst fears of its detractors failed to materialize. Cholera, though it turned up in the Mississippi River valley in 1873 and was reported aboard immigrant ships in New York harbor from time to time, never appeared again in Newark after 1866. Typhoid fever was on the increase, but was not yet epidemic. The board of health, in its annual report for 1881, professed ignorance of any illness resulting from the use of Passaic River water. Similar reservations were expressed in interviews in 1877 of twenty prominent Newark physicians.[47] Furthermore, with the discovery that many epidemic diseases were caused by living organisms, a shadow was cast on the value of chemical analysis in determining the safety of municipal water supplies. Chemical examination of a water supply will reveal the presence of organic matter or its constituents, and thus is useful in detecting fecal contamination, but it will not disclose the presence of microbes.[48] A study of the different methods of analysis of water supplies was made in 1881, at the request of the National Board of Health, by Professor J. W. Mallet of the University of Virginia, who concluded that it was not possible to make a definitive judgment about the wholesomeness or unwholesomeness of a drinking water solely on the basis of chemical analysis. One year later, J. D. Brumley, the Newark health physician, wrote there was no proof that the use of polluted water caused illness.[49]

Nevertheless, most Newark officials were cognizant of the dangers of fecal contamination and of the necessity, at the very least, of improving the physical qualities—color, smell, and taste—of Newark's drinking water. By the time the report of the state water commission had been released, a new plan for protecting the purity of the Passaic River had already been put into effect by the authorities of Newark and Jersey City.

The plan had its genesis in a water scare that struck Newark in 1880. Complaints were received from all sections of the city that the water smelled like creosote, tasted bad, and had an odd color.[50] Upon investigation it was found the water was being contaminated by carbolic acid from the Kingsland Paper Mill on the Third River, some two miles above the Newark intake. An indictment was brought against the mill for creating a public nuisance, and the company was forced to stop discharging its wastes into the river. Encouraged by this success, Newark and Jersey City joined forces to prevent further pollution of the Passaic River. On October 27, 1881, the Board of Inspection of the Pollution of the Passaic River and Its Tributaries, composed of members of the Newark Aqueduct Board and Boards of Public Works and Finance of Jersey City, was organized. Authority for the board's activities was found in section 192 of the Crimes Act, which made public nuisances misdemeanors punishable by up to two years imprisonment or a fine not exceeding five hundred dollars, or both; in an act passed March 21, 1873, which prohibited the discharge of petroleum, rock oil, or coal tar into the Passaic River within Essex and Hudson counties; and in a law passed February 27, 1880, which prohibited individuals and manufacturers from polluting waterways used for drinking water.[51] To implement the board's work, Leeds was instructed to take water samples from selected stations along the river, and a sanitary patrol was instituted of the waterway and its tributaries.

The work of the board began with much fanfare and amid great promise. The chief engineer of Jersey City confidently predicted that in a few years the water would return "to its original state of purity," and both Jersey City and Newark would "have the best, purest and most abundant source of water supply of any city within 500 miles."[52] The board's accomplishments during its first years of operation provided ample reason for the optimism of its supporters. Leeds reported:

> The rigid inspection of the streams has succeeded in keeping it free from car-casses of dead animals, from its being used as a dumping place for night soil, offal and refuse of all description. It has caused the removal of [water] closets and drains which formerly carried the excreta of thousands of [mill and factory] operatives and [river bank inhabitants] directly into the Passaic or some of its tributaries. It has caused the smaller communities located on Second and Third rivers to give up the project of converting these streams into sewers, and instead to resort to systems of sewage utilization. . . . It has caused so large a community as that of the town of Passaic to seriously con-sider the problem of disposing of its sewage by a method which would return the effluent waters in a purified condition to the Passaic.[53]

Leeds was encouraged by the samples he examined, and the infor-mation obtained would suggest new methods for protecting the water's safety. In his first report, dated November 1881, in which the water was described as "tolerably wholesome," Leeds analyzed the contami-nation at the Newark and Jersey City intakes. Noting that the samples improved as he left Paterson and moved downstream, Leeds concluded that the natural settling, dilution, and oxidation of pollutants in the course of the river's flow had purified the water.

Leeds's explanation for this phenomenon, which he referred to "as the power inherent in a flowing stream to purify itself after a sufficient number of miles of flow," was in accord with the best scientific opinion of the day.[54] Nevertheless, little was known about the self-purification of streams other than that water that flowed over pebbly beds or cas-caded over rocky falls had been extolled throughout the ages for its taste and purity. Aeration alone, however, might not be sufficient to render contaminated water safe. Moreover, the Passaic River below

Paterson was a deep, smooth-flowing stream, and Leeds was almost certainly wrong about its self-cleansing capabilities.[55]

As Leeds approached the Newark pumping station, the water became much worse, the result of the tide, which twice daily carried Newark's sewage past the plant's water intake.[56] Leeds's report induced the board of pollution to introduce a bill in the legislature in 1882 to build a dam across the river, which, as already related, was defeated. In his second annual report, dated December 27, 1882, Leeds studied the effects of season and weather on the water's purity. The water was discovered to have been at its worst in September and October, owing to a severe drought during the summer and autumn.[57] In 1883 the water was reported to be of much better quality than in previous years, and in 1884 was said to be vastly improved over what it had been in 1883.[58]

By 1884 Leeds was ready to announce a plan for ending the pollution of the Passaic River. He proposed to make Passaic River water safe by: (1) requiring manufacturers and communities to remove 50 percent of the organic impurities from their sewage before allowing it to enter the river; (2) relying on the river's own powers of self-purification; and (3) purifying the water before it entered the reservoirs of the two cities.[59]

Leeds sought to purify the water by a combination of filtration and aeration, a plan he had put into effect in Hoboken in 1884. Here water that had been "so nauseous that it was unfit for use" had been made so wholesome, Leeds claimed, that its excellence was commented upon by strangers. Leeds, who was the chief adovcate in the United States of forced aeration as a means of removing organic matter from water, may have had a personal interest in the matter, for he would soon take out patents on several systems of forced aeration. Though systems of forced aeration were used successfully in a few waterworks to retard the growth of algae, Leeds's attempt to accelerate nature's method of oxidizing organic matter in municipal water supplies was declared a failure by the Massachusetts State Board of Health, the nation's leading center for the study of water and sewage purification.[60] In any case, the pollution of the Passaic River was a challenge to even Leeds's ability, for he admitted that though he could make Passaic River water safe, "he would not like to have it as a regular drink."[61]

In fact, the gains made by the board of pollution could not be secured. The population of the lower Passaic River valley in 1880 was 250,000; by 1918 it would reach 800,000. Communities the board had hoped would use other methods of sewage disposal, such as Passaic and Belleville, found it easier to empty their wastes into the nearby Passaic River or its tributaries, and cities that had always used the Passaic River for this purpose, such as Paterson and Newark, contributed ever-increasing loads.[62]

After some initial successes, the board was unable to prevent factory owners from polluting the river. "Legal notices and warnings are unheeded by them," reported Thomas W. Leak, river inspector for the board of pollution, "and it will be a useless task for me to try to stop them until legal action is instituted against them."[63] But civil proceedings were slow, and when the board threatened to bring criminal action against polluters, the owners banded together, "determined to sustain one another against any one of them."[64]

The board was also experiencing organizational difficulties. When asked by a reporter why polluters had not been prosecuted, board officials proceeded to blame one another. The river inspector stated he only had the power to give notice to end pollution. The counsel for the board replied he had not received orders to prosecute. And the president of the board blamed the chemist for having failed to provide data that was needed in court. In October 1886 Albert Leeds was dismissed from the Newark Aqueduct Board for having "placed the Board [of Pollution] in a bad light before the public."[65] At the time, Leeds was in England studying bacteriological techniques of water analysis, and apparently through some mixup his assistants had failed to turn in their reports.[66] Newark officials and newspapers placed part of the responsibility for the board of pollution's inaction on the cupidity of Jersey City officials, charging they were more concerned with acquiring patronage on the board than with ending pollution.[67]

"INSPECTION IN VAIN, A DO-NOTHING POLLUTION BOARD," proclaimed the *Newark Evening News* in a front-page headline. The source of the story, which appeared in September 1886, was inspector Leak, who "candidly admitted that very little had been accomplished . . . and that the water was being polluted every day."[68] In a follow-up interview held the next year, Leak stated he had stopped residents along the river from emptying cesspools and water closets into the waterway, "but with the chief transgressors [communities and industrial establishments] . . . had been unable to do anything."[69]

The board's failure to end the pollution of the Passaic River led to renewed agitation for reform. In 1885 the president of the Newark Board of Trade warned that Newark could never expect to attain commercial eminence while the specter of pestilence hung over the city.[70] It is "unquestionable," wrote the *Sunday Call*, "that Newark has managed to obtain a reputation for possessing the most unhealthful water supply in the Union."[71] A resolution in favor of a new water supply was adopted in September 1885 at a meeting of delegates from Newark's civic-improvement ward associations; one delegate called for a referendum on the issue. In the fall of 1886, the local Democratic and Republican parties put themselves on record in favor of abandoning the Passaic River.[72] The Newark Aqueduct Board acknowledged that the subject of a new water supply was being publicly debated but refused to take any action unless directed to do so by the city's elected political authorities.[73]

By 1884 the board of pollution had reached the pinnacle of its success; thereafter, the quality of Passaic River water was to decline precipitately. Professor Leeds's final report, for the year 1885, showed an enormous increase in the carbon dioxide content of the water and a corresponding decrease in the oxygen level.[74] In 1886 the state geologist described the water as "disgustingly impure."[75] The most graphic account of the defilement of the Passaic River was furnished by Leeds himself in 1887. Starting at Paterson and working his way some sixteen miles downstream to Newark, Leeds listed and commented upon the principal sources of pollution.

1. Paterson, population 70,000; cotton mills, woolen manufacturers, locomotive works, jute mills, and silk and silk-dyeing establishments pouring their wastes into the Passaic River; city rapidly extending its sewer system.

2. Oil seepage from storage tanks opposite Passaic and oil from a burst pipeline crossing Saddle River; oil can be seen for miles.

3. Passaic, population 10,000; river being contaminated by six mills and a chemical plant; city proceeding with plans for new sewers which will drain into the Passaic River.

4. Third River; once a mountain stream, now an open sewer. The stream receives the drainage of the town of Franklin and parts of Belleville, and the refuse of woolen and paper mills; stream joins the Passaic River at a point just one and a quarter miles above the Newark intake and two miles above the Jersey City intake.

5. Belleville, population 3,500; no sewers, but a large number of drains that discharge into the river.

6. Second River; one of the worst sources of pollution; outlet for the sewage of Orange, Montclair, Bloomfield, Ridgewood, and Soho, and the many varied industries along its banks.

7. Newark and East Newark; sewage and wastes from combined population of about 180,000; heavily industrial area.[76]

Leeds, who according to one newspaper was the "foremost water chemist in the country," had compiled the list in responding to the first of four questions put to him by the residents of Jersey City acting through a newspaper of that city, the *Sunday Eagle*. Leeds was asked if the pollution was worsening, and he answered affirmatively. Is it dangerous, he was asked, to which he replied: "This is as though I were asked is drinking sewage dangerous to health? I believe it to be not merely dangerous, but so fatal that thousands of people are killed by sewage-drinking every year."[77] Queried about the best method of obtaining a pure water supply, Leeds dealt a severe blow to those who still clung to his original plans for filtration and aeration of Passaic River water by recommending instead the tapping of the upper Passaic River watershed.

Perhaps the most alarming note was struck by Professors Peter T. Austin and F. A. Wilbur of Rutgers College, the chemists who succeeded Leeds, in their report to the board of pollution dated June 1887.[78] They stated:

> During the greater part of the year the water . . . is contaminated with filth, sewage and manufacturing waste, and is unfit for drinking purposes. In the summer the water reaches a degree of pollution which makes its use dangerous beyond a doubt. Should the water during these months become impregnated with the seeds of typhoid, cholera or other zymotic diseases, the most disastrous results may be expected. . . . We have no doubt that the use of a pure water in the cities of Newark and Jersey City would be attended by a most marked decrease in the death rate, especially that of children.[79]

The board of pollution, for obvious reasons, did not publish the report.

Ezra M. Hunt, the secretary of the New Jersey Board of Health, in an article titled "The Passaic River as Related to Water Supply and Death Rates," which appeared in the annual report of the state board of health for 1887, hammered the last nail in the coffin of the river's apologists. The article was written at the request of the *Sunday Call* after interviews with leading physicians of Newark had shown them divided on the safety of Passaic River water.[80] Hunt summarized the testimony offered by chemists, engineers, and the state geologist over the course of the preceding nine years and recounted the unsuccessful attempts of the board of pollution to cleanse the river. Through analysis of state mortality data for this period, he demonstrated that Newark and Jersey City, with 20 percent of New Jersey's population, accounted for 33 percent of the state's deaths from typhoid fever and diarrheal diseases. Hunt dismissed the opinions of the Newark physicians who believed that the river's water was safe for drinking, on the grounds that most physicians were not well versed in the science of public health.[81]

While city and state officials discussed the health risks posed by the Passaic River's pollution, the people of Newark struggled as best they could to cope with the water problem. Many physicians advised their patients to filter and boil the water before using it, and thousands of Newarkers never drank Passaic River water under any circumstances. In its place they drank well water, which usually was polluted; spring water; distilled water; mineral water; aerated beverages; and beer. One popular beverage, Poland Spring Water, sold for the exorbitant price of $8 per forty gallons. About $250,000 was spent annually on water substitutes, enough to pay the interest on the debt that would be incurred in obtaining a new water supply.[82]

The fortunes of Newark's largest water consumers, its extensive industrial establishments, were inexorably bound up with the water crisis. Newark's sizable lager beer industry, in particular, was threatened by lack of suitable water for brewing. Brewers needed water of exceptional quality to produce the distinctive taste of their product. They also needed soft water for bottling and cask washing and water for cooling.[83] To avoid paying large water bills, several manufacturing concerns drove wells into the underlying red sandstone strata. The water thus obtained was used for condensing or cooling hot substances. Because the water was hard, it could not be used in steam boilers or for washing and rinsing whenever heat or soap were required and was not recommended for drinking or domestic use.[84]

As the reports of Leeds, Hunt, and Austin and Wilbur became general knowledge, it became imperative that the Passaic River be abandoned. The events leading to the acquisition of a new water supply began with a trip by Mayor Joseph E. Haynes to the Pequannock watershed in 1886. Haynes had been invited to inspect the watershed by Julius Pratt, a New Jersey industrialist and land speculator. He was immediately captivated by the unspoiled beauty of this mountain wilderness and by the sparkling purity of its waters. By the time Haynes had returned home he had decided to direct all his energies toward acquiring the Pequannock River for Newark. In the next few years, Haynes's leadership would be decisive in securing for Newark one of the nation's best water supplies.[85]

In his annual message to the common council for 1887 Mayor Haynes said that the Passaic River was the natural sewage outlet for Paterson, Passaic, Belleville, Montclair, Bloomfield, and the Oranges, and therefore could not be protected against pollution. Many persons in the past had been dissuaded from living in Newark because of its water supply, and many more would bypass the city in the future. Now was the time to act![86]

By now even the Newark Aqueduct Board was beginning to feel the pressure. "Charged with an unwillingness to listen to the publicly expressed wishes of the people of our city in favor of a new water supply, and of an unreasonable and stubborn refusal to take the necessary official action to give the people of Newark pure and wholesome water,"[87] the board called a public meeting on January 19, 1987, to discuss the water situation. At a second such meeting, held a week later, a resolution was adopted requesting the mayor to appoint a citizens committee to act in conjunction with the aqueduct board.[88]

At the joint meetings of the citizens committee and the aqueduct board, Haynes fought hard for the acquisition of the Pequannock watershed. He also introduced a note of urgency into the discussions by warning that the waterworks, which had a capacity of supplying about fourteen million gallons of water a day, was being taxed to its limit and one and a half million dollars would have to be spent in the next three years in expanding the physical plant.[89]

The momentum for a new water supply was becoming irresistible. On April 10, 1888, the Reverend Horace F. Barnes of the Fairmount Avenue Baptist Church presented a petition "four or five yards of paper" in length to the board of trade, calling for the abandonment of the Passaic River.[90] Three days later the common council appointed a committee to act with the aqueduct board as a joint committee on a new water supply.[91] In June the *Sunday Call,* Newark's financial watchdog, concluded it would be more dangerous for the city to continue with its present supply than to incur a large new debt.[92]

Another obstacle now presented itself, for it appeared the city would have to make a deal with private interests to secure a new water supply. Following the publication of the Croes and Howell report in 1879, land speculators had attempted to get the state to bar Newark from going beyond its corporate boundaries to obtain a municipally owned water supply.[93] In 1882 the Society for Establishing Useful Manufactures succeeded in inducing the state legislature to grant it powers of condemnation. By impounding the waters of the upper Passaic River watershed, the society planned to obtain a monopoly over the future water supplies of Newark and Jersey City. When Governor Ludlow vetoed the bill the society's agent, Garrett A. Hobart, a state senator from Paterson (and later the vice-president of the United States in the first administration of William McKinley), interested a New York syndicate headed by John R. Bartlett in the scheme. Bartlett's syndicate, acting in conjunction with the society, now began buying large tracts of land in the Pequannock watershed.[94] To avoid arousing suspicion, the sales were recorded in Morris and Sussex counties.[95] In light of this brazen behavior, the press, civic leaders, and the mayor "appeared to be irrevocably committed to the policy of municipal construction and ownership."[96] Their statements convey their bitterness and determination not to deal with speculators: "I [Mayor Haynes] want to say emphatically and positively, that Bartlett and his gang of monopolists have no power at all to touch a drop of that water in spite of all their boasts. It lies there awaiting the cities, and when Newark wants, Newark can go and take it."[97] The editors of the *Newark Evening News* and the *Sunday Call* commented:

> To contemplate a bargain which would compel the 175,000 inhabitants of Newark . . . to purchase water filtered through the fingers of a dozen or more speculators is too preposterous to discuss.[98]
>
> . . . nothing but the grossest corruption could secure its adoption by the city.[99]

Meanwhile, a crisis was developing at the Belleville plant. The city's pumping and storage capacities were unable to satisfy the demands of Newark's booming industries and rapidly growing population. Newark had not suffered from a drought for nearly seven years. Should a drought occur during the summer, the reservoirs would be emptied in ten days.[100]

At the same time, the final act in the drama was being enacted at the meetings of the Joint Water Committee. The committee, which included the members of the Newark Aqueduct Board, the mayor, the city counsel, and five members of the common council, worked in secrecy to prevent speculators from capitalizing on its plans. Its first task was to determine the legal standing of the claims of various individuals and corporations to water rights in the upper Passaic River watershed. When it discovered that private interests had gained control of the watershed, the committee discarded plans for a municipally owned water supply and concentrated its attention on the relative merits of the propositions presented by three private corporations: the Bartlett Company, the Lehigh Valley Railroad Company, and the Pratt Company.

The Bartlett Company offered to sell Newark a daily supply of fifty million gallons at forty dollars per million gallons.

The Lehigh Valley Railroad Company proposed to sell the same amount of water at the rate of thirty-six to thirty-nine dollars per million gallons with an option to purchase the plant upon expiration of the contract for $5 million.

The Pratt Company, which owned a small but strategically located plot in the Pequannock watershed, proposed a bid of twenty-five million gallons per day at thirty dollars per million gallons, with an option to buy the waterworks for just under $4 million. The Pratt offer further stipulated the company's acquisition of additional watershed property to insure a total capacity of fifty million gallons per day, the land to be bought by Newark as needed.[101]

As an alternative to private development of the Pequannock watershed, the Pratt Company, which was thought to have the inside track in the negotiations with the city because of Haynes's friendship with Pratt, offered to sell its water parcel for seventy-five thousand dollars. Though eager to have the city build its own waterworks, the Joint Water Committee, acting "with a special knowledge of the situation," saw "the folly of appealing to the law-making body of the State" for gaining the needed condemnation privileges and bonding powers, and declined the offer. Rather, it preferred to let the Pratt Company fight it out in the legislature against the other "great and hungry corporate interests," aiding the company as best it could. Included in the terms of the proposed agreement with the Pratt Company was a clause permitting the company to use the city's name, should it become necessary, to invoke the power of eminent domain in obtaining additional parcels.[102]

On December 22, 1888, the joint committee announced its acceptance of the Pratt offer. However, the terms of the settlement were criticized in the press, and consequently the companies were asked to submit new bids.[103] In the interim, Hobart persuaded the Bartlett Company to merge its interests with those of the Lehigh Valley Railroad Company, the new combination taking the name of the East Jersey Water Company. Though the Pratt Company's new offer was still the lower of the two bids submitted,[104] it was rejected when Ferdinand H. Wismer, the water commissioner of the Newark Aqueduct Board, questioned the ability of the company to fulfill the terms of the contract. Specifically, it appeared that the Pratt Company might have difficulty in furnishing a daily supply of twenty-five million gallons and would face lengthy litigation if it tried to expand its holdings to provide more than that amount. Moreover, there were doubts cast about the company's solvency.[105]

While these deliberations were proceeding, on July 22, 1889, Newark's last hope that the Passaic River could be protected against pollution was shattered when the Court of Chancery of New Jersey refused to issue a preliminary injunction to prevent the city of Passaic from discharging sewage into the river at a point four miles above the Belleville plant. The chancellor ruled that since there was conflicting evidence as to whether the discharge of Passaic's sewage would create a nuisance, he could not issue an injunction. Passaic based its case on the testimony of Henry Wurtz, the former state chemist of New Jersey, who some years earlier had expressed alarm about the pollution of the Passaic River.[106] He now argued that if the sewage from Paterson, with a population of fifty thousand, disappeared in a flow of four and a half miles (therefore, could not be detected chemically), then the sewage in question, from a population of only ten thousand, would almost certainly vanish in the greater volume of Passaic River water near the Newark waterworks intake. The chancellor asked why, if the danger of drinking sewage-contaminated water was as great as Newark claimed, had there been no waterborne epidemics in the city? Faced with the prospect of having to endure an epidemic in order to win its case, the city decided it would be more prudent to bargain with the East Jersey Water Company for a new water supply.[107]

Under the terms of the contract signed on September 24, 1889, the East Jersey Water Company was required to supply Newark with Pequannock River water at a price of thirty-six to thirty-nine dollars per million gallons, delivery to begin by May 1, 1892. The company further agreed to furnish a water plant in the Pequannock watershed capable of supplying Newark with fifty million gallons a day, and to give Newark the option of buying the works, upon completion, for six million dollars. If Newark exercised this option, then payment of one-third of the cost would be deferred until 1900, in return for which the company would be given the right to divert all water in excess of 27.5 million gallons until that time.[108] This last provision was inserted because of the enormous cost of the undertaking: six million dollars. The bonded debt of the city was only half that amount, while the city's total revenues for 1889 amounted to less than two and a half million dollars.

While the story of Newark's quest for a safe and abundant water supply is already very lengthy, an epilogue must be added. To begin with, the controversy surrounding the water issue continued even after

Figure 1
Typhoid Fever in Newark, 1869–1922

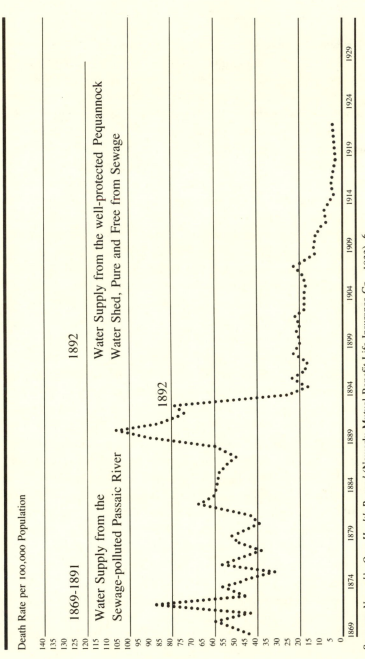

Death Rate per 100,000 Population

1869-1891

Water Supply from the
Sewage-polluted Passaic River

1892

1892

Water Supply from the well-protected Pequannock
Water Shed, Pure and Free from Sewage

SOURCE: *Newark's Own Health Record* (Newark: Mutual Benefit Life Insurance Co., 1923), 6.

the signing of the contract. Haynes had played a somewhat devious role in the events leading to the settlement. His public statements had led the people of Newark to believe he was unalterably opposed to dealing with water speculators, whereas for some time he had been secretly negotiating with them. The *Sunday Call* turned against Haynes, calling him "the New Haynes." The *Call* asserted a deal had been made between the Democratic political bosses who, it was charged, stood to gain from the contract, and Haynes, who needed the bosses' support in the next mayoral election. The boss of the Democratic party in Newark was the brewer Gottfried Krueger. He was also the head of the Brewers' Association of Newark, "which exerted considerable influence on the Democratic Party,"[109] and which had a large stake in the water question. Nevertheless, Haynes was reelected.[110]

Any misgivings anyone might have had about the city's acquisition of a new water supply vanished during the events of the following years. In 1891 Newark was ravaged by a severe typhoid fever epidemic. The death rate for typhoid fever in 1890, the last nonepidemic year Passaic River water was used exclusively, was 107 per 100,000 population; in 1893, the first year Pequannock River water was solely relied upon, it was 30 per 100,000 population. In Jersey City, which continued to use the Passaic River, typhoid fever in the years 1892–1897 annually accounted for an average of 79.9 deaths per 100,000 persons. In the seven years following Jersey City's abandonment of the river, the disease killed only about one-third that number (see Figure 1).[111] The introduction of pure water also lowered the incidence of deaths from diarrheal diseases in infants and young children and was an important factor in the decline in Newark's death rate that began in the mid-1890s. Finally, besides improving the public health, the purity of the new water supply would become a source of civic pride in a city that up until that time had almost no public works projects to which it could point with pride.[112]

CONCLUSION

THE IMPACT OF ACUTE, COMMUNICABLE DISEASES ON the life of a nineteenth-century urban community is exemplified by Newark's response to the public health problems that beset it in the years 1832–1895. Throughout the period, communicable diseases were rampant, tuberculosis, pneumonia, and diseases of infancy and early childhood accounting for the most deaths. As industrialization and rapid population growth compounded the dangers posed by urban living conditions, the municipal authorities slowly began to assume responsibility for protecting the public health.

At first there was little organized community effort to prevent disease. Though three times ravaged by cholera in the year preceding the Civil War, Newark did not have a permanent public health entity until 1857. Nevertheless, the salubrity of the city surpassed that of many larger cities. The water supply was drawn principally from uncontaminated brooks and streams. Foods were produced on nearby farms and dairies, insuring their freshness and wholesomeness. Open spaces and better housing afforded most Newark residents a degree of health protection not found in the congested immigrant districts of the nation's leading seaports. With the exception of the years when cholera was epidemic, Newark's death rate before the Civil War seldom exceeded 20 per 1,000 population.

For nearly two centuries following the establishment of Newark in 1666, fear of public censure deterred residents from dirtying the environment. But with the arrival of thousands of Irish and German immigrants in the 1840s and 1850s, the homogeneity of the community was destroyed and the salubrity of the city declined. Public health codes had to be enacted in order to achieve what public opinion previously had effected. Moreover, as "privatism," or the search for individual fortune, replaced the Puritan vision of a Bible commonwealth knit together in a common purpose, an earlier concern for the health hazards presented by crowded urban living conditions was sacrificed.

In the years following the Civil War, Newark experienced many of the health problems that had attended unbridled development in New York, Philadelphia, and Baltimore during the first half of the century. Sewers emptied into sluggish tidal creeks not far from major population centers. Offal and stagnant pools provided numerous breeding places for flies, mosquitoes, and other insect vectors. In need of a vastly enlarged water supply, Newark turned to the Passaic River at just the same time that neighboring communities and factory owners started using it as a repository for their wastes, Newark's own sewerage contributing substantially to the river's pollution. Regulation of privately provided municipal services was almost nonexistent. Nearly all municipally furnished services were underfinanced and unplanned. The board of health was enmeshed in partisan politics and was generally not well regarded. And because the etiology of disease was poorly understood, the board's principal methods of combating epidemics—isolation of persons with pestilential diseases and emergency sanitary campaigns— seldom were effective. Eleven times in the years 1859–1879 Newark's death rate surpassed 25 per 1,000 population.

The root cause of Newark's unsalubrious condition was its rapid, unplanned growth.[1] Industrialization and immigration created sudden demands on the environment that could not be dealt with by city leaders. Newark's weak government, battered by partisan politics and petty haggling, was ill prepared to undertake sanitary projects that required large capital expenditures, technical expertise, and constant attention. Then, too, the rampant individualism of the day made Newarkers suspicious of increased government powers and forestalled any thought of comprehensive urban planning. This was true of other cities as well. Jon Peterson writes that "city growth, in short, was a helter-skelter process—haphazard, unregulated, and uncoordinated. Municipal officials commonly reinforced this pattern, ordering streets widened, sewer and water mains laid, and other public works undertaken on a piecemeal basis as need arose."[2]

Most Americans viewed the filthy skies and waterways in their cities with equanimity. Pollution was seen as a necessary evil, a by-product of economic growth. Indeed, factory smoke and dust-covered workrooms elicited favorable responses, for they were regarded as signs of productivity. Americans believed that increased production and consumption would enable them to enjoy a life of affluence and individual freedom. Environmental quality was treated as a free resource for manufacturers and cities to exploit as they strove to reduce the cost of giving urban residents the amenities and services they desired. This could be seen most clearly in Newark in its feeble attempt to safeguard the Passaic River from pollution during the period it was used to provide water for the city, an effort doomed to failure by the widely shared belief that the river was there to be utilized by the cities and industries along its banks in whatever ways best served their immediate economic interests.

It was widely thought that whatever harm might result from pollution would be rectified eventually through technology. Just as technology and scientific management had solved the problem of scarcity and made available an abundance of material goods for the first time in history, so too could they be applied to solving the problems of waste removal and providing pure and copious water supplies. But for much of the nineteenth century, cities were saddled with primitive means of eliminating the ever-growing mountains of wastes that threatened to engulf them. Garbage was disposed of by feeding it to scavenging pigs, by erecting garbage dumps, or by unloading it at sea. The movement of people and goods within the city was done by horses, each of which produced from fifteen to twenty-two pounds of manure daily. The manure fell on unpaved streets, where it attracted flies and emitted a sickening stench. The city's privies and cesspools elicited numerous citizen complaints and endangered the public health.

Since no one challenged the desirability of increased production and consumption, little thought was given to altering American attitudes that promoted waste and pollution. Instead, Americans waited for science and technology to deliver them from the filth that threatened their possessions. By the turn of the century their wait appeared over as new technologies succeeded in removing many irritants from urban life. The invention of the internal combustion engine led to the disappearance of the horse from American cities. Reduction and incineration held out the promise of more sanitary means of garbage disposal. The acquisition of safe municipal water supplies and the development of water-carriage sewerage eliminated polluted wells and outhouses.

Some of these "solutions" were to lead to new problems of environmental pollution, as in the case of the automobile, but it has only been in the last two decades that any appreciable number of Americans have come to question the wisdom of relying so heavily on technology and economic growth to solve social problems.

Many, if not most, of the Newark Board of Health's programs were opposed by the urban masses. In this connection, board member Dr. Edward E. Worl's comment that the board was more unpopular than the tax office is very revealing.[3] "Sanitary reform," noted one New York authority, "is of slow growth, for every improvement is an attack more or less imposed upon the prejudices or property of a considerable number of citizens and taxpayers, and is, therefore, vigorously resisted."[4] Initially, proposals to do away with cesspools and polluted wells were strenuously resisted by the poor. Most individuals were not cognizant of the dangers in their backyards. Often privy vaults and cesspools caused no immediate and self-evident injury to the health of persons living in their midst. Similarly, many persons drank from polluted wells without apparent harm. The intrusion of politics into the board of health's work served to stiffen the resistance of homeowners, since everyone seemed to know of cases in which politically influential landlords had been permitted to allow their property to run down while other property owners had been required to make costly repairs.[5]

In London, Paris, and New York the poor frequently opposed urban renewal projects because of their well-founded fear that they would not be able to find affordable dwellings to replace their condemned homes. Since the rental market in these cities was very tight, the destruction of any housing stock, even slum rookeries, might leave the poor worse off than they already were. The enforcement of laws against overcrowding, the tearing down of rear tenements, and the building of parks were goals sought by middle-class reformers. It is instructive that in the late nineteenth century socialists and labor leaders in Europe's and America's largest cities, with the notable exception of London's local trade union leaders, paid little attention to housing reform, instead focusing their efforts on securing higher wages, better working conditions, and a greater voice in government for workers.[6]

The most resented actions of the Newark Board of Health involved its efforts to prevent the spread of pestilential diseases. The forcible vaccination of persons who had been exposed to smallpox, the removal of cholera and smallpox victims to the hated pesthouse, and the placarding and quarantining of homes containing an infectious disease, often done in a callous and sometimes brutal manner, imposed emotional and economic hardships on the persons affected and were regarded by many Americans as violations of basic American rights.

Not all public health reforms were opposed by Newark's poor. The adoption of a new water supply was widely supported, as it was in nearly every city with a polluted water supply.[7] As early as the mid-nineteenth century, pure water had come to be regarded as so essential to the public welfare as to warrant government ownership and large municipal expenditures. Public support for sewers lagged behind but by 1900 was widespread as individuals came to realize their health benefits and as indoor plumbing became commonplace.[8]

The attitude of the poor toward public health reform can best be analyzed by refracting it through a cost-benefit prism. The poor responded to the initiatives of health officials, representing the so-called "better elements" of society, according to how they would be affected. As in the case of education and other public services, they supported whatever they thought would benefit them regardless of who proposed it or why. Thus the poor usually took advantage of the opportunity to be vaccinated without cost at public dispensaries because they did not wish to be without protection against smallpox. Similarly, they supported business leaders in their efforts to obtain pure, abundant water supplies even though it meant higher taxes, because a good water supply was worth the cost.

On the other hand, the urban poor opposed most other sanitary reforms because the evidence that cleanliness would prevent disease was inconclusive. Pneumonia, tuberculosis, scarlet fever, and diphtheria struck the rich as well as the poor, and many persons living in grimy, filthy neighborhoods enjoyed robust health. It was observed repeatedly that persons who should have been ill if the miasmatic theory of disease was valid were surprisingly fit. Public health historian Howard D. Kramer writes that "the 'disappointedly' good health of the inmates of the most unsanitary dwellings destroyed faith in filth as the originating cause of disease."⁹ Since the etiology of communicable diseases was poorly understood in the nineteenth century, the most common ailments of the period appeared to most laymen to be capricious in nature. Given the unpredictable behavior of such diseases, the poor were unwilling to incur costly sanitary improvements unless they offered some other significant improvement in their lives. It was only when an epidemic of cholera or yellow fever devastated their run-down neighborhoods that they demanded the health authorities institute sanitary reform. Once the epidemic ceased, so usually did their demands. In short, the poor responded to the sanitary reforms sponsored by health officials and city leaders on the basis of an inchoate calculus of material self-interest. Examined in this light, the behavior of the poor was rational and consistent, if not always in their best interest.

As Judith W. Leavitt has shown in her study of Milwaukee,¹⁰ medical science determined the parameters of municipal health reform, but politics dictated the movements of the actors. The public health battlefield was a sea of subtle and shifting currents, and health officials had to be politically astute to navigate in these tricky waters. Economic conditions, patronage, personalities, the interests of different constituencies, and the nearness of municipal elections all had to be taken into consideration when going before the common council for more money or new powers. At first the Newark Board of Health was inept at politics and its entire program suffered as a result. Because health reform was politically determined, programs were adopted piecemeal and progress was erratic. Frequently health reform followed a zigzag course, moving forward, faltering, and then moving ahead again.

What little public health reform there was in Newark during the nineteenth century was spurred in part by fear of epidemics and by humanitarianism, but principally by concern that the city's poor health reputation would hurt business. Newark business leaders supported municipal improvements out of a sense of civic pride and because it was important that the city project an image of being progressive and up-to-date in all its facilities and amenities. The board of trade therefore lobbied for the completion of the city's sanitary infrastructure, for without the availability of sewerage and a pure and abundant water supply, businesses and individuals would be deterred from coming to

Newark. In advocating sanitary reform the board had to overcome strong resistance from conservative businessmen and property owners who objected to its high cost.[11]

Public water supply systems and water-carriage sewerage were just two of the many technological innovations that transformed American cities from overgrown villages into modern metropolises in the late nineteenth century. However, whereas electricity, gas, telephone, and trolley service were provided on a fee-for-service basis, the sanitary infrastructure was built and financed by the city at great cost to taxpayers. In fact, municipal waterworks and sewerage were the most ambitious and expensive capital improvements undertaken by nineteenth-century cities.[12]

Joel A. Tarr, the nation's foremost authority on the evolution of urban wastewater technology, writes: "It is clear that much infrastructure construction . . . was related to commerce and development."[13] Water-carriage sewerage enhanced the value of urban real estate, and by the turn of the century middle-class home purchasers regarded it as indispensable. Of paramount importance, cities competed with one another to attract newcomers, and as one United States public health official observed, disease and unsanitary means of disposing of human wastes were poor advertising.[14] In the late 1890s, sanitary engineer Moses N. Baker commented that "a village or town without waterworks and sewers is at a great disadvantage as compared with communities having these conveniences and safeguards. Industries and population are not so quickly attracted to it."[15] Public health historians have generally credited the local boards of health with the few improvements in municipal health that were made in the nineteenth century. But since they equate health reform with the activities of the board of health and ignore water supply and sewerage, they overlook the most important public health advances of the period, developments in which the business community usually played the dominant role.

In city after city businessmen spearheaded the movement to obtain sanitary services. Nelson Blake attributes the adoption of municipally owned water supplies in the great northeastern seaports in the early nineteenth century to fear of fire and epidemic diseases. The business community supported municipal water service for this reason and because it affected the welfare of numerous industries. Eugene P. Moehring, in his discussion of the Croton River water supply system, argues that New York City's business community was in the forefront of the battle to have it built. Fire insurance companies were anxious to avoid a repetition of the huge financial losses they had incurred in past conflagrations. Chemical manufacturers, candle and soapmakers, and tanners and dyers whose wells were going dry sought a plentiful supply of water, while bakers, sugar refiners, and brewers who were concerned about the growing pollution of local ground supplies insisted that the city make available water that was pure.[16]

In Chicago, the Citizens' Association, a municipal improvement organization comprised of leading businessmen, was instrumental in protecting the city's water supply and in solving its sewage pollution problem.[17] Carol E. Hoffecker, in her history of Wilmington, Delaware, writes; "It was the business leaders' commitment to their city more than any other single factor that made industrial Wilmington a liveable city for most of its residents."[18] In Pittsburgh, which in the 1890s had the highest typhoid mortality rate of any major American city, an alarmed chamber of commerce established a water supply committee, which succeeded in getting the common council to filter the city's water supply.[19] In the post–Civil War South, merchants and industrialists took the lead in cleansing their cities of organic filth in the belief that a clean city would be less vulnerable to epidemics of yellow fever, which in the past had severely retarded the region's development. John Ellis, the historian of the movement, writes that southern business leaders "thought of public works on sewerage and water supply as business investments in the projection of a favorable urban image."[20]

Whereas the business community as a whole profited from improvements in the city's reputation for salubrity, individual firms that were threatened by the introduction of a particular new technology or by municipal assumption of responsibility for their service resisted calls for sanitary improvements. In Baltimore the politically powerful odorless excavator companies, which cleaned the city's privies, delayed development of a sewer system until 1906. In Milwaukee scavenger firms bribed politicians for the city's garbage-hauling business. And when

private industry failed to remove the municipality's garbage in a satisfactory manner, the scavengers flexed their political muscle in an
unsuccessful attempt to prevent the construction of a city-owned incinerator.[21]

In dealing with the issue of municipal health reform businessmen,
like the poor, acted on the basis of self-interest. Even within particular
industries businessmen sometimes took opposing positions on proposals for improving the city's sanitary infrastructure depending on how
they would be affected. For example, suburban developers in Boston
championed the extension of water and sewer lines to their communities in order to make their properties more marketable, while in tenement districts in New York, Newark, and Atlanta landlords refused to
pay for the cost of laterals and hookups that would enable their tenants
to make full use of the municipal sewer system.[22]

Nevertheless, because of the city-building role assumed by business
organizations, the opposition of business interests adversely affected by
specific public health initiatives was more than offset by the support the
business community gave to sanitary reform generally. American cities, as Daniel J. Boorstin has brilliantly argued, gave rise to a new type
of businessman: the businessman as civic booster. On the frontier developers laid out new cities in the hope of getting rich from the sale of
real estate lots when the cities they began started to prosper. Sheer
speculative mania swept the West as more cities were planned than
could be supported by the region's economy. For new cities to survive
they had to make themselves more attractive than their rivals, both as
places in which to do business and as residential communities. Cities
that failed to provide modern amenities such as schools, good roads,
and water would be unable to attract new residents and would stagnate.
Consequently, businessmen had to take an active role in public affairs,
since their economic fortunes were tied to the welfare of their cities.[23]

As Boorstin observes, it is misleading to describe the American
businessman "as simply a man engaged in mercantile transactions. We
might better characterize him as a peculiarly American type of community maker and community leader. His starting belief was the interfus-
ing of public and private property."[24] Hence, in the new cities of the
West and South, and to a lesser extent in the established cities of the

Northeast, businessmen took the initiative in developing water supplies, sewerage, and other public improvements that would promote their cities' well-being.

THE BOOM IN THE CONSTRUCTION OF CANALS, RAILroads, and urban water supplies that began after the War of 1812 created a huge demand for civil engineers. Since there were no schools of engineering in the United States, American engineers received their training through apprenticeship and on-the-job training. In time engineering schools such as Rensselaer Polytechnic Institute, Stevens Institute, and Massachusetts Institute of Technology were established. Whereas before the Civil War the technology that made possible advances in transportation and sanitation originated in Europe, by the end of the century American research centers, such as the Lawrence, Massachusetts, State Board of Health Experiment Station, were doing pioneering work in sewage treatment and filtration of water supplies.[25]

In most nineteenth-century American cities the engineers, chemists, and biologists employed in municipal bureaucracies or on a consulting basis were simply hired help, technical resource persons who provided the politicians and business leaders with the financial estimates and engineering data they needed for making decisions about the city's sanitary services. In some instances, however, they willingly allowed their skills to be appropriated for partisan political purposes. As a member of boss George Cox's political machine in Cincinnati, chief engineer Horace J. Stanley used his control over sewer construction to reward loyal wards and supporters with service, while other parts of the city were neglected. Though Stanley's competence was not questioned by reformers who wished to see public works removed from politics, his independence and professional integrity were challenged. Thus when a reform mayor was elected in 1897, Stanley and his assistants were fired and then rehired when Cox came back into power in 1900.[26]

In Massachusetts engineers and public health professionals enjoyed considerable independence and played a prominent role in promoting, planning, and developing water supplies and sewerage for the Boston metropolitan area. In Boston the question of water supply had been removed from politics as early as 1848, when the Cochituate water supply system was completed, providing Bostonians with abundant sweet water from the uplands of western Massachusetts. The excellent service provided by the Cochituate Water Board, together with Boston's relative freedom from cholera, conferred status upon the engineers and created a situation in which wide latitude was given to them to make decisions for the city in this critical area.[27]

Memphis provides another example of a nineteenth-century city in which sanitary engineers were allowed to make momentous decisions for the entire community. After having its economy all but destroyed by epidemics of yellow fever in the 1870s, the city fathers called in the short-lived National Board of Health (1879–1883) to study the matter. As a member of that board the noted sanitary reformer George E. Waring, Jr., proposed the construction of what became known as the separate or "Waring" system of sewerage, which employed two sets of drain pipes, one for household wastes and the other for stormwater.[28] Though most of the larger cities subsequently adopted the "combined system" of sewerage because it was less expensive, the favorable publicity generated by the marked improvement in Memphis's sanitary condition spurred sewer construction all across the nation. Leonard Metcalf and Harrison P. Eddy, two prominent sanitary engineers who championed the "combined system," subsequently revealed the motivation behind the sewering of Tennessee's largest city when they declared that "the Memphis system was the most conspicuous [of its type], although a comparative failure, a fact that the people of the city naturally suppressed for business reasons for many years."[29]

Jon Peterson argues that late nineteenth-century sanitary reform provided the inspiration for the more comprehensive urban planning movement of the early twentieth century. However, he qualifies this by observing:

> As planners, sanitary engineers operated as technical specialists, and their reports to localities consistently focused upon the precise workings of their proposed schemes, not broad issues of civic layout.[30]
>
> The sanitary environment, not the urban environment, represented the real concern; . . . sanitary reformers should be seen as health planners by design

and as urban planners by historical necessity—namely the fact that nineteenth-century urban populations suffered so often from epidemics attributed to filth conditions.[31]

With a few notable exceptions, municipal sanitary engineers in the nineteenth century designed water and sewer systems to the specifications determined by political officials. They rarely questioned the purposes to which ends their talents were being employed.[32]

Pollution is not a respecter of political boundaries. Since it was recognized that water supply and sewerage had to be considered on a regional basis, plans were made to centralize administration of these services. The big cities acted first; examples include the Chicago Sanitary District (1889), the Boston Metropolitan Sewerage Commission (1889), and the Passaic Valley Sewerage Commission (1902). With the establishment of metropolitan water and sewer districts around the turn of the century, the ability of engineers to plan the physical environment of the city and its suburbs increased enormously.[33]

Not everyone benefited equally from the development of municipal services. Since water supply and sewerage were expensive, the affluent had first claims on them. Municipal improvements were intially limited to the central business district. The extension of sanitary services to poorer sections of the city waited upon a general improvement in the standard of living and consequently lagged behind by several decades. Thus while downtown property owners had the use of municipal water and sewerage in the 1850s, these life-supporting services were still not available to thousands of Newarkers fifty years later. Similarly, because the well off could purchase private medical care or could travel to New York City for the specialized health services they required, Newark's municipal leaders put off the establishment of a public hospital until 1882. While the wealthy were catered to in their homes and in well-run private medical facilities, the indigent sick were forced to undergo a humiliating means test before they could receive aid at the city dispensary. Those least able to provide for themselves were consigned to Newark's squalid, disease-ridden poorhouse. Nineteenth-century Newark was a dangerous place in which to be sick or poor.

In other cities as well, class distinctions determined the availability of municipal services. In Milwaukee's affluent suburbs urban services usually came in advance of population, whereas in outlying areas inhabited by poor Polish immigrants the installation of sewer and water mains was delayed until residential streets were partially occupied. Christine Meisner Rosen has found that in the years immediately following the great fires that destroyed much of downtown Chicago and Boston in the early 1870s, suburban developers and affluent homeowners induced their aldermanic boards and public works departments to extend water service, sewerage, and paved streets to outlying areas at the expense of inner-city districts that needed redevelopment of their water and transportation infrastructures. She attributes this development to the suburbanites' economic clout and political savvy, whereas the poor who inhabited the inner wards were politically weak, inarticulate, and unsophisticated. Similarly, in New York, Memphis, and Atlanta blacks, immigrants, and the poor were the last ones to benefit from improvements in municipal services.[34]

While the introduction of pure water and a sanitary means of disposing of bodily wastes unquestionably reduced the death rate,[35] often the energies of health reformers were dissipated in a broadside attack on filth. Thus health officials devoted considerable efforts to sanitary matters that were of only marginal importance, such as clean streets. At the same time, dangerous sanitary conditions, such as the existence of pools of stagnant water around houses, were often overlooked. It would not be until the advent of bacteriology in the 1890s that a more scientific approach to public health was adopted.

Except for the occasional issuance of a resolution in support of vaccination, the Essex County Medical Society, as was true of most medical associations in the United States and England,[36] did not play an active role in municipal health reform before 1900. The society's name seldom appeared on public health memorials, and its voice was not heard in government councils. The proceedings of the society were largely taken up with the admittance of new members, the election of delegates, the reports of officers, and other routine business matters. Substantive concerns were narrowly construed. Under attack from "irregular" (sectarian) physicians for maintaining a monopoly in medical practice, and in public disfavor because of medicine's inability to cure most illnesses, the societies of the "regular" physicians, or allopaths, were forced to fight a rear-guard action against the inroads in medical practice being made by unqualified practitioners. Though limited in scope, the protection thus afforded the American people against quacks and incompetent physicians was not without merit or importance.[37]

To be sure, medical papers—mainly on epidemics and unusual cases and cures—were presented at the meetings of the allopaths, and the physicians who attended were able to share experiences and to exchange ideas at a time when many physicians had no other medium for such discussion. In this manner the meetings of county and state medical societies provided postgraduate training of a sort to physicians not affiliated with a medical school or a hospital. The gatherings of the medical fraternity also served a social function. But these concerns were peripheral to the allopaths' overriding preoccupation with preventing sectarian physicians from entering the medical profession.

Little of the altruism traditionally associated with the practice of medicine is evidenced in the minutes of the Essex County Medical Society. In 1859 a resolution was introduced denying membership in the society to persons who sold or endorsed the use of nostrums and patent medicines. While there was general agreement that such traffic was dangerous to the welfare of the community, the members would not deny themselves this lucrative source of income. Generally the society remained aloof from community affairs except when the financial interests and professional prerogatives of physicians were at stake. Thus in 1861 it attempted to limit medical practice in the New Jersey militia to "regular" physicians, and in 1902 it conducted an extensive investigation into suspected public abuse of the county's medical charities.[38] In an address delivered in 1907 on the dangers besetting the public health, Archibald Mercer, the president of the society, suggested "that in the future the Society might better justify its existence by aiding in the correction of these evils."[39] But if the society was motivated largely by self-interest, its members often made outstanding individual contributions. Physicians studied the health problems endangering their communities and established medical facilities for treating the poor, proof that at least a part of the profession continued to recognize its societal obligations.

In his article "The American Medical Profession and Public Health: From Support to Ambivalence," John Duffy surveys the relationship of organized medicine to health reform from the early 1800s to the Great Depression. He states that in the pre–Civil War era the medical profession was too weak to have much impact on public policy. However, as James H. Cassedy has recently shown, local and state medical societies did play a leading role in the semisuccessful movement of the mid-nineteenth century for compulsory reporting of vital statistics.[40]

In 1872 a small group of physicians employed in municipal health work who believed that the medical profession placed too much emphasis on treatment of disease and not enough on preventive measures organized the American Public Health Association. The establishment of the association followed closely the successes of the United States Sanitary Association in providing for the health and welfare of Union soldiers during the Civil War and the New York Metropolitan Board of Health in turning back an attack of cholera in 1866. The favorable publicity engendered by these events aroused interest in preventive medicine at all levels of government. In the 1870s, state medical societies championed the creation of state boards of health. A National Board of Health was established in 1879 to help combat epidemics of yellow fever but was allowed to die in 1883.[41]

But in the decades that followed up until the Progressive Era the medical profession lost interest in preventive medicine. As public health became synonymous with environmental santitation, and as the fight for municipal health reform was taken over by businessmen, engineers, and public officials, organized medicine withdrew from the battlefield. The average family practitioner was too busy trying to support himself to take time out from his practice to engage in protracted political battles for sanitary reform. Similarly, the leaders of the American medical profession were too committed to efforts to reform medical education and to improve the status and influence of organized medicine to render much help.[42] Historians Stanley K. Schultz and Clay McShane state that boards of health and physicians who sought to ameliorate the living conditions of the urban poor supported tenement house legislation, municipal regulation of foodstuffs, adoption of pure water supplies, and sewer construction, "but rarely, except in times of epidemics, did public health officers and sanitarians exert influence over most matters of public policy and administration. Customarily, political clout in matters of public health lay with businessmen."[43]

While the medical profession was sympathetic to the idea of sanitary reform, it seldom participated in the political campaigns of the late nineteenth century for improved water supplies, sewer construction, and more sanitary means of garbage disposal. This was not as true of the medical community of New York City, which helped undertake a sanitary survey of working-class neighborhoods in 1864 and provided support for tenement house reform. But in Chicago and Philadelphia, the nation's second and third largest cities, organized medicine largely ignored the environmental hazards that threatened people's health. Likewise, in the urban South and in northern industrial centers such as Wilmington, Pittsburgh, and Newark, the medical profession stood on the sidelines while boards of trade and business-dominated civic organizations fought to establish sanitary infrastructures.[44] Duffy comments that "although physicians continued to claim credit for the passage of health legislation, it is clear that medical societies played only a supportive role."[45]

Though Newark's health fortunes had seemingly reached their nadir in 1890, when the United States Census reported that Newark was the nation's unhealthiest city, events were occurring that presaged a better future. For one thing, after much difficulty, in 1889 Newark had succeeded in obtaining a safe water supply. The substitution of Pequannock River water for Passaic River water ended a twenty-year period in which typhoid fever, dysentery, and other waterborne diseases reached near epidemic heights in Newark. With the abandonment of the Passaic River, the single most important environmental and, therefore, remediable cause of Newark's high death rate was eliminated. Also, the purity of the new water supply induced Newark homeowners to abandon their wells. By 1915 nearly all wells in Newark used for potable water, except for a few wells in outlying and recently annexed areas, had been abandoned. At about the same time, the sewer system was completed.[46]

Ironically, just as the Newark Board of Health started to realize its sanitary objectives, it began to lose interest in them. During the 1890s public health practice in the United States was revolutionized by the ascendancy of the germ theory of disease. As specific causes of disease were identified, public health officials became less concerned about filthy environmental conditions and began to focus their efforts on the bacteriological laboratories that were established to wage war against the microbial agents of disease. Sanitary measures were not completely forgotten, but the shotgun approach to sanitary reform was discarded. Henceforth, public health officials would be able to distinguish between those aspects of sanitation that have a direct bearing on disease and those that are primarily of aesthetic concern to the community. More important, the new science of bacteriology would open up new vistas of public health work. Diseases that sanitarians had labored in vain to contain, such as diphtheria, would be brought under control, while concerns that boards of health had not even attempted to deal with before, such as tuberculosis and infant mortality, would be made the objects of intensive public health campaigns. The dark era in Newark's public health history was coming to an end.

NOTES

INTRODUCTION

1. Barbara Gutmann Rosenkrantz, *Public Health and the State: Changing Views in Massachusetts, 1842–1936* (Cambridge, Mass.: Harvard University Press, 1972), 11, 18–19; Roy Lubove, *The Progressives and the Slums: Tenement House Reform in New York City, 1870–1917* (1962; reprint, Westport, Conn.: Greenwood Press, 1974), 56, 72; Carol E. Hoffecker, *Wilmington, Delaware: Portrait of an Industrial City, 1830–1910* (Charlottesville: University Press of Virginia, 1974), 15.

2. Rosenkrantz, *Public Health and the State*, 31, 35; George Rosen, "Historical Trends and Future Prospects in Public Health," *Medical History and Medical Care: A Symposium of Perspectives*, ed. Gordon McLachlan and Thomas McKeown (London: Oxford University Press, 1971), 61.

3. Sam Alewitz, "Sanitation and Public Health: Philadelphia, 1870–1910" (Ph.D. diss., Case Western Reserve University, 1981); Nelson Manfred Blake, *Water for the Cities: A History of the Urban Water Supply Problem in the United States* (Syracuse, N.Y.: Syracuse University Press, 1956); Louis P. Cain, *Sanitation Strategy for a Lakefront Metropolis: The Case of Chicago* (Dekalb: Northern Illinois University Press, 1978); Jacqueline Karnell Corn, "Municipal Organization for Public Health in Pittsburgh, 1851–1895" (D.A. diss., Carnegie-Mellon University, 1972); John Duffy, *A History of Public Health in New York City*, vol. 1, *1625–1866*, vol. 2, *1866–1966* (New York: Russell Sage Foundation, 1974); Dennis East II, "Health and Wealth: Goals of the New Orleans Public Health Movement, 1879–1884," *Louisiana History* 9 (Summer 1968):245–275; John H. Ellis, "Businessmen and Public Health in the Urban South During the Nineteenth Century: New Orleans, Memphis, and Atlanta," *Bulletin of the History of Medicine* 44, no. 3 (May–June 1970):197–211, no. 4 (July–August 1970):346–371; John Ellis and Stuart Galishoff, "Atlanta's Water Supply, 1865–1918," *Maryland Historian* 8 (Spring 1977):5–22; Geoffrey Giglierano, "The City and the System: Developing a Municipal Service, 1800–1915," *Cincinnati Historical Society Bulletin* 35 (Winter 1977):223–247; Carol E. Hoffecker, *Water and Sewage Works in Wilmington, Delaware, 1810–1910: Essays in Public Works History*, no. 12 (Chicago: Public Works Historical Society; 1981);

Richard J. Hopkins, "Public Health in Atlanta: The Formative Years, 1865–1879," *Georgia Historical Quarterly* 53 (September 1969):287–304; William Travis Howard, Jr., *Public Health Administration and the Natural History of Disease in Baltimore, Maryland: 1797–1920* (Washington, D.C.: Carnegie Institution of Washington, 1924); Duncan B. Jamieson, "Toward a Cleaner New York: John H. Griscom and New York's Public Health, 1830–1870" (Ph.D. diss., Michigan State University, 1972); Judith Walzer Leavitt, *The Healthiest City: Milwaukee and the Politics of Health Reform* (Princeton, N.J.: Princeton University Press, 1982); Alan I. Marcus, "The Strange Career of Municipal Health Initiatives: Cincinnati and City Government in the Early Nineteenth Century," *Journal of Urban History* 7 (November 1980):3–29; Fern L. Nesson, *Great Water: A History of Boston's Water Supply* (Hanover, N.H.: University Press of New England, 1983); James C. O'Connell, *Chicago's Quest for Pure Water: Essays in Public Works History,* no. 1 (Washington, D.C.: Public Works Historical Society, 1976); Dorothy T. Scanlon, "The Public Health Movement in Boston, 1870–1910" (Ph.D. diss., Boston University, 1956); William Wright Sorrels, *Memphis' Greatest Debate: A Question of Water* (Memphis, Tenn.: Memphis State University Press, 1970); Mark Tierno, "The Search for Pure Water in Pittsburgh: The Urban Response to Water Pollution, 1893–1914," *Western Pennsylvania Historical Magazine* 60 (January 1977):23–36; Charles H. Weidner, *Water for a City: A History of New York City's Water Problem from the Beginning to the Delaware River System* (New Brunswick, N.J.: Rutgers University Press, 1974). This comprises only the literature on specific cities. For other works see the endnotes for the chapters of this book.

4. *The First American Medical Association Reports on Public Hygiene in American Cities;* reprinted from *Transactions of the American Medical Association* 2 (1849); *Public Health in America,* ed. Barbara Gutmann Rosenkrantz (New York: Arno Press, 1977); hereafter referred to as *AMA Reports on Public Hygiene.* Elisha Harris, "Report on the Public Health Service in the Principal Cities and the Progress of Sanitary Works in the United States," American Public Health Association, *Public Health Reports and Papers* 2 (1874–1875):151–182; Henry I. Bowditch, *Public Hygiene in America* (Boston: Little, Brown, 1877); Albert H. Buck, ed., *A Treatise on Hygiene and Public Health,* 2 vols. (1879; reprinted, New York: Arno Press, 1977); George E. Waring, Jr., *The Sanitary Drainage of Houses and Towns,* 6th ed. (Boston: Houghton, Mifflin, 1884); U.S. Bureau of the Census, *Tenth Census of the United States, 1880,* vols. 18–19, *Report on the Social Statistics of Cities* (Washington, D.C.: Government Printing Office, 1886–1887); George

W. Rafter and Moses N. Baker, *Sewage Disposal in the United States* (New York: D. Van Nostrand, 1893); Samuel W. Abbott, *The Past and Present Condition of Public Hygiene and State Medicine in the United States*, vol. 19 of *Monographs on American Social Economics*, ed. Herbert B. Adams (Boston: Wright and Potter, 1900); Charles V. Chapin, *Municipal Sanitation in the United States* (Providence, R.I.: Snow and Farnham, 1901); Frederick L. Hoffman, "The General Death Rate of Large American Cities, 1871–1904," *Publications of the American Statistical Association* 10, n.s., no. 73 (March 1906):1–75; George Chandler Whipple, *Typhoid Fever, Its Causation, Transmission, and Prevention* (New York: John Wiley, 1908); Leonard Metcalf and Harrison P. Eddy, *American Sewerage Practice*, 3 vols. (New York: McGraw-Hill, 1914); Charles Zeublin, *American Municipal Progress*, rev. ed. (New York: Macmillan, 1916); Mazÿck Porcher Ravenel, ed., *A Half Century of Public Health: Jubilee Historical Volume of the American Public Health Association* (New York: American Public Health Association, 1921).

5. Blake McKelvey, *The Urbanization of America, 1860–1915* (New Brunswick, N.J.: Rutgers University Press, 1963), 86–91, 105–106.

6. Stuart Galishoff, "Triumph and Failure: The American Response to the Urban Water Supply Problem, 1860–1923," in *Pollution and Reform in American Cities, 1870–1930*, ed. Martin V. Melosi (Austin: University of Texas Press, 1980), 35, 44–45, 51; Charles Edward-Amory Winslow, *The Evolution and Significance of the Modern Public Health Campaign* (New Haven, Conn.: Yale University Press, 1923), 38; U.S. Public Health Service, *Public Health Bulletin No. 164: Municipal Health Department Practice for the Year 1923 Based upon Surveys of the 100 Largest Cities in the United States* (Washington, D.C.: Government Printing Office, 1926), 474–477.

7. *AMA Reports on Public Hygiene*, 433–434; Joel A. Tarr, James McCurley, and Terry F. Yosie, "The Development and Impact of Urban Wastewater Technology: Changing Concepts of Water Quality Control, 1850–1930," in *Pollution and Reform in American Cities*, 59–64; McKelvey, *Urbanization of America*, 90; J. J. Cosgrove, *History of Sanitation* (Pittsburgh, Pa.: Standard Sanitary Manufacturing Co., 1909), 86; Metcalf and Eddy, *American Sewerage Practice*, 1:17–21; U.S. Public Health Service, *Public Health Bulletin No. 136: Report of the Committee on Municipal Health Department Practice* (Washington, D.C.: Government Printing Office, 1923), 219.

8. Sam Bass Warner, Jr., *The Urban Wilderness: A History of the American City* (New York: Harper and Row, 1972), 288.

9. Edward F. Meeker, "The Improving Health of the United States, 1850–

1915," *Explorations in Economic History* 9 (Summer 1972):367–371; Rosen, "Historical Trends in Public Health," 61–64.

10. *Safeguarding the Public Health: Newark, 1895–1918* (Westport, Conn.: Greenwood Press, 1975).

11. Thomas McKeown, "Determinants of Health," *Human Nature* (April 1978):60, 62–64. The argument is made most fully in Thomas McKeown, *The Modern Rise of Population* (London: Edward Arnold, 1976). For a different view, see Samuel H. Preston, *Mortality Patterns in National Populations; with Specific Reference to Recorded Causes of Death* (New York: Academic Press, 1976), 81–83.

12. McKeown, "Determinants of Public Health," 63; George Rosen, *A History of Public Health* (New York: MD Publications, 1958), 201–206; Frederick L. Hoffman, "American Mortality Progress During the Last Half Century," *A Half Century of Public Health: Jubilee Historical Volume of the American Public Health Association*, ed. Mazÿck P. Ravenel (New York: American Public Health Association, 1921), 101–104; Wilson G. Smillie, *Public Health, Its Promise for the Future: A Chronicle of the Development of Public Health in the United States, 1607–1914* (New York: Macmillan, 1955), 113–117.

13. Rosen, *A History of Public Health*, 236–237; Galishoff, "Urban Water Supply Problem," 36, 40, 45; Jon A. Peterson, "The Impact of Sanitary Reform upon American Urban Planning, 1840–1890," *Journal of Social History* 13 (Fall 1979):87–88; Joel A. Tarr, "The Search for the Ultimate Sink: Urban Air, Land, and Water Pollution in Historical Perspective," the 1981 Letitia Woods Brown Memorial Lecture, *Records of the Columbia Historical Society of Washington, D.C.* 51 (1984):7.

14. Joel A. Tarr with James McCurley III, Francis C. McMichael, and Terry Yosie, "Water and Wastes: A Retrospective Assessment of Wastewater Technology in the United States, 1800–1932," *Technology and Culture* 25 (April 1984):234; Tarr, "The Search for the Ultimate Sink," 7.

I   A VILLAGE BECOMES A CITY

1. Susan Eleanor Hirsch Bloomberg, "Industrialization and Skilled Workers: Newark, 1828–1860" (Ph.D. diss., University of Michigan, 1974), 9, 30.

2. John T. Cunningham, *Newark* (Newark: New Jersey Historical Society, 1966), 13–19.

3. Frank John Urquhart, *A History of the City of Newark, New Jersey*, 3 vols. (New York: Lewis Historical Publishing Co., 1913), 1:238–241.

4. Martha B. Lamb, "Newark," *Harper's New Monthly Magazine* (October 1876):667.

5. Quoted in Raymond Michael Ralph, "From Village to Industrial City: The Urbanization of Newark, New Jersey, 1830–1860" (Ph.D. diss., New York University, 1978), 16.

6. Ibid., 15; Bloomberg, "Industrialization and Skilled Workers," 19–20.

7. Samuel Harry Popper, "Newark, N.J., 1870–1910: Chapters in the Evolution of an American Metropolis" (Ph.D. diss., New York University, 1952), 9–13, 122–123, 125; Urquhart, *History of Newark*, 1:577–579; Cunningham, *Newark*, 84–85, 100–101, 106–108; Bloomberg, "Industrialization and Skilled Workers," 19, 28.

8. Cunningham, *Newark*, 101–102, 116.

9. Ralph, "From Village to Industrial City," 142, 149.

10. Ibid., 142.

11. Ibid., 148–149. Bloomberg sees the movement toward class segregation beginning in the 1850s. "Industrialization and Skilled Workers," 192.

12. Ralph, "From Village to Industrial City," 179–181.

13. Ibid., 201.

14. *Newark Daily Mercury*, April 21, 1853.

15. Cunningham, *Newark*, 136–137; Ralph, "From Village to Industrial City," 200–201.

16. *Records of the Town of Newark, New Jersey from Its Settlement in 1666 to Its Incorporation as a City in 1836* (Newark: Newark Daily Advertiser, 1864), passim; Ralph, "From Village to Industrial City," 219–221; Susan Eleanor Hirsch, "Newark in Its Prime, 1828–1860: Private Wealth and Public Policy," *Cities of the Garden State: Essays in the Urban and Suburban History of New Jersey*, ed. Joel Schwartz and Daniel Prosser (Dubuque, Iowa: Kendall Hunt, 1977), 4.

17. J. Wilmer Kennedy, *Newark in the Public Schools of Newark: A Course of Study on Newark, Its Geography, Civics and History, with Biographical Sketches and a Reference Index* (Newark: Newark Board of Education, 1911), 105–107; Urquhart, *History of Newark*, 2:851–852.

18. Ralph, "From Village to Industrial City," 104–106.

19. *Newark Daily Mercury*, June 12, 1857.

20. Ralph, "From Village to Industrial City," 220–223, 250.

21. Ibid., 234–235; *Newark Daily Mercury*, August 19, 1857.

22. *Newark Daily Mercury*, March 13, 1849.

23. Ibid., April 27, 1853.

24. Ibid., August 18, 1853.

25. Ibid., March 25, 1853.

26. Newark, *Reports of the Health Physician, Secretary of the Dispensary Board, and the District Physicians to the Board of Health Together with the Plan of Reorganization of the Newark City Dispensary, 1860* (Newark: Newark Daily Advertiser, 1860), 19–22 (hereafter referred to as *Report of the Health Physician*).

27. *Newark Daily Advertiser*, May 5, 1853.

28. *Report of the Health Physician, 1858*, 8–9.

29. Ibid., *1860*, 20.

30. *Newark Daily Mercury*, January 5, 1861.

31. Urquhart, *History of Newark*, 1:563–564, 567–568; Cunningham, *Newark*, 124–125.

32. Author's calculation based on mortality statistics found in Newark city directories and annual reports of the New Jersey secretary of state.

33. Frederick L. Hoffman, "American Mortality Progress during the Last Half Century," *A Half Century of Public Health: Jubilee Historical Volume of the American Public Health Association*, ed. Mazÿck P. Ravenel (New York: American Public Health Association, 1921), 101–104.

34. William Wirt Sikes, "About Newark," *Northern Monthly* 1 (September 1867):392.

35. *Newark Daily Advertiser*, May 11, 18, September 14, 1852.

36. The death rate curve is derived from mortality statistics in Newark city directories and annual reports of the New Jersey secretary of state.

37. New Jersey Mosquito Extermination Association, *Proceedings of the Annual Meeting, 1916*, 86.

38. Howard D. Kramer, "The Beginnings of the Public Health Movement in the United States," *Bulletin of the History of Medicine* 21 (May–June 1947):357; *Charter of the City of Newark with the Ordinances and By-laws Passed by the Common Council* (1838), *Ordinances*, 112–114; Fred B. Rogers and A. Reasoner Sayre, *The Healing Art: A History of the Medical Society of New Jersey* (Trenton: Medical Society of New Jersey, 1966), 104; *Charter of Newark and Revised Ordinances* (1858), *Ordinances*, 237–241. For further comment on the inadequacies of early bills of mortality, see John B. Blake, *Public Health in the Town of Boston, 1630–1822* (Cambridge, Mass.: Harvard University Press, 1959), 216; James H. Cassedy, *American Medi-*

cine and Statistical Thinking, 1800–1860 (Cambridge, Mass.: Harvard University Press, 1984), 17–19, 179–181, 190, 194–197, 203.

39. *Newark Daily Advertiser,* March 11, 1857; *Sentinel of Freedom,* April 30, 1844; Cunningham, *Newark,* 98; *Charter of the City of Newark and Laws of New Jersey Relating to Said City with the Ordinances Passed by the Common Council* (1850), *Laws of New Jersey,* 6–7, *Ordinances,* 120; *Charter of Newark and Revised Ordinances* (1858), *1857 Charter of the City of Newark,* 23–24, *Ordinances,* 237–241; David L. Pierson, *Narratives of Newark, 1866–1916* (Newark: Pierson, 1917), 334–337.

40. Thomas Bender, "The 'Rural' Cemetery Movement: Urban Travail and the Appeal of Nature," *New England Quarterly* 47 (June 1974):196, 204, 210.

41. Cassedy, *American Medicine and Statistical Thinking,* 179–180.

42. Ralph, "From Village to Industrial City," 236–37; Lamb, "Newark," 671.

43. *Newark Daily Mercury,* July 21, September 4, 1855.

44. Ibid., July 21, 1855.

45. Ibid., May 7, 1857.

46. William H. Shaw, comp., *History of Essex and Hudson Counties, New Jersey,* 2 vols. (Philadelphia: Everts and Peck, 1884), 1:309; *Charter of the City of Newark with the Ordinances and By-laws Passed by the Common Council* (1838), 52–53, *Ordinances,* 114–116.

47. *Newark Daily Advertiser,* December 30, 1854, April 30, June 5, December 14, 1857, in Samuel Berg, comp., "Medical Practice and Hospital Development in Newark, N.J., 1850–1887, as Reported in *Newark Daily Advertiser,*" Newark Public Library, New Jersey Reference Division.

48. Ibid., January 14, 1852.

49. *Newark Daily Mercury,* November 3, 1855.

50. Ibid., December 8, 1855. In New York and a few other big cities the large number of sick inmates in the almshouses led to their assuming the functions of a municipal hospital. Charles E. Rosenberg, "And Heal the Sick: The Hospital and the Patient in 19th Century America," *Journal of Social History* 10 (June 1977):430.

51. *Newark Daily Mercury,* January 5–6, 1856.

52. Ibid., June 6, July 1, 1857.

53. Ibid., July 2, 1857.

54. Urquhart, *History of Newark,* Appendix A, "Chronological History of Newark," 2:851–853; *Newark Daily Advertiser,* May 19, 1849, May 4, 1850; *The City Charter and Ordinances of the City of Newark Together with Miscellaneous Acts of the Legislature Relating to the City with an Appendix*

(1858), *Appendix*, 360–361; *Newark Daily Advertiser*, July 15, 1868, in Berg, "Medical Practice and Hospital Development in Newark, 1850–1887."

55. Cassedy, *American Medicine and Statistical Thinking*, 34.
56. Ibid., 32–35.
57. See Chapter 3, "Cholera."
58. *Charter of Newark and Revised Ordinances* (1858), *1857 Charter of the City of Newark*, 23.
59. Ibid., *Ordinances*, 167–173.
60. Newark, *Supplements to the Charter of Newark and Revised Ordinances* (1865), *Ordinances*, 127; New Jersey, *Legislative Acts* (1871), 325–326; U.S. Bureau of the Census, *Tenth Census of the United States, 1880: Social Statistics of Cities*, pt. 1, p. 712; *Sentinel of Freedom*, December 14, 1875.
61. *Newark Daily Advertiser*, February 14, 1859, in Berg, "Medical Practice and Hospital Development in Newark, N.J., 1850–1887."

2   PUBLIC HEALTH, DRAINAGE, AND WATER SUPPLY

1. Frank John Urquhart, *A History of the City of Newark, New Jersey*, 3 vols. (New York: Lewis Historical Publishing Co., 1913), 1:563–564.
2. *Charter of the City of Newark with the Ordinances and By-laws Passed by the Common Council* (1838), *Ordinances*, 70. Newark's first tax on dogs, adopted in 1808, was intended to protect sheep. *Records of the Town of Newark, New Jersey from Its Settlement in 1666 to Its Incorporation as a City in 1836* (Newark: Newark Daily Advertiser, 1864), 195–196.
3. *Charter of the City of Newark and Laws of New Jersey Relating to Said City with the Ordinances Passed by the Common Council* (1850), *Ordinances*, 116-118.
4. *Newark Daily Mercury*, April 17, 1857.
5. Ibid., April 14, 17, 1857.
6. Ibid., April 17, 1857.
7. Ibid., April 18, 1857.
8. Ibid., April 23, 27, 1857.
9. Ibid., July 3, 13–15, 1857.
10. Ibid., July 14–17, 1857.
11. Ibid., July 16–17, 1857.
12. Ibid., July 31, 1857.
13. Ibid., February 8, 1858.

14. Ibid.

15. Ibid., August 11, 16, 1859.

16. Ibid., June 9, 1860.

17. *Charter of the City of Newark with the Ordinances and By-laws Passed by the Common Council* (1838), *1836 Charter of the City of Newark*, 15, *Ordinances*, 97-99; *Newark Daily Advertiser*, October 18, 1847.

18. *Charter of the City of Newark and Laws of New Jersey Relating to Said City with the Ordinances Passed by the Common Council* (1850), 73-74, 97-98, 107-108. Charles R. Adrian and Earnest S. Griffith, *A History of American City Government: The Formation of Traditions, 1775-1870* (New York: Praeger, 1976), 74-75.

19. Charles N. Glaab and A. Theodore Brown, *A History of Urban America*, 2d ed. (New York: Macmillan, 1976), 68-69; Adrian and Griffith, *A History of American City Government*, 98; Urquhart, *History of Newark*, 1:563-564.

20. Cunningham, *Newark* (Newark: New Jersey Historical Society, 1966), 20; *Newark Daily Advertiser*, January 4, 6, 1847, April 17, 1852.

21. *Newark Daily Mercury*, June 29, 1855, September 21, 1855.

22. *Newark Daily Advertiser*, January 4, 1847.

23. *Newark Daily Mercury*, January 25, 1853.

24. *Newark Daily Advertiser*, April 9-10, 15, 1853.

25. *Charter of the City of Newark with the Ordinances and By-laws Passed by the Common Council* (1838), *1836 Charter of the City of Newark*, 13-14, 17, 21-22, 24-25, *Ordinances*, 53-56; Cunningham, *Newark*, 124.

26. *Newark Daily Advertiser*, June 1, 4, August 7, 1852; *Newark Daily Mercury*, June 29, 1855, September 21, 1855.

27. *Newark Daily Advertiser*, August 7, 1852, August 13, 1853.

28. *Newark Daily Mercury*, October 19, 1850.

29. Ibid., August 8-9, 13, 1853.

30. Ibid., June 3, 1854.

31. R. A. Lewis, *Edwin Chadwick and the Public Health Movement, 1832-1854* (Reprints of Economic Classics; New York: Augustus M. Kelley, 1970), 48; *AMA Reports on Public Hygiene*, 433, 472; *Newark Daily Advertiser*, August 7, 1852, August 13, 1853.

32. *Newark Daily Advertiser*, August 7, 1852, August 13, 1853.

33. Ibid., August 7-16, 1853.

34. See Chapter 3, "Cholera."

35. *Newark Daily Advertiser*, May 13, 18, 1852.

36. David L. Pierson, *Narratives of Newark, 1866-1916* (Newark: Pierson, 1917), 276.

37. *Newark Daily Advertiser,* May 14, 18, 1852.

38. Ibid., July 29, 1852.

39. Ibid.

40. Ibid., August 7, 1852.

41. S. E. Finer, *The Life and Times of Sir Edwin Chadwick* (New York: Barnes and Noble, 1952), 221–222; Jon A. Peterson, "The Impact of Sanitary Reform upon American Urban Planning, 1840–1890," *Journal of Social History* 13 (Fall 1979):86; *AMA Reports on Public Hygiene,* 432–433, 583–584; Leonard Metcalf and Harrison P. Eddy, *American Sewerage Practice,* 3 vols. (New York: McGraw-Hill, 1914), 1:11; J. J. Cosgrove, *History of Sanitation* (Pittsburgh, Pa.: Standard Manufacturing Co., 1909), 86.

42. *Newark Daily Advertiser,* August 7, 1852.

43. *The City Charter and Ordinances of the City of Newark Together with Miscellaneous Acts of the Legislature Relating to the City with an Appendix* (1858), *Appendix,* 357–359.

44. *Newark Daily Mercury,* September 21, 1855.

45. Ibid.

46. Ibid., January 6, 1857.

47. Ibid., January 9, 1856, January 5, 1859, January 5, 1860.

48. Edward S. Rankin, *The Running Brooks and Other Sketches of Early Newark* (Somerville, N.J.: Unionist Gazette, 1930), 15. With the exception of a few sluggish tidal creeks on the meadows and three large streams on the city's borders, these waterways have since been filled.

49. Newark Department of Public Works, Annual Report of the Division of Water, 1941, *Early History of Newark's Water Supply System,* 7 (hereafter referred to as Division of Water, *Early History of Newark's Water Supply*).

50. Ibid., 7–9.

51. Edward S. Rankin, *Indian Trails and City Streets* (Montclair, N.J.: Globe Press, 1927), 53; *Newark Daily Advertiser,* May 9, 1848, May 11, 1853.

52. Urquhart, *History of Newark,* 2:594–596.

53. Ibid., 2:632–633; Cunningham, *Newark,* 111–112; *Newark Evening News,* July 24, 1949.

54. Division of Water, *Early History of Newark's Water Supply,* 9; Pierson, *Narratives of Newark,* 339; *Sunday Call,* March 29, 1936; Newark, *The Mayor's Message, Together with the Reports of the City Officers of the City of Newark, N.J., 1892, Annual Report of the Board of Street and Water Commissioners,* 7. Some reports of city officers were published separately as well. When citing a report of a city department that was published with the accounts of other municipal agencies, the citation will appear as *Newark Annual Reports,* and will include the year and name of the reporting unit.

55. *Newark Daily Advertiser,* May 11, July 21, 1853, January 22, 1857; Pierson, *Narratives of Newark,* 342.

56. *Newark Daily Mercury,* April 7, 1855.

57. *Newark Annual Reports, 1892, Board of Street and Water Commissioners,* 9.

58. *Newark Daily Mercury,* September 6, 1856, February 3, 1859.

59. Ibid., January 4, 1860.

60. Ibid., January 5, 1859.

61. Ibid., February 3, 1859.

62. *Newark Daily Mercury,* March 2, 1861; *Newark Evening News,* May 23, 1884; Hugh Holmes, *Reminiscences of 75 Years of Belleville, Franklin, and Newark,* 2d ed. (1895 or 1896), 53–54.

63. Urquhart, *History of Newark,* 2:669–672; *Newark Athletic Club News* (February 1921), 19–20; *Sunday Call,* February 19, 1933; *Newark Evening News,* April 17, 1949, April 22, 1956; *Newark Star-Ledger,* July 20, 1946.

64. *Newark Daily Mercury,* January 9, 1861.

65. Ibid., August 18, 1860.

66. Ibid.

67. *Newark Annual Reports, 1892, Board of Street and Water Commissioners,* 9–18; Division of Water, *Early History of Newark's Water Supply,* 9–10; Pierson, *Narratives of Newark,* 343.

3   CHOLERA

1. Charles E. Rosenberg, *The Cholera Years: The United States in 1831, 1849, and 1866* (Chicago: University of Chicago Press, *1962*). For accounts of cholera in particular cities, see William K. Beatty, "When Cholera Scourged Chicago," *Chicago History* 11, no. 1 (1982):2–13; Robert E. Brill, "The Sabbath-day Summer: Madison, Indiana, and the 1849 Cholera Epidemic," *Indiana Medical History Quarterly* 8 (September 1982):3–16; Patrick F. McLear, "The St. Louis Cholera Epidemic of 1849," *Missouri Historical Review* 63 (January 1969):171–181; Margaret M. Phaneuf, "Sanitation and Cholera: Springfield and the 1866 Epidemic," *Historical Journal of Western Massachusetts* 8, no. 1 (1980):26–36; Charles E. Rosenberg, "The Cholera Epidemic of 1832 in New York City," *Bulletin of the History of Medicine* 33 (January–February 1959):37–49.

2. James A. Doull, "Cholera," in Kenneth F. Maxcy and Milton J. Rosenau, *Preventive Medicine and Public Health,* ed. Philip E. Sartwell, 9th ed. (New York: Appleton-Century-Crofts, 1965), 243; Rosenberg, *Cholera,* 2.

3. S. H. Pennington, "Report for the Eastern District," *Transactions of the Med-*

ical Society of New Jersey, 1807–1858, 306 (hereafter referred to as *Trans. MSNJ*).

4. Doull, "Cholera," 243, 246–247; Rosenberg, *Cholera,* 2. In 1960 it was discovered that not all cases of cholera are severe and sometimes the symptoms are so innocuous that the diagnosis is not made. Nineteenth-century physicians saw only acute cases and most considered themselves fortunate if no more than 50 percent of their patients died. An investigation of 7,356 cases in the Mississippi River valley in 1873 revealed a case fatality rate of 52 percent. Todd L. Savitt, *Medicine and Slavery: The Diseases and Health Care of Blacks in Antebellum Virginia* (Urbana: University of Illinois Press, 1978), 226, n. 15; James H. Cassedy, *American Medicine and Statistical Thinking, 1800–1860* (Cambridge, Mass.: Harvard University Press, 1984), 185, 187; John Shaw Billings, Ely McClellan, and John C. Peters, *The Cholera Epidemic of 1873 in the United States,* 43rd Cong., 2d sess., Document 95 (Washington, D.C., 1875), 32.

5. Doull, "Cholera," 245–247.

6. The following sections on the impact of cholera in the United States are based on Rosenberg, *Cholera,* passim.

7. Alex W. Rogers, "Abstract of Report from Essex and Passaic," *Trans. MSNJ, 1807–1858,* 505.

8. John T. Cunningham, *Newark* (Newark: New Jersey Historical Society, 1966), 86–87, 89.

9. *Newark Daily Advertiser,* June 21, 23, 1832.

10. *Sentinel of Freedom,* June 19, 1832.

11. *Newark Daily Advertiser,* June 23, 1832.

12. Ibid., June 25, 28, July 2–3, 1832; *Sentinel of Freedom,* June 26, 1832.

13. Pennington, "Report for the Eastern District," 301–302.

14. Ibid.

15. Ibid.

16. *Newark Daily Advertiser,* July 17, 1832.

17. Pennington, "Report for the Eastern District," 302.

18. *Newark Daily Advertiser,* July 16, 1832.

19. Ibid., August 11, 1832.

20. *Newark Daily Advertiser,* July 19, August 11, 1832; Pennington, "Report for the Eastern District," 303; J. Henry Clark, "History of the 'Cholera' Epidemic, as It Appeared in the City of Newark, N.J., from June to October 1849," *New York Journal of Medicine,* n.s., 4 (1850):223.

21. *Newark Daily Advertiser,* July 19, 1832.

22. Ibid.

23. Ibid., July 28, 1832.

24. Ibid., July 25, 1832.

25. Pennington, "Report for the Eastern District," 303–304.

26. Ibid., 303.

27. *Newark Daily Advertiser*, July 28, 1832.

28. Pennington, "Report for the Eastern District," 308.

29. Ibid., 304.

30. Rosenberg, *Cholera*, 56–57, 114, n.35.

31. *Sentinel of Freedom*, June 19, 1849.

32. Ibid.

33. Rogers, "Report from Essex and Passaic," 504.

34. Clark, "History of the 'Cholera' Epidemic," 223.

35. *Trans. MSNJ, 1861*, 64.

36. *New Jersey Board of Health, Annual Report for 1880*, 106–107 (hereafter cited as *ARNJBH*). Other municipal poorhouses were also stricken with the disease. In Baltimore's almshouse, ninety-six persons died from the disease in 1849, and in Buffalo's county poorhouse the mortality in the 1854 epidemic was said to be "frightful." Billings, McClellan, and Peters, *Cholera Epidemic of 1873*, 612–613, 637.

37. *Sentinel of Freedom*, August 14, 1849.

38. Clark, "History of the 'Cholera' Epidemic," 214.

39. Ibid., 213–214, 220–221; Rogers, "Report from Essex and Passaic," 504.

40. Rosenberg, *Cholera*, 114–116; John Sharpe Chambers, *The Conquest of Cholera: America's Greatest Scourge* (New York: Macmillan, 1938), 238; Billings, McClellan, and Peters, *Cholera Epidemic of 1873*, 619; Brill, "Madison and the 1849 Cholera Epidemic," 8–12.

41. Chambers, *Conquest of Cholera*, 27, 43, 63–64, 118, 148–169; Billings, McClellan, and Peters, *Cholera Epidemic of 1873*, 568, 584; Rosenberg, "Cholera in New York City," 39.

42. Pennington, "Report for the Eastern District," 307.

43. Ibid.; Rogers, "Report from Passaic and Essex," 506.

44. Letter, Dr. W.C.J. Thompson to Health Committee, October 12, 1854, Newark Public Library, Archives.

45. Rosenberg, *Cholera*, 143, 149.

46. Clark, "History of the 'Cholera' Epidemic," 222.

47. Letter, Thompson to Health Committee, Newark Public Library, Archives.

48. Rosenberg, *Cholera*, 168–172; Clark, "History of the 'Cholera' Epidemic," 222.

49. Clark, "History of the 'Cholera' Epidemic," 215.

50. *Newark Daily Advertiser*, July 3, 1854; *Sentinel of Freedom*, July 4, 1854.

51. Report of the Health Committee (1854), Newark Public Library, Archives.

52. *Newark Daily Advertiser*, July 6, 1854.

53. Ibid., July 8, 24, 1854; William H. Shaw, comp., *History of Essex and Hudson Counties, New Jersey, 2* vols. (Philadelphia: Everts and Peck, 1884), 1:321.

54. *Newark Daily Advertiser*, July 12, 24, 28, August 24, 1854; Report of the Health Committee (1854), Newark Public Library, Archives.

55. Report of the Health Committee to the Common Council, September 1, 1854, Newark Public Library, Archives; Report of the Health Committee, September 25, 1854, Newark Public Library, Archives.

56. Report of the Health Committee [n.d.], Newark Public Library, Archives. In other cities as well the poor were removed from unsanitary dwellings and temporarily housed in less exposed quarters. Rosenberg, *Cholera,* 34, 88–89.

57. *Newark Daily Advertiser*, July 23, 1854. Throughout the nation, community opposition to the establishment of cholera hospitals was intense and "neighbors resorted to everything from humble petitions to arsons in their efforts to have them removed." Rosenberg, *Cholera,* 94.

58. Report of the Health Committee (1854), Newark Public Library, Archives.

59. Ibid.

60. *Newark Daily Advertiser*, July 24, 1854.

61. Report of the Health Committee (1854), Newark Public Library, Archives.

62. *Sentinel of Freedom*, August 29, 1854.

63. *Newark Daily Advertiser*, August 30, 1854.

64. These reports were probably prompted by the fact that other than in Newark, cholera was not virulent in the Northeast in 1854. There were only 128 cholera deaths in New York City, 88 in Philadelphia, and a few cases in Baltimore and Washington. However, when the pestilence reached the West, it caused great havoc. Saint Louis was the most seriously afflicted, with 3,547 deaths. Billings, McClellan, and Peters, *Cholera Epidemic of 1873,* 635–636; Chambers, *Conquest of Cholera,* 255.

65. *Newark Daily Advertiser*, August 30, 1854; *Sentinel of Freedom*, September 5, 1854.

66. *Trans. MSNJ, 1861,* 64.

67. *Newark Daily Advertiser*, July 29, 1854.

68. George H. Bailey, *Report to the Newark Aqueduct Board upon the Subject of a Supply of a Water for the City of Newark* (Newark: Newark Daily Advertiser, 1861), 6.

69. *Newark Daily Advertiser*, August 10, 1854.

70. Ibid., September 14, 1854.

71. Charles-Edward Amory Winslow, *Man and Epidemics* (Princeton, N.J.: Princeton University Press, 1952), 271–276; Rosenberg, *Cholera*, 193–194.

72. Rosenberg, *Cholera*, 195–234.

73. *Trans. MSNJ, 1867*, 253–255.

74. *Newark Daily Advertiser*, August 4, 1866; *Sentinel of Freedom*, August 7, 1866.

75. *Trans. MSNJ, 1867*, 253–255; *Sentinel of Freedom*, July 31, 1866. Other cities were not so fortunate. Saint Louis had 8,500 deaths; Cincinnati, 1406; and Chicago, 990. Billings, McClellan, and Peters, *Cholera Epidemic of 1873*, 672.

4   AN AGE OF GIANTS

1. John T. Cunningham, *Newark* (Newark: New Jersey Historical Society, 1966), 152–155, 158–159; Samuel Harry Popper, "Newark, N.J., 1870–1910: Chapters in the Evolution of an American Metropolis" (Ph.D. diss., New York University, 1952), 12–24.

2. Popper, "Newark," 12–14.

3. Raymond Michael Ralph, "From Village to Industrial City: The Urbanization of Newark, New Jersey, 1830–1860" (Ph.D. diss., New York University, 1978), 41, 63, 65; Chalres Stephenson, "The Process of Community: Class, Culture, and Ethnicity in Nineteenth-Century Newark," in *New Jersey's Ethnic Heritage: Papers Presented at the Eighth Annual New Jersey History Symposium, December 4, 1976*, ed. Paul A. Stellhorn (Trenton: New Jersey History Commission, 1978), 95; Popper, "Newark," 79–85.

4. Popper, "Newark," 13–15.

5. Ibid.

6. Cunningham, *Newark*, 174–184.

7. Ibid., 201–208; Popper, "Newark," 63, 126–135.

8. Ralph, "From Village to Industrial City," 180–182; Popper, "Newark," 160–165.

9. Popper, "Newark," 166–171.

10. Cunningham, *Newark*, 222–223; Popper, "Newark," 270.

11. Frank John Urquhart, *A History of the City of Newark, New Jersey*, 3 vols. (New York: Lewis Historical Publishing Co., 1913), 2:858, 861.

12. The Thirteenth Ward Improvement Association of the City of Newark, N.J., *Secretary's Annual Report for 1885* (Newark: Kerr's Print, 1886).

13. *A History of the Old Burying Ground as Contained in the Case of the Attorney-General Against the City of Newark, 1888* (Newark: Ward and Tichenor, 1888), 25–26; Ralph, "From Village to Industrial City," 237–238.

14. Quoted in Popper, "Newark," 289.

15. Ibid., 288–291.

16. Ibid., 166–171.

17. Ibid., 173–175; Newark Board of Education, *Newark Study Leaflets* (1914), no. 37, *Newark Advantages*, 2.

18. Cunningham, *Newark,* 189–196; Popper, "Newark," 223–228.

19. *Newark Daily Advertiser,* March 17, June 5, 1857; *Charter of Newark and Revised Ordinances* (1858), *1857 Charter of the City of Newark,* 23, 167–173.

20. *Newark Daily Advertiser,* May 5, 1858, in Samuel Berg comp., "Medical Practice and Hospital Development in Newark, N.J., 1850–1887, as Reported in Newark Daily Advertiser," Newark Public Library, New Jersey Reference Division.

21. Ibid., October 27, 1853, December 30, 1854, March 17, April 30, June 5, December 14, 1857, February 14, 1859.

22. Ibid., October 27, 1853; May 6, 9, June 3, 5, 1854.

23. Ibid., March 19, April 22, 25, 1857; *Newark Daily Mercury,* January 27, February 27, 1857.

24. *Report of the Health Physician, 1860,* 34. Newark was not the only city of its size without a municipal hospital. Milwaukee did not establish a creditable, general purpose municipal hospital until the second decade of the twentieth century. Judith Walzer Leavitt, *The Healthiest City: Milwaukee and the Politics of Health Reform* (Princeton, N.J.: Princeton University Press, 1982), 67–70, 203, 216.

25. David L. Pierson, *Narratives of Newark, 1866–1916* (Newark: Pierson, 1917), 299–302.

26. *Newark Daily Advertiser,* August 14, December 10, 1869, March 27, 1875, in Berg, "Medical Practice and Hospital Development in Newark, N.J., 1850–1887."

27. Ibid., June 18, 1868; *The Message: Hospital of Saint Barnabas* 21 (March 1949):18.

28. *Newark Daily Advertiser,* June 13, 1870, in Berg, "Medical Practice and Hospital Development in Newark, N.J., 1850–1877."

29. Ibid.

30. Ibid., June 12, 1871.

31. Ibid.

32. Ibid., June 5, 1874.

33. Rosary S. Gilheany, "Early Newark Hospitals," *Proceedings of the New Jersey Historical Society* (January 1965):14.

34. *Newark Daily Advertiser,* April 27, May 3, August 9, 1869, April 24, May 8, 1871, in Berg, "Medical Practice and Hospital Development in Newark, N.J., 1850–1887"; Saint Michael's Hospital, Newark, N.J., *Diamond Jubilee, 1867–1942,* 18.

35. *Newark Daily Advertiser,* May 26, 1869, May 21, 1870, January 23, 1871, in Berg, "Medical Practice and Hospital Development in Newark, N.J., 1850–1887."

36. Ibid.

37. Ibid., February 10, 1873.

38. Gilheany, "Early Newark Hospitals," 18.

39. *Newark Daily Advertiser,* February 16, 1880, in Berg, "Medical Practice and Hospital Development in Newark, N.J., 1850–1887"; Gilheany, "Early Newark Hospitals," 18.

40. John T. Cunningham, *Clara Maass: A Nurse, a Hospital, a Spirit* (Cedar Grove, N.J.: Rae, 1968), 13.

41. Ibid., 15–16.

42. Ibid.; *Newark Daily Advertiser,* January 20, December 9, 1868, in Berg, "Medical Practice and Hospital Development in Newark, N.J., 1850–1887."

43. Cunningham, *Clara Maass,* 17–18.

44. Ibid., 18–24.

45. Ibid., 26; *Newark Daily Advertiser,* December 11, 1878, in Berg, "Medical Practices and Hospital Development in Newark, N.J., 1850–1887."

46. Cunningham, *Clara Maass,* 29.

47. Ibid., 26; Gilheany, "Early Newark Hospitals," 19; *Newark Daily Advertiser,* December 22, 1884, in Berg, "Medical Practice and Hospital Development in Newark, N.J., 1850–1887."

48. Cunningham, *Clara Maass,* 29.

49. Ibid.

50. Ibid., 30–31; Gilheany, "Early Newark Hospitals," 21.

51. *Quarter-Century's Progress of New Jersey's Leading Manufacturing Centers* (New York: International Publishing Co., 1887), 49; Urquhart, *History of Newark,* 2:63.

52. *Newark Daily Advertiser,* January 26, February 2, April 8, 1880, in Berg, "Medical Practice and Hospital Development in Newark, N.J., 1850–1887."

53. Ibid., February 18, 1881, February 23, 1882, February 25, 1884, March 16, 1885.

54. Ibid., March 13, 1876; Urquhart, *History of Newark,* 2:885.

55. *Newark Daily Advertiser,* January 5, December 3, 1880, in Berg, "Medical Practice and Hospital Development in Newark, N.J., 1850–1887."

56. Ibid., December 3, 1880.

57. Ibid., January 6, 1880, February 25, 1883.

58. Ibid., June 14, September 1, 1870, August 7, 1872, December 27, 1878, March 24, 1882.

59. Ibid., February 13, 1875, June 30, 1882, March 10, 1883.

60. Ibid., July 14, 25, 1882, March 15, 1883; *Newark Annual Reports, 1883, Newark City Hospital,* 672.

61. *Newark Daily Advertiser,* March 24, August 12, 1882, January 3, 1883, November 21, 1884, in Berg, "Medical Practice and Hospital Development in Newark, N.J., 1850–1887"; Bureau of Municipal Research, New York, "A Survey of the Government, Finances and Administration of the City of Newark, N.J." (November 1, 1919), 230, 301–302, Newark Public Library, New Jersey Reference Division (hereafter referred to as Bureau of Municipal Research, N.Y., "Survey").

62. *Newark Daily Advertiser,* June 14, 1883.

63. Frederick L. Hoffman, "The General Death Rate of Large American Cities, 1871–1904," *Publications of the American Statistical Association* 10, n.s., no. 73 (March 1906):5, 49.

64. Ezra M. Hunt, "A Study of Consumption as a Preventable Disease," *ARNJBH, 1881,* 245.

65. U.S. Bureau of the Census, *Eleventh Census of the United States, 1890: Report on Vital and Social Statistics,* 1:588, 2:276–283. A positive correlation of congestion and foreign birth with high mortality was an article of faith of nineteenth-century sanitary and housing reformers. However, geographer David Ward has shown that Jewish immigrants who shared the same wretched housing as Italian newcomers had much lower mortality rates and concludes from this that cultural and biological factors, especially those arising from the Jews' previous urban experience, probably explain much of the difference in mortality rates. Historian Judith Leavitt has found that in Milwaukee the inhabitants of crowded dwellings were not significantly at risk from contracting tuberculosis or pneumonia. Nevertheless, she writes that "the highest correlates of general death rates in both 1890 and 1900 were density within dwelling and foreign nativity. . . . The more congested the housing and the larger the percentage of foreign-born in a given ward, the greater the chance of high mortality rates." David Ward, "The Internal Spatial Structure of Immigrant Residential Districts in the Late 19th Century," *Geographical Analysis* 1 (1969):337–353; Leavitt, *Milwaukee and the Politics of*

Health Reform, 30–31. See also Clayton R. Koppes and William P. Norris, "Ethnicity, Class, and Mortality in the Industrial City: A Case Study of Typhoid Fever in Pittsburgh, 1890–1910," *Journal of Urban History* 11 (May 1985):259–279.

66. Ezra Mundy Hunt, "The Passaic River as Related to Water Supply and Death Rates," *ARNJBH, 1887, 317–358*.

67. Author's calculations based on mortality statistics contained in the annual reports of the New Jersey Board of Health.

68. Ibid.

69. Cunningham, *Newark*, 222.

70. Ibid., 222–223; Popper, "Newark," 270; Ernest S. Griffith, *A History of American City Government: The Conspicuous Failure, 1870–1900* (New York: Praeger, 1974), 69.

71. *Newark Daily Journal*, August 7, 9, 11, 1883.

72. Ibid., September 1, 1883.

73. Popper, "Newark," 79–85.

74. In some communities Prohibition was regarded as a public health issue, but not in Newark, where it was viewed primarily in moral and religious terms.

5   BOARD OF HEALTH

1. U.S. Bureau of the Census, *Tenth Census of the United States, 1880: Social Statistics of Cities*, pt. 1, pp. 711–712; *Newark Annual Reports, 1879, Board of Health*, 403–408, *1880*, 427–441. Until 1881 the city's public health agency was known as the "Board of Health"; from 1881 to 1884 as the "Local Board of Health"; from 1885 to 1893 as the "Board of Health"; and from 1897 on as the "Department of Public Health." The governing council of the agency was called the "Board of Health." The chief executive officer was referred to variously as the "Health Physician" and the "Health Officer." Frank Pierce Hill and Varnum Lansing Collins, comp., *Books, Pamphlets and Newspapers Printed at Newark, N.J., 1776–1900* (privately press of Courtier-Citizen Co., 1902), 164.

2. Elisha Harris, "Report on the Public Health Service in the Principal Cities, and the Progress of Sanitary Works in the United States," American Public Health Association, *Public Health Reports and Papers* 2 (1874–1875):169. For accounts of other nineteenth-century municipal departments of health, see Sam Alewitz, "Sanitation and Public Health: Philadelphia, 1870–1910"

(Ph.D. diss., Case Western Reserve University, 1981); James H. Cassedy, *Charles V. Chapin and the Public Health Movement* (Cambridge, Mass.: Harvard University Press, 1962); Jacqueline Karnell Corn, "Municipal Organization for Public Health in Pittsburgh, 1851–1895" (D.A. diss., Carnegie-Mellon University, 1972); John Duffy, *A History of Public Health in New York City,* vol. *1, 1625–1866,* vol. *2, 1866–1966* (New York: Russell Sage Foundation, 1974); Duncan R. Jamieson, "Toward a Cleaner New York: John H. Griscom and New York's Public Health, 1830–1870" (Ph.D. diss., Michigan State University, 1972); Judith Walzer Leavitt, *The Healthiest City: Milwaukee and the Politics of Health Reform* (Princeton, N.J.: Princeton University Press, 1982); Alan I. Marcus, "In Sickness and in Health: The Marriage of the Municipal Corporation to the Public Interest and the Problem of Public Health, 1820–1870. The Case of Cincinnati" (Ph.D. diss., University of Cincinnati, 1979); Dorothy T. Scanlon, "The Public Health Movement in Boston, 1870–1910" (Ph.D. diss., Boston University, 1956).

3. *Newark Evening News,* March 13, 1884.

4. Ibid., November 6, 1883.

5. *Newark Evening News,* September 6, 1883.

6. Alan I. Marcus, "The Strange Career of Municipal Health Initiatives; Cincinnati and City Government in the Early Nineteenth Century," *Journal of Urban History* 7 (November 1980):3–14.

7. Ibid.

8. David R. Goldfield, "The Business of Health Planning: Disease Prevention in the Old South," *Journal of Southern History* 42 (November 1976):559, 568.

9. Ibid., 560–563; Richard Harrison Shryock, *The Development of Modern Medicine: An Interpretation of the Social and Scientific Factors Involved* (New York: Alfred A. Knopf, 1947), 216–217.

10. Goldfield, "The Business of Health Planning," 564–566.

11. Ibid.

12. George Rosen, *A History of Public Health* (New York: MD Publications, 1958), 201–206; Wilson G. Smillie, *Public Health, Its Promise for the Future: A Chronicle of the Development of Public Health in the United States, 1607–1914* (New York: Macmillan, 1955), 123–127; Howard D. Kramer, "The Beginnings of the Public Health Movement in the United States," *Bulletin of the History of Medicine* 21 (May–June 1947):355–358.

13. Rosen, *History of Public Health,* 200–201, 234–240.

14. Ibid., 213–214.

15. Ibid., 206–216.

16. Kramer, "The Beginnings of the Public Health Movement in the United States," 352–376.

17. Ibid., 363.

18. Howard D. Kramer, "Early Municipal and State Boards of Health," *Bulletin of the History of Medicine* 24 (November–December 1950):504.

19. James H. Cassedy, *American Medicine and Statistical Thinking, 1800–1860* (Cambridge, Mass.: Harvard University Press, 1984), 222–229.

20. Smillie, *Chronicle of the Development of Public Health*, 352; Kramer, "Early Municipal and State Boards of Health," 504.

21. Quoted in Smillie, *Chronicle of the Development of Public Health*, 289.

22. Ibid., 291–292.

23. Ibid., 292–295; Rosen, *History of Public Health*, 244–248; Charles E. Rosenberg, *The Cholera Years: The United States in 1832, 1849, and 1866* (Chicago: University of Chicago Press, 1958), 211–212, 227; Kramer, "Early Municipal and State Boards of Health," 509–513, 516–525.

24. Smillie, *Chronicle of the Development of Public Health*, 294; Kramer, "Early Municipal and State Boards of Health," 515; John Duffy, *A History of Public Health in New York City*, 2 vols. (New York: Russell Sage Foundation, 1974), 2:49–53, 67–68, 92–93, 239, 250–251, 257, 261, 276.

25. Howard D. Kramer, "The Germ Theory and the Early Public Health Program in the United States," *Bulletin of the History of Medicine* 22 (May–June 1948):237; Sam Alewitz, "Sanitation and Public Health: Philadelphia, 1870–1900" (Ph.D. diss., Case Western Reserve University, 1981), 103.

26. Alewitz, "Sanitation and Public Health: Philadelphia, 1870–1900," 101–106.

27. Charles V. Chapin, *Municipal Sanitation in the United States* (Providence, R.I.: Snow and Farnham, 1901), 30.

28. Stanley K. Schultz and Clay McShane, "To Engineer the Metropolis: Sewers, Sanitation, and City Planning in Late-Nineteenth Century America," *Journal of American History* 65 (September 1978):397–398.

29. Ibid., 398.

30. Ibid., 395.

31. Ibid., 399.

32. Barbara Gutmann Rosenkrantz, *Public Health and the State: Changing Views in Massachusetts, 1842–1936* (Cambridge, Mass.: Harvard University Press, 1972), 74.

33. Cassedy, *Charles V. Chapin and the Public Health Movement*, 41.

34. Corn, "Municipal Organization for Public Health in Pittsburgh, 1851–1895," 24.

35. *Newark Annual Reports, 1870, Mayor's Message*, 17, *1872*, 27.

36. Lott Southard, "Drainage and Sewerage of the City of Newark and Their Relation to the Causation of Disease," *Trans. MSNJ, 1877*, 192. Antebellum

health reformers generally maintained that a third of all urban deaths were preventable. Post–Civil War sanitarians commonly estimated that one-half of all disease occurrences could be avoided and the death rate reduced to 15 per 1,000 population through adoption of better modes of personal and public hygiene. Cassedy, *American Medicine and Statistical Thinking,* 207; John S. Billings, "Introduction," *A Treatise on Hygiene and Public Health,* ed. Albert H. Buck, 2 vols. (1879; reprint, New York: Arno Press, 1977), 1:5.

37. *Annual Report of the Board of Trade, 1880,* 8.

38. Howard D. Kramer, "History of the Public Health Movement in the United States, 1850 to 1900" (Ph.D. diss., State University of Iowa, 1942), 182–183.

39. Frederick L. Hoffman, "The General Death Rate of Large American Cities, 1871–1904," *Publications of the American Statistical Association* 10, n.s., no. 73 (March 1906):11.

40. James H. Cassedy, "The Registration Area and American Vital Statistics: Development of a Health Research Resource, 1885–1915," *Bulletin of the History of Medicine* 39 (March–April 1965):221–222, 226–227; Kramer, "History of Public Health," 182–183.

41. From the Greek word for fermentation, *zymōtikos.*

42. Edgar Holden, *Mortality and Sanitary Record of Newark, N.J.*[1859–1879]: *A Report Presented to the President and Directors of the Mutual Benefit Life Insurance Company, January, 1880* (Newark, 1880), 5.

43. Ibid.

44. David L. Cowen, *Medicine and Health in New Jersey: A History,* vol. 16 of *The New Jersey Historical Series,* ed. Richard M. Huber and Wheaton J. Lane (New Brunswick, N.J.: Rutgers University Press, 1964), 85–87; New Jersey, *Legislative Acts, 1881,* 160, *1882,* 217–223, *1883,* 237–238.

45. *Newark Daily Advertiser,* April 26, May 8, 1883.

46. Ibid., June 14, 1883.

47. *Newark Evening News,* November 15, 1883.

48. *Newark Daily Journal,* July 19, August 2, 7–9, 11, 15, 18, 20, 22, 25, 29, September 1, 6, 20, 26, October 10, 1883.

49. Ibid., August 2, 1883.

50. Ibid., August 7, 1883.

51. Ibid., September 1, 1883.

52. Ibid., August 11, 1883.

53. Ibid., August 29, 1883.

54. Ibid., September 20, 1883.

55. Ibid., September 1, 1883.

56. Quoted in *Newark Daily Advertiser*, October 12, 1883.

57. *Newark Annual Reports, 1884, Mayor's Message*, 35–36.

58. *Newark Evening News*, March 13, July 16, 25–27, August 29, 1884, February 4, 1885; *Sunday Call*, April 26, May 3, 1885; *Newark Daily Advertiser*, May 1, 1885; *Newark Annual Reports, 1885, Mayor's Message*, 81–82; *ARNJBH, 1885*, 31, 270.

59. *Newark Annual Reports, 1885, Mayor's Message*, 50–52, *1886*, 83–84, *1889*, 73–74.

60. The tax appropriation for 1889 was $13,000. An additional $6,000 was made available through permit receipts, fees, licenses, and transfers from other accounts.

61. *Annual Report of the Board of Health, 1889*, 18–19.

62. Hill and Collins, *Books, Pamphlets and Newspapers Printed at Newark*, 164; *Newark Evening News*, October 30, 1895.

63. *Newark Daily Advertiser*, May 8, 1883; *Newark Evening News*, July 29, 1886; *Sunday Call*, September 16, 1888.

64. See Chapter 8, "Smallpox."

65. *Sunday Call*, January 21, 1923.

66. U.S. Bureau of the Census, *Eleventh Census of the United States, 1890: Report on Vital and Social Statistics*, 2:2–4, 21–22, 75, 78, 85, 88, 96, 99.

67. *Newark Evening News*, March 31, 1890.

68. *Sunday Call*, February 16, 1890.

69. The two incidents are described in *Newark Annual Reports, 1890, Mayor's Message*, 47–53; *Newark Evening News*, March 31, April 4, May 1, 6, 8, June 7, 1890; *Sunday Call*, February 16, May 18, June 8, 1890.

70. *Newark Evening News*, June 27, 1890.

71. *Annual Report of the Newark Board of Health, 1898*, 25; *Newark Annual Reports, 1891, Mayor's Message*, 58; *Newark Evening News*, August 20, 1891.

72. *Newark Evening News*, August 20, 22, 26–28, September 3, 1891; *Sunday Call*, August 23, 30, September 6, November 8, 1891.

73. *Newark Annual Reports, 1891, Mayor's Message*, 57.

74. *Newark Evening News*, March 2, 1892.

75. Ibid., July 3, 1893.

76. *Sunday Call*, January 27, 1895; *Newark Evening News*, January 28, 1895. What Mayor Lebkuecher really appears to have been upset about, however, was the board of health's success in getting the common council to override his veto of a measure to establish a bacteriological laboratory to produce diphtheria antitoxin.

77. *Newark Annual Reports, 1885, Board of Health*, 573, 624, *1887*, 478–479.

78. *Newark Annual Reports, 1917, Board of Health*, 147, 173–179.

79. *Annual Report of the Newark Board of Health, 1894*, 49–51; *Sunday Call*, September 12, 1888; George B. Ford and E. P. Goodrich, *Housing Report,* [Reports of] *The City Plan Commission, Newark, N.J.* (Newark: Mathias Plum, 1913), 46–49; Bureau of Municipal Research, N.Y., "A Survey of the Government, Finances and Administration of the City of Newark, New Jersey" (November 1, 1919), 268–272 (hereafter referred to as Bureau of Municipal Research, N.Y., "Survey"), Newark Public Library, New Jersey Reference Division.

80. See Willard D. Price, *The Ironbound District: A Study of a District of Newark, N.J.* (Newark, 1912), 24–25 (made by Willard D. Price for the Neighborhood House).

81. Ford and Goodrich, *Housing Report*, 46–49; Bureau of Municipal Research, N.Y., "Survey," 268–272.

82. *Newark Annual Reports, 1885, Board of Health*, 597.

83. *Sunday Call*, March 1, 1885.

84. Southard, "Drainage and Sewerage of . . . Newark," 198–199.

85. *Sunday Call*, March 1, 1885. The board of health was also critical of the situation. See *Newark Annual Reports, 1886, Board of Health*, 564–567.

86. William H. Ford, "Soil and Water," *A Treatise on Hygiene and Public Health*, ed. Albert H. Buck, 1:518–522; Joel A. Tarr, "Out of Sight, Out of Mind," *American History Illustrated* 10 (January 1976):41–42.

87. Newark, *The Sanitary Code Adopted by the Board of Health of the City of Newark, New Jersey* (June 1888), 9–13, 18–19.

88. *Newark Evening News*, August 21, 1891; *ARNJBH, 1901*, 344–345. The fertilizer was made by mixing night soil with gypsum or earth.

89. Ford and Goodrich, *Housing Report*, 9, 12.

90. *Newark Annual Reports, 1915, Board of Health*, 974–975.

91. Frank John Urquhart, *A History of the City of Newark, New Jersey*, 3 vols. (New York: Lewis Historical Publishing Co., 1913), 2:594–596; George H. Bailey, *Report to the Newark Aqueduct Board upon the Subject of a Supply of Water for the City of Newark* (Newark: Newark Daily Advertiser, 1861), 5–6; Southard, "Drainage and Sewerage of . . . Newark," 192.

92. Southard, "Drainage and Sewerage of . . . Newark," 194, 196.

93. See Chapter 3, "Cholera."

94. *Annual Report of the Aqueduct Board, 1873*, 40.

95. *Newark Annual Reports, 1883, Board of Health*, 428–429.

96. *Newark Evening News*, August 30, 1884.

97. Ibid.; *Sunday Call*, July 25, 1884, June 27, 1915.

98. *Sunday Call*, June 29, 1915.

99. Ibid., October 17, 1884.

100. *Newark Annual Reports, 1887, Board of Health,* 478–479; *Sunday Call,* June 27, 1915; *Annual Report of the Board of Health, 1894,* 43–45.

101. *Annual Report of the Board of Health, 1894,* 43–45.

102. *Newark Annual Reports, 1887, Board of Health,* 476–477.

103. A similar code had been adopted in New York nine years earlier. May N. Stone, "The Plumbing Paradox: American Attitudes toward Late Nineteenth-Century Domestic Sanitary Arrangements," *Winterthur Portfolio* (Autumn 1979):295.

104. William Travis Howard, Jr., *Public Health Administration and the Natural History of Disease in Baltimore, Maryland, 1797–1920* (Washington, D.C.: Carnegie Institution of Washington, 1924), 164–165; *Newark Daily Journal,* August 20, 22, 1883; *Annual Report of the Newark Board of Health, 1888,* 9, *1894,* 47–48; Newark, *Supplement to the Sanitary Code of the City of Newark, N.J., to Compel, Prescribe, Regulate and Control the Plumbing, Ventilation and Drainage of All Buildings . . .* (1890), passim.

105. *Newark Annual Reports, Board of Health, 1883,* 438.

106. *Newark Annual Reports, Board of Health, 1881,* 414–418, *1883,* 438–440; *1885,* 601–602, *1887,* 479, 482–483.

107. Roger S. Tracy, "Public Nuisances," *A Treatise on Hygiene and Public Health,* ed. Albert H. Buck, 2:390–391, 402–407, 422–423; Emmons Clark, "Sanitary Improvement in New York during the Last Quarter of a Century," *Popular Science Monthly* 39 (1891):321–322, 326–327; F. Garvin Davenport, "The Sanitation Revolution in Illinois, 1870–1900," *Journal of the Illinois State Historical Society* 66 (Autumn 1973):321–324; Duffy, *Public Health in New York,* 2:128–132.

108. Kenneth F. Maxcy and Milton J. Rosenau, *Preventive Medicine and Public Health,* ed. Philip E. Sartwell, 9th ed. (New York: Appleton-Century-Crofts, 1965), 324–325, 366–369, 372–374, 378–383.

109. N.J. Board of Agriculture, *Annual Report, 1883–1884,* 186, *1884–1885,* 191, *1897,* 185–187 (hereafter referred to as *ARNJBA*).

110. *Newark Annual Reports, Board of Health, 1883,* 438–440.

111. Ibid., *1886,* 582–585. The board, in its annual report for 1885, stated incorrectly that Gerth had resigned to become state veterinarian of Nebraska.

112. *Newark Annual Reports, Board of Health, 1885,* 620; *Annual Report of the Board of Health, 1901,* 14; *Newark Evening News,* June 5, 1913; Bureau of Municipal Research, N.Y., "Survey," 277–278.

113. Cassedy, *American Medicine and Statistical Thinking,* 12–13.

114. *Annual Report of the Newark Board of Health, 1894*, 18, *1897*, 29–30; Chapin, *Municipal Sanitation*, 53.

115. I have been influenced in my thinking here by John B. Blake, *Public Health in the Town of Boston, 1630–1822* (Cambridge, Mass.: Harvard University Press, 1969), 241–242.

6   SEWERAGE

1. U.S. Bureau of the Census, *Tenth Census of the United States, 1880: Social Statistics of Cities*, pt. 1, pp. 708–709.

2. Report of the Engineers to the Special Committee on Sewerage, August 1, 1884 (Newark, 1884), 8–9; Popper, "Newark," 306.

3. Newark, *Charter of Newark and Revised Ordinances* (1858), *1857 Charter of the City of Newark*, 58; *Ordinances*, 212–221.

4. *Newark and Its Leading Businessmen* (Newark: 1891), 12.

5. Samuel Harry Popper, "Newark, N.J., 1870–1910: Chapters in the Evolution of an American Metropolis" (Ph.D. diss., New York University, 1952), 305.

6. John T. Cunningham, *Newark* (Newark: New Jersey Historical Society, 1966), 222; *Newark Annual Reports, 1886, Mayor's Message*, 44–45.

7. *Newark Evening News*, January 10, 1884.

8. The history of sewerage and wastewater treatment in the United States is described in Joel A. Tarr, James McCurley, and Terry F. Yosie, "The Development and Impact of Urban Wastewater Technology: Changing Concepts of Water Quality Control, 1850–1930," in *Pollution and Reform in American Cities, 1870–1930*, ed. Martin V. Melosi (Austin: University of Texas Press, 1980), 59–82; Joel A. Tarr, with James McCurley III, Francis C. Michael, and Terry Yosie, "Water and Wastes: A Retrospective Assessment of Wastewater Technology in the United States, 1800–1932," *Technology and Culture* 25 (April 1984):226–263; Ellis L. Armstrong, ed., *History of Public Works in the United States, 1776–1976* (Chicago: American Public Works Association, 1976), 399–430. For accounts of the development of sewer systems in individual cities, see Sam Alewitz, "Sanitation and Public Health: Philadelphia, 1870–1900" (Ph.D. diss., Case Western Reserve University, 1981), 157–173; Alan D. Anderson, *The Origin and Resolution of an Urban Crisis: Baltimore, 1890–1930* (Baltimore, Md.: Johns Hopkins University Press, 1977), 66–70; Geoffrey Giglierano, "The City and the System: Developing a Municipal Service, 1800–1915," *Cincinnati Historical Society Bul-*

letin 35 (Winter 1977):223–247; Lynette B. Wrenn, "The Memphis Sewer Experiment," *Tennessee Historical Quarterly* 44 (Fall 1985):340–349.

9. Richard Harrison Shryock, *Medicine and Society in America: 1660–1860* (New York: New York University Press, 1960), 100, 134, 161.

10. Wilson G. Smillie, *Public Health, Its Promise for the Future: A Chronicle of the Development of Public Health in the United States, 1607–1914* (New York: Macmillan, 1955), 342–350.

11. Charles-Edward Amory Winslow, *The Conquest of Epidemic Diseases: A Chapter in the History of Ideas* (Princeton, N.J.: Princeton University Press, 1943), 311, 316; Charles E. Rosenberg, *The Cholera Years: The United States in 1832, 1849, and 1866* (Chicago: University of Chicago Press, 1962), 194.

12. George Rosen, *A History of Public Health* (New York: MD Publications, 1957), 258–259, 287–288, 311–321.

13. Leonard Metcalf and Harrison P. Eddy, *American Sewerage Practice*, 3 vols. (New York: McGraw-Hill, 1914), 1:1.

14. Stuart Galishoff, "Triumph and Failure: The American Response to the Urban Water Supply Problem, 1860–1923," in *Pollution and Reform in American Cities, 1870–1930*, 35–36, 42–43; Alewitz, "Sanitation and Public Health: Philadelphia, 1870–1900," 213.

15. Tarr, McCurley, and Yosie, "Development and Impact of Urban Wastewater Technology," 62.

16. Tarr, et al., "Water and Wastes," 229–230; Letty Anderson, "The Diffusion of Technology in the Nineteenth Century American City: Municipal Water Supply Investments" (Ph.D. diss., Northwestern University, 1980), 123; Alewitz, "Sanitation and Public Health: Philadelphia, 1870–1900," 52, 139; May N. Stone, "The Plumbing Paradox: American Attitudes toward Late Nineteenth-Century Domestic Sanitary Arrangements," *Winterthur Portfolio* 14 (1979):283–309; Tarr, McCurley, and Yosie, "Development and Impact of Urban Wastewater Technology," 62.

17. Stone, "The Plumbing Paradox," 286; Alewitz, "Sanitation and Public Health in Philadelphia: 1870–1900," 148, 155–156, 163; Tarr, McCurley, and Yosie, "Impact and Development of Urban Wastewater Technology," 61–63; Tarr et al., "Water and Wastes," 234–235; Ernest S. Griffith, *A History of American City Government: The Conspicuous Failure, 1877–1900* (New York: Praeger, 1974), 8; Metcalf and Eddy, *American Sewerage Practice*, 1:15.

18. Tarr, McCurley, and Yosie, "Impact and Development of Urban Wastewater Technology," 61–64; Tarr et al., "Water and Wastes," 232–233; J. J.

Cosgrove, *History of Sanitation* (Pittsburgh, Pa.: Standard Sanitary Manufacturing Co., 1909), 85–86; Anderson, *Baltimore, 1890–1930,* 66–69; Alewitz, "Sanitation and Public Health in Philadelphia: 1870–1900," 156; Jon Peterson, "The Impact of Sanitary Reform upon American Urban Planning, 1840–1890," *Journal of Social History* 13 (Fall 1979):84–89.

19. The establishment of plumbing as a licensed trade with recognized standards is described in Stone, "The Plumbing Paradox," 283–309.

20. Tarr et al., "Water and Wastes," 233–237; Alewitz, "Sanitation and Public Health in Philadelphia: 1870–1900," 168; Melcalf and Eddy, *American Sewerage Practice,* 1:17–21.

21. Edgar Holden, *Mortality and Sanitary Record of Newark, N.J., 1859–1879: A Report Presented to the President and Directors of the Mutual Benefit Life Insurance Company, January, 1880* (Newark, 1880), 113–114.

22. *Newark Annual Reports, 1878, Board of Health,* 28.

23. Holden, *Mortality and Sanitary Record of Newark,* 24ff.

24. Ibid., 24.

25. Roseville Improvement Association, *Annual Report of the Secretary, 1883,* 2–3.

26. *Sunday Call,* August 8, 1886.

27. Ibid., December 28, 1884.

28. *Newark Daily Journal,* August 7, 9, 1883; *Newark Annual Reports, 1883, Board of Health,* 426.

29. *Newark Annual Reports, 1887, Board of Health,* 475–476.

30. New Jersey, *Legislative Acts* (1882), 60–65, (1886), 119–120; *Newark Annual Reports, 1886, Mayor's Message,* 44–45; *1892,* 7.

31. *Newark Annual Reports, 1883, Board of Health,* 401.

32. New Jersey, *Legislative Acts* (1882), 60–65; *Sunday Call,* December 28, 1884.

33. *Newark Annual Reports, 1885, Board of Health,* 803, *1890, Mayor's Message,* 10, *1910, Board of Health,* 847; *Annual Report of the Newark Board of Health, 1894,* 21.

34. Popper, "Newark," 309.

35. *Sunday Call,* December 28, 1884, August 26, 1888, February 8, 1891; *Newark Evening News,* November 19, 1889.

36. *Sunday Call,* December 28, 1884.

37. Ibid.; Bureau of Municipal Research, N.Y., "Survey," 318–319.

38. *Sunday Call,* February 5, 1911.

39. Ibid.

40. *Annual Report of the Newark Board of Health, 1894,* 19.

41. Popper, "Newark," 305.

42. *Report of the Engineers*, 28.

43. *Newark Evening News*, April 24, 1886, June 18, 1887, June 30, 1889; *Newark Annual Reports, 1885, Board of Health*, 803.

44. Lott Southard, "Drainage and Sewerage of the City of Newark and Their Relation to the Causation of Disease," *Trans. MSNJ, 1877*, 198–199; *Newark Annual Reports, 1883, Board of Health*, 426; *Newark Evening News*, June 18, 1887.

45. *Annual Report of the Newark Board of Health, 1894*, 21.

46. *ARNJBH, 1880*, 124; *Newark Daily Advertiser*, May 8, 1885; *Newark Annual Reports, 1883, Board of Health*, 43–45.

47. *Newark Daily Advertiser*, May 8, 1885.

48. *Newark Evening News*, June 10, 1884.

49. Ibid.

50. *ARNJBH, 1884*, 13–14, 189–190, *1887*, 187; *Newark Evening News*, June 18, 1884, June 18, 1887.

51. *ARNJBH, 1884*, 189–190; *Newark Daily Advertiser*, January 9, 1889; *Newark Evening News*, June 18, 1887. In 1891 it was revealed that shoddy construction had caused numerous breaks in the sewer. There were also suggestions of impropriety in the awarding of the contract.

52. *Newark Daily Journal*, August 7, 9, 1883; *Annual Report of the Board of Health, 1894*, 20.

53. *Annual Report of the Newark Board of Health, 1894*, 5.

54. Newark, *Supplement to the Sanitary Code . . . 1889*, sec. 5.

55. *Annual Report of the Newark Board of Health, 1894*, 20; *Newark Annual Reports, 1910, Board of Health*, 574. In Milwaukee, a city of roughly the same size and population of Newark, but without its large, uninhabited meadows, the number of miles of sewerage increased from 195.8 in 1890 to 428 in 1910. Roger David Simon, "The Expansion of an Industrial City: Milwaukee, 1880–1910" (Ph.D. diss., University of Wisconsin, 1971), 110.

56. Frank John Urquhart, *A History of the City of Newark, New Jersey*, 3 vols. (New York: Lewis Historical Publishing Co., 1913), 2:630; Bureau of Municipal Research, N.Y., "Survey," 588–601.

57. Bureau of Municipal Research, N.Y., "Survey," 588.

58. In other cities as well, developers put in water and sewer lines in new middle- and upper-class neighborhoods and added the cost to the price of their properties. Carl V. Harris, *Political Power in Birmingham, 1871–1921* (Knoxville: University of Tennessee Press, 1977), 149–153; Roger D. Simon, *The City-Building Process: Housing and Services in New Milwaukee Neighborhoods, 1880–1910* (Philadelphia: American Philosophical Society, 1978), 40.

59. Willard D. Price, *The Ironbound Dictrict: A Study of a District in Newark*,

N.J. (Newark 1912), 24–25 (made by Willard D. Price for the Neighborhood House).

60. Everywhere in the nation the poor were the last to benefit from sanitary improvements. Sam Bass Warner, Jr., *The Urban Wilderness: A History of the American City* (New York: Harper and Row, 1972), 202–205.

7   GARBAGE DISPOSAL

1. *Sentinel of Freedom,* April 15, 1873; *Sunday Call,* July 31. 1881.
2. Samuel Harry Popper, "Newark, N.J., 1870–1910: Chapters in the Evolution of an American Metropolis" (Ph.D. diss., New York University, 1952), 298–299.
3. *Newark Evening News,* March 20, 1887.
4. New Jersey, *Legislative Acts* (1902), 52, 200–201, *Annual Report of the Board of Health, 1888,* 9–10; *Newark Evening News,* July 1, 1908, November 5, 1915.
5. *Newark Evening News,* March 20, 1887, March 13, 1908, January 4, 1913, February 5, 25, 1914, July 18, 1916; *Annual Report of the Board of Health, 1894,* 50–51; *Yearbook of the Board of Trade, 1910,* 112; George B. Ford and E. P. Goodrich, *Housing Report,* [Report of] *The City Plan Commission, Newark* (Newark: Matthias Plum, 1913), 15–16.
6. *Annual Report of the Board of Health, 1888,* 9.
7. Ibid., July 23, 1903, May 7, 1913, August 19, 1916.
8. *Newark Evening News,* July 23, 1903.
9. The history of grabage disposal in the United States, especially during the late nineteenth and early twentieth centuries, is analyzed in Martin V. Melosi, *Garbage in the Cities: Refuse, Reform, and the Environment, 1880–1980* (College Station: Texas A & M University Press, 1981). The best study of garbage disposal in a single city is found in Judith Walzer Leavitt, *The Healthiest City: Milwaukee and the Politics of Health Reform* (Princeton, N.J.: Princeton University Press, 1982), 122–155.
10. "First Report of the Committee on Public Hygiene of the American Medical Association," *Transactions of the American Medical Association* 2 (1849):472; Charles V. Chapin, *Municipal Sanitation in the United States* (Providence, R.I.: Snow and Farnham, 1901), 193–194; Leavitt, *Milwaukee and the Politics of Health Reform,* 123; Otto L. Bettman, *The Good Old Days—They Were Terrible!* (New York: Random House, 1974), 7.
11. Martin V. Melosi, "'Out of Sight, Out of Mind'; The Environment and Disposal of Municipal Refuse, 1860–1920," *Historian* 35 (August 1973):622;

Joel A. Tarr, "Urban Pollution—Many Long Years Ago," *American Heritage,* 22 (October 1971):65–66, 106; Bettman, *The Good Old Days,* 3; H. Wayne Morgan, "America's First Environmental Challenge, 1865–1920," in *Essays on the Gilded Age,* ed. Margaret Francine Morris (Austin: University of Texas Press, 1973), 99–100.

12. "First Report of the Committee on Public Hygiene of the American Medical Association," 472, 558–559; Charles E. Rosenberg, *The Cholera Years: The United States in 1832, 1849, and 1866* (Chicago: University of Chicago Press, 1962), 103; Stanley K. Schultz and Clay McShane, "Pollution and Political Reform in Urban America: The Role of Municipal Engineers, 1840–1920," in *Pollution and Reform in American Cities, 1870–1930,* ed. Martin V. Melosi (Austin: University of Texas Press, 1980), 156; Leavitt, *Milwaukee and the Politics of Health Reform,* 122–127.

13. Melosi, *Garbage in the Cities,* 107; Ernest S. Griffith, *A History of American City Government: The Conspicuous Failure, 1877–1900* (New York: Praeger, 1974), 167; Chapin, *Municipal Sanitation,* 694.

14. Chapin, *Municipal Sanitation,* 698; Joel A. Tarr, "The Search for the Ultimate Sink: Urban Air, Land, and Water Pollution in Historical Perspective," The 1981 Letitia Woods Brown Memorial Lecture, *Records of the Columbia Historical Society of Washington, D.C.* 51 (1984):18–19.

15. Martin V. Melosi, "Refuse, Pollution and Municipal Reform: The Waste Problem in America, 1880–1917," *Pollution and Reform in American Cities, 1870–1930,* ed. Martin V. Melosi (Austin: University of Texas Press, 1980), 110.

16. Melosi, *Garbage in the Cities,* 176–181; Chapin, *Municipal Sanitation,* 701–704.

17. Rudolph Hering, "Sewage and Solid Refuse Removal," *A Half Century of Public Health: Jubilee Historical Volume of the American Public Health Association,* ed. Mazÿck Porcher Ravenel (New York: American Public Health Association, 1921), 189–194; Melosi, *Garbage in the Cities,* 184–187; Ellis L. Armstrong, ed., *History of Public Works in the United States, 1776–1976* (Chicago: American Public Works Association, 1976), 449–450.

18. Martin V. Melosi, *Pragmatic Environmentalist: Sanitary Engineer George E. Waring, Jr. Essays in Public Works History,* no. 4 (Chicago: Public Works Historical Society, 1977), 12–17.

19. Leavitt, *Milwaukee and the Politics of Health Reform,* 124, 150–154.

20. Harrison P. Eddy, "Historic Review of the Development of Sanitary Engineering in the United States during the Past One Hundred and Fifty Years," *Transactions of the American Society of Civil Engineers* 92 (1928):1299.

21. Melosi, "Refuse, Pollution and Municipal Reform," 123–125; Melosi, *Gar-*

bage in the Cities, 156–157; Leavitt, *Milwaukee and the Politics of Health Reform,* 135, 143.

22. Newark, *The Sanitary Code . . . 1888,* secs. 48–54, 17–19.

23. *Annual Report of the Newark Board of Health, 1897,* 16–17; Ford and Goodrich, *Housing Report,* 17.

24. *Newark Evening News,* March 20, 1887; *Annual Report of the Board of Health, 1888,* 9.

25. *Newark Annual Reports, 1890, Mayor's Message,* 53–54, 93–94.

26. *Annual Report of the Newark Board of Health, 1894,* 50–51, *1897,* 16–20.

27. *Sunday Call,* April 14, 1876; *Newark Evening News,* August 17, 1896.

28. Popper, "Newark," 299.

29. *Newark Evening News,* July 21, 1901; Frank John Urquhart, *A History of the City of Newark, New Jersey,* 3 vols. (New York: Lewis Historical Publishing Co., 1913), 2:637.

30. *Newark Evening News,* July 21, 1901, March 19, 1902, January 17, 1913; *Sunday Call,* April 6, 1902; New Jersey, *Legislative Acts* (1902), 51, 200–201.

31. Newark Board of Street and Water Commissioners, *Scavenger Contract* (1902); Newark, *Revised Ordinances* (1902), "Relating to Garbage, etc.," 567–569.

32. *Newark Evening News,* June 21, 1903.

33. Rudolph Hering, "Sewage and Solid Refuse Removal," 191–192; Charles Edward-Amory Winslow, *Man and Epidemics* (Princeton, N.J.: Princeton University Press, 1952), 108.

34. I was unable to determine the exact date. *Newark Evening News,* March 20, 1909; J. C. Hallock and F. O. Runyon, *Report on Disposal of Refuse for the City of Newark, New Jersey, 1912.*

35. Popper, "Newark," 298–300.

36. *Newark Evening News,* June 21, July 23, 1903, March 20, 1909, June 23, 1911; Ford and Goodrich, *Housing Report,* 15.

37. *Yearbook of the Board of Trade, 1908,* 110–111.

38. Hallock and Runyon, *Report on Disposal of Refuse,* 17–19.

39. Ibid., 19–26.

40. *Newark Evening News,* October 1, 1912, January 18, 1915.

41. Ibid., January 4, February 5, May 7, 1913; February 25, December 29–30, 1914, January 19, 1915; Ford and Goodrich, *Housing Report,* 5–6.

42. *Newark Evening News,* January 18, 1915.

43. Ibid., November 5, 1915.

44. Ibid., December 24, 1915.

45. *Sunday Call,* March 26, 1916.

46. Ibid.

47. *Newark Evening News,* July 18, 1916.

48. Ibid., August 2, 1916.

49. Ibid., August 16, 22, 1916.

50. Ibid., August 4, 1916.

51. Ibid., August 22–25, 1916.

52. Ibid., August 24, 1916.

53. Ibid.

54. Ibid., September 1, 1916.

55. Ibid., September 8, 1916.

56. Ibid., February 21, 23, 1917.

57. Ibid., July 28, 1917.

58. Bureau of Municipal Research, N.Y., "Survey," 644–645.

59. *Newark Evening News,* August 15, 1917; Bureau of Municipal Research, N.Y., "Survey," 642–645.

8 SMALLPOX

1. Donald Hopkins, *Princes and Peasants: Smallpox in History* (Chicago: University of Chicago Press, 1983), 3–4; M. V. Ball, "Death Rate from Smallpox in Various Cities and States," *American Medicine* 5 (1903):450; Cyril William Dixon, *Smallpox* (London: J & A Churchill, 1962), 104–105.

2. John Duffy, *Epidemics in Colonial America* (Baton Rouge: Louisiana State University Press, 1953), 104.

3. Ibid., 110–111; Richard Harrison Shryock, *Medicine and Society in America: 1660–1860* (New York: New York University Press, 1960), 82–84, 94.

4. The impact of smallpox on colonial America and the introduction of inoculation and, later, vaccination are treated at length in John B. Blake, *Public Health in the Town of Boston, 1630–1822* (Cambridge, Mass.: Harvard University Press, 1959), 52–98, 177–191; idem, *Benjamin Waterhouse and the Introduction of Vaccination: A Reappraisal* (Philadelphia: University of Pennsylvania Press, 1957); Duffy, *Epidemics in Colonial America;* Genevieve Miller, *The Adoption of Inoculation for Smallpox in England and France* (Philadelphia: University of Pennsylvania Press, 1957); Ola Elizabeth Winslow, *A Destroying Angel: The Conquest of Smallpox in Colonial Boston* (Boston: Houghton, Mifflin, 1974).

Once effective methods of preventing smallpox became available, Americans lost interest in the disease and so too did historians. The experience of Virginia blacks during the antebellum period is described in Todd L. Savitt, *Medicine and Slavery: The Diseases and Health Care of Blacks in Antebellum Virginia* (Urbana: University of Illinois Press, 1978), 219–226. For an excellent account of one city's encounter with smallpox, see Judith Walzer Leavitt, *The Healthiest City: Milwaukee and the Politics of Health Reform* (Princeton, N.J.: Princeton University Press, 1982), 76–121. The controversies engendered by compulsory vaccination are discussed in John Duffy, "School Vaccination: The Precursor to School Medical Inspection," *Journal of the History of Medicine and Allied Sciences* 33 (July 1978):344–355; Martin Kaufman, "The Antivaccinationists and Their Arguments," *Bulletin of the History of Medicine* 41 (September–October 1967):463–478; Joan Retsinas, "Smallpox Vaccination: A Leap of Faith," *Rhode Island History* 38 (November 1979):113–124.

5. Miller, *Inoculation*, 42–43, 45–99; Blake, *Public Health in Boston*, 52–73. Since around 1910 the term "vaccination" has been used generically to refer to any instance in which a person is injected with an immunizing substance. Milton J. Rosenau, *Preventive Medicine and Hygiene*, 1st ed. (New York: D. Appleton, 1913), 3.

6. Hopkins, *Smallpox in History*, 310.

7. Winston H. Price and James P. Leake, "Smallpox and Vaccinia," in Kenneth F. Maxcy and Milton J. Rosenau, *Preventive Medicine and Public Health*, ed. Philip E. Sartwell, 9th ed. (New York: Appleton-Century-Crofts, 1965), 131–139.

8. *Trans. MSNJ, 1883*, 39–41.

9. Price and Leake, "Smallpox and Vaccinia," 135–138; Allan McLane Hamilton and Bache McE. Emmett, "Smallpox and Other Contagious Diseases," in *A Treatise on Hygiene and Public Health*, ed. Albert H. Buck, 2 vols. (1879; reprint, New York: Arno Press, 1977), 2:526; Charles V. Chapin, *Municipal Sanitation in the United States* (Providence, R.I.: Snow and Farnham, 1901), 597.

10. W. Mortimer Brown, "Report from the Eastern District," *Trans. MSNJ, 1807–1858*, 459.

11. Hopkins, *Smallpox in History*, 85; Leavitt, *Milwaukee and the Politics of Health Reform*, 80–81.

12. *Newark Evening News*, March 23, 1901.

13. Hopkins, *Smallpox in History*, 88.

14. Ibid., 268; Retsinas, "Smallpox Vaccination," 114, 119–120, 122, n. 8.

15. *ARNJBH, 1880,* 302.

16. *Journal of the American Medical Association* 38 (1902):1147; Joseph Mc-Farland, "Tetanus and Vaccination: An Analytical Study of Ninety-five Cases of this Rare Complication," *Journal of Medical Research,* n.s., 2 (1902):474–493.

17. *ARNJBH, 1880,* 301–303; *Trans. MSNJ, 1882,* 93, *1883,* 39–41; George Rosen, *A History of Public Health* (New York: MD Publications, 1957), 279; Wilson G. Smillie, "The Period of Great Epidemics in the United States (1800–1875)," *The History of American Epidemiology,* ed. Franklin H. Top (Saint Louis: C. V. Mosby, 1952), 58; Rosenau, *Preventive Medicine and Hygiene,* 4–5; Alex McAllister, "The Cause of Sore Arms in Vaccination," *Trans. MSNJ, 1902,* 154; Ralph Chester Williams, *The United States Public Health Service, 1798–1950* (Richmond, Va.: Whitlet and Shepperson, 1951), 184; New Jersey, *Legislative Documents* (1875), doc. 24, *Report of the Health Commission for the Year 1874,* 12–14; Chapin, *Municipal Sanitation,* 593–594.

18. Peter Razzell, *The Conquest of Smallpox: The Impact of Inoculation on Smallpox Mortality in Eighteenth Century Britain* (Firle, Sussex: Caliban Books, 1977), 151.

19. Hopkins, *Smallpox in History,* 87–88.

20. Dixon, *Smallpox,* 199.

21. Hamilton and McE. Emmett, "Smallpox and Other Contagious Diseases," 518.

22. *Newark Evening News,* March 27, 1901.

23. *The Rudolph Matas History of Medicine in Louisiana,* ed. John Duffy, 2 vols. (Baton Rouge: Louisiana State University Press, 1958), 2:437.

24. Leavitt, *Milwaukee and the Politics of Health Reform,* 77, n.2.

25. Ibid., 98–115.

26. Ibid., 77, n.2.

27. Ibid., 116, 118.

28. Kaufman, "The Anti-Vaccinationists," 463–478; William Travis Howard, Jr., *Public Health Administration and the Natural History of Disease in Baltimore, Maryland: 1797–1920* (Washington, D.C.: Carnegie Institution of Washington, 1924), 295–296; Wilson G. Smillie, *Public Health, Its Promise for the Future: A Chronicle of the Development of Public Health in the United States, 1607–1914* (New York: Macmillan, 1955), 432; *Newark Evening News,* April 16, 1901, September 11, 14, 1915.

29. Retsinas, "Smallpox Vaccination," 114, 118; Hopkins, *Smallpox in History*, 95.

30. Retsinas, "Smallpox Vaccination," 115–117.

31. Ibid., 115, 118–119.

32. Ibid., 117.

33. Ibid., 116.

34. Duffy, "School Vaccination," 345–351.

35. Ibid., 352–353.

36. Ibid., 355; Chapin, *Municipal Sanitation*, 501.

37. Hopkins, *Smallpox in History*, 292.

38. Ibid.

39. Duffy, "School Vaccination," 346–348; Retsinas, "Smallpox Vaccination," 116.

40. The incidence of smallpox in Newark is derived from a number of sources. For the period 1841–1858, see the mortality statistics in the Newark city directories and the annual reports of the New Jersey secretary of state; for 1859–1879, Edgar Holden, *Mortality and Sanitary Record of Newark, N.J.: A Report Presented to the President and Director of the Mutual Benefit Life Insurance Company, January 1880* (Newark, 1880), 8–16; for 1880–1902, annual reports of the Newark Board of Health and the New Jersey Board of Health.

41. Fred B. Rogers and A. Reasoner Sayre, *The Healing Art: A History of the Medical Society of New Jersey* (Trenton: Medical Society of New Jersey, 1966), 106, 109–110, 135; David L. Cowen, *Medicine and Health in New Jersey: A History*, vol. 16 of *The New Jersey Historical Society Series*, ed. Richard M. Huber and Wheaton J. Lane (Princeton, N.J.: D. Van Nostrand, 1964), 88.

42. *Trans. MSNJ, 1864,* 111.

43. Minutes of the District Medical Society, County of Essex, State of New Jersey, 1816–1920 (hereafter referred to as Minutes ECMS), 2:50–51, 53, Office of the Executive Secretary, Essex County Medical Society.

44. Ibid., 1:163.

45. *Directory of the City of Newark, 1852,* 37.

46. Newark, *Charter of the City of Newark and Laws of New Jersey Relating to Said City with the Ordinances Passed by the Common Council* (1850), Addenda; *Newark Daily Advertiser*, June 12, July 10, 1852.

47. *Report of the Health Physician, 1858,* 3–4, *1859,* 7; Cowen, *Medicine and Health in New Jersey,* 93; *Newark Annual Reports, Board of Health, 1881,* 411, *1885,* 612, *1901,* 33–34.

48. Hamilton and McE. Emmett, "Smallpox and Other Contagious Diseases," 518; Duffy, "School Vaccination," 347.

49. Hopkins, *Smallpox in History*, 95–96.

50. Ibid., 282.

51. Leavitt, *Milwaukee and the Politics of Health Reform*, 80–84, 99–112.

52. *Annual Report of the Board of Education, 1885*, 212; *Sunday Call*, January 21, 1923.

53. It has never been demonstrated that anyone is immune to cowpox vaccine. Dixon, *Smallpox*, 134–136.

54. *Annual Report of the Board of Education, 1895*, 350, *1905*, 162–165; *Newark Evening News*, December 4, 1891.

55. Howard, *Baltimore*, 294–296; *Annual Report of the Board of Health, 1897*, 52.

56. *Newark Evening News*, May 27, 1887, July 23–26, 1894.

57. Hamilton and McE. Emmett, "Smallpox and Other Contagious Diseases," 527; Chapin, *Municipal Sanitation*, 501, 596.

58. Newark, *Charter of Newark and Revised Ordinances* (1858), *Ordinances*, 167–173.

59. *Report of the Health Physician, 1860*, 10.

60. *Trans. MSNJ, 1869*, 139. See also, *Report of the Health Physician, 1860*, 10.

61. Chapin, *Municipal Sanitation*, 502, 607.

62. Evlin L. Kinney, "Smallpox in Provincetown, Massachusetts, 1872–73," *Journal of the History of Medicine and Allied Sciences* 36 (July 1981):334.

63. Ibid., 355.

64. Dixon, *Smallpox*, 73–77; Hamilton and McE. Emmett, "Smallpox and Other Contagious Diseases," 515.

65. *Annual Report of the Board of Health, 1894*, 62–63; *Trans. MSNJ, 1894*, 240.

66. *Newark Annual Reports, Mayor's Message, 1871*, 20, *1882, Board of Health*, 464; *1885*, 609–610, *1886*, 588, *Annual Report of the Board of Health, 1894*, 20, 24, 63; Newark, *Charter of Newark and Revised Ordinances* (1858), *Ordinances*, 169.

67. See n. 40, above.

68. *Annual Report of the Board of Health, 1901*, 33–34; *Newark Evening News*, April 1–2, 19, 1901.

69. *Newark Evening News*, April 19, 1901.

70. Ibid., April 20, 1901.

71. Ibid., September 5, 1901.

72. Ibid., September 4–5, 16, 1901.

73. Ibid., September 24, 26, 29, October 2, 4, 1901.

74. Ibid., November 3, 7–8, 1901.

75. Newark, *The Sanitary Code Adopted by the Board of Health of the City of Newark, N.J., January, 1902*, 86–90; *Newark Evening News*, February 5, 1902.

76. *Annual Report of the Board of Health, 1901*, 33–36; *1902*, 21, 30, 36–37, 40.

77. Hopkins, *Smallpox in History*, 95–96; Chapin, *Municipal Sanitation*, 592, 597; Retsinas, "Smallpox Vaccination," 120.

78. Hopkins, *Smallpox in History*, 5–6, 287–290, 293.

79. Ibid., 290–293; Dixon, *Smallpox*, 205.

9   WATER SUPPLY

1. George H. Bailey, *Report to the Newark Aqueduct Board upon the Subject of a Supply of Water for the City of Newark* (Newark: Newark Daily Advertiser, 1861), 43.

2. Edward S. Rankin, *Indian Trails and City Streets* (Montclair, N.J.: Globe Press, 1927), 55.

3. *Newark Annual Reports, 1892, Board of Street and Water Commissioners*, 18–19.

4. Stuart Galishoff, "Triumph and Failure: The American Response to the Urban Water Supply Problem, 1860–1923," in *Pollution and Reform in American Cities, 1870–1930*, ed. Martin V. Melosi (Austin: University of Texas Press, 1980), 35–36; Letty Anderson, "The Diffusion of Technology in the Nineteenth Century American City: Municipal Water Supply Investments" (Ph.D. diss., Northwestern University, 1980), 105. Unlike other sanitary services, the literature on municipal water supplies is extensive. The development of public water supply systems in the early nineteenth century is described in Nelson Manfred Blake, *Water for the Cities: A History of the Urban Water Supply Problem in the United States* (Syracuse, N.Y.: Syracuse University Press, 1956). The growth of urban water supply systems after the Civil War is taken up in Galishoff and in Anderson, above. There are several histories of individual municipal water supplies, including: Elmer W. Becker, *A Century of Milwaukee Water: A Historical Account of the Origin and Development of the Milwaukee Water Works* (Milwaukee: Privately Printed, 1974); Louis P. Cain, *Sanitation Strategy for a Lakefront Metropolis: The Case of*

Chicago (DeKalb, Ill.: Northern Illinois University Press, 1978); John Ellis and Stuart Galishoff, "Atlanta's Water Supply, 1865–1918," *Maryland Historian* 8 (Spring 1977):5–22; Carol Hoffecker, *Water and Sewage Works in Wilmington, Delaware, 1810–1910: Essays in Public Works History*, no. 12 (Chicago: Public Works Historical Society, 1981); Fern L. Nesson, *Great Waters: A History of Boston's Water Supply* (Hanover, N.H.: University Press of New England, 1983); James C. O'Connell, "Technology and Pollution: Chicago's Water Policy, 1833–1930" (Ph.D. diss., University of Chicago, 1980); William Wright Sorrels, Memphis' Greatest Debate: A Question of Water (Memphis, Tenn.: Memphis State University Press, 1970); Charles H. Weidmer, *Water for a City: A History of New York City's Problem from the Beginning to the Delaware River System* (New Brunswick, N.J.: Rutgers University Press, 1974).

5. Galishoff, "The Urban Water Supply Problem, 1860–1923," 35, 39–40.

6. O'Connell, "Chicago's Water Policy," 80. See also, Charles V. Chapin, *Municipal Sanitation in the United States* (Providence, R.I.: Snow and Farnham, 1901), 265–266.

7. Anderson, "Municipal Water Supply Investments," 71.

8. Sam Alewitz, "Sanitation and Public Health: Philadelphia, 1870–1900," (Ph.D. diss., Case Western Reserve University, 1981), 218–220.

9. Ibid., 221–222.

10. Moses N. Baker, *The Quest for Pure Water: The History of Water Purification from the Earliest Records to the Twentieth Century* (New York: American Water Works Association, 1948), 133–136; Wilson G. Smillie, *Public Health, Its Promise for the Future: A Chronicle of the Development of Public Health in the United States, 1607–1914* (New York: Macmillan, 1955), 344.

11. Galishoff, "The Urban Water Supply Problem, 1860–1923," 37–38, 44; John B. Blake, "The Origins of Public Health in the United States," *American Journal of Public Health* 38 (1947):541.

12. Galishoff, "The Urban Water Supply Problem," 44–45.

13. See ibid., 45; George C. Whipple, "Fifty Years of Water Purification," in *A Half Century of Public Health: Jubilee Historical Volume of the American Public Health Association*, ed. Mazÿck Porcher Ravenel (New York: American Public Health Association, 1921), 165–173.

14. Among the big cities that obtained new water supplies in the 1880s and 1890s were Atlanta, Jersey City, Memphis, and Newark.

15. Bailey, *Report to the Newark Aqueduct Board* (1861), 23–24.

16. Ibid., 43; George H. Bailey, *Report of the Newark Aqueduct Board* (Newark, 1871), 4–5.

17. *Newark Daily Advertiser,* July 2, 1872.
18. Albert R. Leeds, *Shall We Continue to Use the Sewage Polluted Passaic; or Shall We Get Pure Water?* (Jersey City: Jersey City Printing, 1887), 14.
19. Ibid., 14–15.
20. *Annual Report of the Board of Trade, 1872,* 12–13.
21. New Jersey, *Legislative Acts* (1873), 520–526.
22. Henry Wurtz et al., *Reports to the Joint Commission on the Water Supplies of the Cities of Newark and Jersey City* (Jersey City: Pangborn, Dunning, and Dear, 1873), 41–42.
23. Ibid., 45, 51–58.
24. *Annual Report of the Board of Trade, 1874,* 13.
25. Ibid., *1875,* 13.
26. Ibid., 15.
27. New Jersey, *Annual Report of the State Geologist, 1874,* 61, *1876,* 13–14, 18–19 (hereafter referred to as *AR St. Geol.*).
28. *AR St. Geol., 1876,* 13–14.
29. *Newark Daily Advertiser,* August 2, 9, 1874, February 11, 1877; *Annual Report of the Newark Aqueduct Board* (1861), 23–24; *Newark Annual Reports, 1892, Board of Street and Water Commissioners,* 14–15; Bailey, "Water Supply of Newark," 51–58.
30. J. R. Croes and George E. Howell, *Report on Additional Water Supply* (Newark: Newark Aqueduct Board, 1879), 4. The city of Little Falls is located on a small waterfall for which the city is named. Great Falls, which provided the power for Paterson's industries, is sixty-six feet high.
31. Newark Aqueduct Board, *Pollution of the Passaic River: Embracing the Report of the Special Committee Appointed to Represent the Newark Aqueduct Board in the Board of Inspection of the Passaic River and Its Tributaries* (Newark: Ingalls, 1882), 8–9 (hereafter referred to as Newark Aqueduct Board, *Report of the Special Committee*).
32. Croes and Howell, *Report on Additional Water Supply,* 14–15.
33. Ibid., 42–45.
34. Ibid., 62–67.
35. Ibid., 93.
36. Ibid., 79–91.
37. *AR St. Geol., 1882,* 137–138; Croes and Howell, *Report on Additional Water Supply,* 48–62; *Newark Annual Reports, 1881, Board of Health,* 400. A small amount of well water obtained from this source is still used for industrial purposes. N.J. Department of Conservation and Economic Development, Division of Water Policy and Supply, *Special Report 10, Preliminary*

Report on the Geology and Ground Water Supply of the Newark, N.J., Area (1951), 40 (hereafter referred to as *Special Report 10*).

38. Minutes ECMS, 2:120, 142.
39. Edgar Holden, *Mortality and Sanitary Record of Newark, N.J., 1859–1879: A Report Presented to the President and Director of the Mutual Benefit Life Insurance Company, January, 1880* (Newark, 1880), 20.
40. *Newark Annual Reports, 1880, Board of Health*, 429–430.
41. *Sunday Call*, May 30, 1880.
42. *Newark Annual Reports, 1882, Board of Health*, 621; *Annual Report of the Newark Aqueduct Board, 1882*, 21–22.
43. Leeds, *Sewage Polluted Passaic*, 15; Albert R. Leeds, "The Monstrous Pollution of the Water Supply of Jersey City and Newark," *Journal of the American Chemical Society* (1887), 90–94; *AR St. Geol., 1881*, 73–74.
44. *ARNJBH, 1883*, 8–9.
45. New Jersey, *Legislative Documents* (1884), vol. 2, doc. 40, *Report of the Commissioners of State Water Supply of New Jersey, March, 1884*, [along with the *Supplementary Report*], 3–8, 26–27; *ARNJBH, 1882*, 8–9.
46. *Annual Report of the Newark Aqueduct Board, 1884*, 131.
47. Ezra M. Hunt, "The Passaic River as Related to Water-Supply and Death Rates," *ARNJBH, 1887*, 325.
48. *AR St. Geol., 1882*, 130–131.
49. *Newark Annual Reports, 1883, Board of Health*, 399–400.
50. *Sunday Call*, April 25, 1850; Newark Aqueduct Board, *Report of the Special Committee*, 3–6, 12–19.
51. Newark Aqueduct Board, *Report of the Special Committee*, 3–6, 12–19; *Newark Evening News*, June 12, 1886.
52. Hunt, "The Passaic River," 335.
53. *Annual Report of the Newark Aqueduct Board, 1884*, 131–132.
54. Barbara Gutmann Rosenkrantz, *Public Health and the State: Changing Views in Massachusetts, 1842–1936* (Cambridge, Mass.: Harvard University Press, 1972), 81.
55. Daniel Jacobson, "The Pollution Problem of the Passaic River," *Proceedings of the New Jersey Historical Society* (July 1958):194, n.44.
56. *Annual Report of the Newark Aqueduct Board, 1882*, 100–103.
57. Hunt, "The Passaic River," 330.
58. *ARNJBH, 1884*, 188; *Annual Report of the Newark Aqueduct Board, 1884*, 122–124, 131.
59. *Annual Report of the Newark Aqueduct Board, 1884*, 132–134.
60. Moses N. Baker states flatly that Leeds was "influenced by a commercial

bias" in his advocacy of forced aeration. *The Quest for Pure Water*, p. 170. See also, 361–362, 375–379.

61. *Newark Daily Advertiser*, April 2, 1885.

62. Leeds, *Sewage Polluted Passaic*, 10–13; New Jersey, Passaic Valley Sewerage Commissioners, *Brief Description of Passaic Valley Sewerage Commission* [by William Gavin Taylor] (n.p., 1916), 3.

63. *Newark Evening News*, September 2, 1887.

64. Ibid.

65. Ibid., September 9, 1886; October 12, 1886.

66. Ibid., January 20, 1887.

67. Ibid., December 23, 1886, March 9, 1887.

68. Ibid., September 9, 1886.

69. Ibid., September 2, 1886.

70. Ibid., *Annual Report of the Board of Trade, 1885*, 12.

71. *Sunday Call*, May 23, 1886.

72. *Annual Report of the Newark Aqueduct Board, 1887*, 17.

73. Ibid., *1885*, 14.

74. Ibid., 15–19; Hunt, "The Passaic River," 335.

75. *AR St. Geol., 1886*, 210–211.

76. Leeds, *Sewage Polluted Passaic*, 3–14.

77. Ibid., 23.

78. Hunt, "The Passaic River," 336, 346, 351–352; *Newark Evening News*, June 16, 1887.

79. Cited in Hunt, "The Passaic River," 346.

80. *Sunday Call*, March 18, 1888.

81. Hunt, "The Passaic River," passim.

82. *Sunday Call*, June 26, 1887, February 10, 1889; *Newark Evening News*, June 4, 1887.

83. Samuel Harry Popper, "Newark, N.J., 1870–1910: Chapters in the Evolution of an American Metropolis" (Ph.D. diss., New York University, 1952), 279; Eugene P. Moehring, *Public Works and the Patterns of Urban Real Estate Growth in Manhattan, 1853–1894* (New York: Arno Press, 1981), 34.

84. *AR St. Geol., 1882*, 141–143; *Sunday Call*, May 15, 1887. Except for the eastern section of the city, Newark's groundwater resources are meager. Mainly they are used for general industrial purposes. *Special Report 10*, 11, 28, 36–37.

85. *Sunday Call*, September 22, 1901; Julius Howard Pratt, *Reminiscences, Personal and Otherwise* (published by the author, 1910), 183; *Annual Report of the Board of Trade, 1886*, 38–39.

86. *Newark Evening News*, January 5, 1887.

87. *Annual Report of the Newark Aqueduct Board, 1887,* 18.
88. Ibid., 18–20; *Newark Evening News,* March 10, 1887.
89. *Newark Evening News,* January 30, 1887.
90. Ibid., June 14, 1888.
91. *Annual Report of the Newark Aqueduct Board, 1888,* 11.
92. *Sunday Call,* June 17, 1888.
93. Newark, Department of Public Works, *Water Supply of Newark, N.J.* (Newark: Department of Public Works, 1949), 5.
94. *Sunday Call,* September 22, 1901; Newark, *Report of the Special Committee of the Common Council Appointed to Confer with the Commissioners of the Aqueduct Board in Relation to a New Water Supply for the City of Newark Together with the Proceedings of the Joint Committee,* December 19, 1888 (Newark: Ward and Tichenor, 1888), 24 (hereafter referred to as *Proceedings of the Joint Committee*). In the guise of perpetual leases, the Society for the Establishment of Useful Manufactures had sold the average flow of the Passaic River to Paterson millers. Though this water could not be diverted, the society was empowered to build storage reservoirs to divert the surplus flood waters of the river. John R. Bartlett and Associates, *Outline of Plans . . . for Furnishing an Abundant Supply of Water to the City of New York* (published by the author, 1888), 5–6.
95. *Newark Evening News,* April 14, 1936.
96. *Sunday Call,* September 22, 1901.
97. *Newark Evening News,* December 12, 1888.
98. Ibid.
99. *Sunday Call,* June 17, 1888.
100. *Annual Report of the Newark Aqueduct Board, 1888,* 11.
101. *Proceedings of the Joint Committee,* 3–5, 28–31.
102. Ibid., 23–25, 30–31, 38–39; *Newark Evening News,* December 24, 1888; Pratt, *Reminiscences,* 184.
103. *Newark Evening News,* December 24, 1888.
104. Ibid., January 3, 10, 1889; Newark, *Report of the Aqueduct Board of the City of Newark to the Common Council of Its Proceedings and Action on the Subject of New Water Supply, January 15, 1889* (Newark: Ward and Tichenor, 1889), 3, 5–17.
105. *Newark Evening News,* January 15, 1889, January 8, 1890; *Report of the Aqueduct Board . . . to the Common Council,* 17–35.
106. See the earlier part of this chapter.
107. George W. Rafter and M. N. Baker, *Sewage Disposal in the United States* (New York: D. Van Nostrand, 1893), Appendix V, 579–585.
108. *Agreement between the Lehigh Valley Railroad Company, the East Jersey*

Water Company, and the Newark Aqueduct Board and the Mayor and Com-mon Council of the City of Newark, September 24, 1889. Since state law for-bade Newark from obtaining water from an out-of-state company, the Lehigh Valley Railroad Company, which was incorporated in Pennsylvania, created the East Jersey Water Company to consummate the agreement.

109. Rudolph J. Vecoli, *The People of New Jersey,* supplementary volume of *The New Jersey Historical Series,* ed. Richard M. Huber and Wheaton J. Lane (Princteon, N.J.: D. Van Nostrand, 1964), 167.

110. *Sunday Call,* September 29, October 7, 1889.

111. *Annual Report of the Board of Health, 1899,* 7, 106, *1900,* 71; William T. Sedgwick and J. Scott MacNutt, *On the Mills-Reincke Phenomenon and Hazen's Theorem Concerning the Decrease in Mortality from Diseases Other than Typhoid Fever Following the Purification of Public Water-Supplies,* re-printed from *The Journal of Infectious Diseases* 8, no. 4 (August 1910), in *Clean Water and the Health of the Cities, Public Health in America,* ed. Bar-bara Gutmann Rosenkrantz (New York: Arno Press, 1977), 507–510; Ros-enkrantz, *Public Health and the State,* 102–103. After 1895, the impact of bacteriology on public health work in Newark and a higher standard of living, together with a safe water supply and other sanitary improvements, brought about a sharp decline in the city's death rate.

112. See, e.g., *Sunday Call,* July 10, 1904; *Newark Annual Reports, 1916, Board of Health,* 1327.

CONCLUSION

1. I have been guided in my thinking here by H. Wayne Morgan, "America's First Environmental Challenge, 1865–1920," in *Essays on the Gilded Age,* ed. Margaret Francine Morris (Austin: University of Texas Press, 1973), 87–108.

2. Jon Peterson, "The Impact of Sanitary Reform upon American Urban Plan-ning, 1840–1890," Journal of Social History 13 (Fall 1979):84.

3. See Chapter 5, "Board of Health."

4. Emmons Clark, "Sanitary Improvement in New York during the Last Quarter of a Century," *The Popular Science Monthly* 39 (1891):322.

5. John Shaw Billings, "Sewage Disposal in Cities," *Harper's New Monthly* 71 (1885):579; Charles F. Wingate, "The City's Health-Sanitary Construction," *Municipal Affairs* 21 (1898):262.

6. Roy Lubove, *The Progressives and the Slums: Tenement House Reform in*

New York City, 1890–1917 (1962; reprint, Westport, Conn.: Greenwood Press, 1974), 96–97; Ann-Louise Shapiro, *Housing the Poor of Paris, 1850–1902* (Madison: University of Wisconsin Press, 1985), 32–42, 111–114, 133; Anthony S. Wohl, *The Eternal Slum: Housing and Social Policy in Victorian London* (Montreal: McGill-Queen's University Press, 1977), 322–330.

7. Nelson Manfred Blake, *Water for the Cities: A History of the Urban Water Supply Problem in the United States* (Syracuse, N.Y.: Syracuse University Press, 1956), 142, 181, 185, 197–198, 239; John Ellis and Stuart Galishoff, "Atlanta's Water Supply, 1865–1918," *The Maryland Historian* 8 (Spring 1977):18; James C. O'Connell, *Chicago's Quest for Pure Water: Essays in Public Works History*, no. 1 (Washington, D.C.: Public Works Historical Society, 1976), 14; William Wright Sorrels, *Memphis' Greatest Debate: A Question of Water* (Memphis, Tenn.: Memphis State University Press, 1970), 19.

8. Billings, "Sewage Disposal," 584; Charles V. Chapin, *Municipal Sanitation in the United States* (Providence, R.I.: Snow and Farnham, 1901), 296–297.

9. Howard D. Kramer, "The Germ Theory and the Early Public Health Program in the United States," *Bulletin of the History of Medicine* 22 (May–June 1948):239.

10. Judith Walzer Leavitt, "Public Health in Milwaukee, 1867–1910" (Ph.D. diss., University of Chicago, 1975), 331–332.

11. The same holds true for Atlanta, Chicago, Memphis, New Orleans, and Wilmington, Delaware. See Dennis East II, "Health and Wealth: Goals of the New Orleans Public Health Movement, 1879–1884," *Louisiana History* 9 (Summer 1968): 248–249; John H. Ellis, "Businessmen and Public Health in the Urban South during the Nineteenth Century: New Orleans, Memphis and Atlanta," *Bulletin of the History of Medicine* 44, no. 3 (May–June 1970):197–198, no. 4 (July–August 1970), 349–350; Carol E. Hoffecker, *Wilmington, Delaware: Portrait of an Industrial City, 1830–1910* (Charlottesville: University Press of Virginia, 1974), xv, 52–59; O'Connell, *Chicago's Quest for Pure Water*, 6–7.

12. Joel A. Tarr, James McCurley, and Terry F. Yosie, "The Development and Impact of Urban Wastewater Technology: Changing Concepts of Water Quality Control, 1850–1930," in *Pollution and Reform in American Cities, 1870–1930*, ed. Martin V. Melosi (Austin: University of Texas Press, 1980), 64.

13. Joel A. Tarr, "The Evolution of the Urban Infrastructure in the Nineteenth and Twentieth Centuries," in *Perspectives on Urban Infrastructure*, ed. Royce Hanson (Washington, D.C.: National Academy Press, 1984), 10.

14. Carl V. Harris, *Political Power in Birmingham, 1871–1921* (Knoxville: University of Tennessee Press, 1977), 155.

15. Moses N. Baker, *Sewerage and Sewage Purification* (New York: Macmillan, 1896), 11.

16. Blake, *Water for the Cities*, passim; Eugene P. Moehring, *Public Works and the Patterns of Urban Real Estate Growth in Manhattan, 1835–1894* (New York: Arno Press, 1981), 28–37.

17. O'Connell, *Chicago's Quest for Pure Water*, 5–14.

18. Hoffecker, *Wilmington*, xv.

19. Eugene P. Moehring, *Public Works and Urban History: Recent Trends and New Directions; Essays in Public Works History*, no. 13 (Chicago: Public Works Historical Society, 1982), 11.

20. Ellis, "Businessmen and Public Health," 386. See also, Lynette B. Wrenn, "The Memphis Sewer Experiment," *Tennessee Historical Quarterly* 44 (Fall 1985): 340–342.

21. Tarr, McCurley, and Yosie, "Development and Impact of Urban Wastewater Technology," 67; Joel A. Tarr, with James McCurley III, Francis C. Michael, and Terry F. Yosie, "Water and Wastes: A Retrospective Assessment of Wastewater Technology in the United States, 1800–1932," *Technology and Culture* 25 (April 1984):234, 235, n. 25; Judith Walzer Leavitt, *The Healthiest City: Milwaukee and the Politics of Health Reform* (Princeton, N.J.: Princeton University Press, 1982), 133–155.

22. Sam Bass Warner, Jr., *Streetcar Suburbs: The Process of Growth in Boston, 1870–1900* (Cambridge, Mass.: Harvard University Press and MIT Press, 1962), 149–153; Moehring, *Public Works and Urban Real Estate Growth in Manhattan*, 296–299; Stuart Galishoff, "Germs Know No Color Line: Black Health and Public Policy in Atlanta, 1900–1918," *Journal of the History of Medicine and Allied Sciences* 40 (January 1985):40–41.

23. Daniel J. Boorstin, *The Americans: The National Experience* (New York: Random House, 1965), 115–123.

24. Ibid., 115–116.

25. Fern L. Nesson, *Great Waters: A History of Boston's Water Supply* (Hanover, N.H.: University Press of New England, 1983), 3–4, 52–53; Tarr, "Evolution of the Urban Infrastructure," 18–26.

26. Geoffrey Giglierano, "The City and the System: Developing a Municipal Service, 1800–1915," *Cincinnati Historical Bulletin* 35 (Winter 1977):234–238.

27. Nesson, *Boston's Water Supply*, viii, 7–8.

28. Martin V. Melosi, *Pragmatic Environmentalist: Sanitary Engineer George*

E. Waring, Jr., Essays in Public Works History, no. 4 (Washington, D.C.: Public Works History Society, 1977), 10; Tarr, McCurley, and Yosie, "Development and Impact of Urban Wastewater Technology," 68–69. However, on Waring's recommendation, Memphis relied mainly on its creeks to remove storm water. Wrenn, "The Memphis Sewer Experiment," 344.

29. Quoted in Melosi, *Pragmatic Environmentalist,* 10. The sewerage problems are described in Wrenn, The Memphis Experiment," 345–347.

30. Peterson, "Impact of Sanitary Reform upon American Urban Planning," 89.

31. Ibid., 91.

32. Ibid., 89–91.

33. Tarr, "Water and Wastes: A Retrospective Assessment of Wastewater Technology," 250–252; Stanley K. Schultz and Clay McShane, "To Engineer the Metropolis: Sewers, Sanitation, and City Planning in Late-Nineteenth Century America," *Journal of American History* 65 (September 1978):398–399.

34. Roger David Simon, "The Expansion of an Industrial City: Milwaukee, 1880–1910" (Ph.D. diss., University of Wisconsin, 1971), iv–v; Wrenn, "The Memphis Sewer Experiment," 348. Chrintine Meisner Rosen, "Infrastructural Improvement in Nineteenth-Century Cities: A Conceptual Framework and Cases," *Journal of Urban History* 12 (May 1986):211–213, 240–248. Everywhere, the poor, the immigrants, and the blacks were the last ones to benefit from additions to the city's sanitary infrastructure.

35. Edward F. Meeker, "The Improving Health of the United States, 1850–1915," *Explorations In Economic History* 9 (Summer 1972):366–367; Thomas Mckeown and R. G. Record, "Reasons for the Decline of Mortality in England and Wales during the Nineteenth Century," *Population Studies* 16 (November 1967):109–110, 118–120.

36. George Rosen, "Historical Trends and Future Prospects in Public Health," *Medical History and Medical Care: A Symposium of Perspectives,* ed. Gordon McLachlan and Thomas McKeown (London: Oxford University Press, 1971), 66.

37. Minutes ECMS, 4:3; James Gordon Burrow, *A.M.A.: Voice of American Medicine* (Baltimore; Johns Hopkins University Press, 1963), 21–26.

38. Minutes ECMS, 1:39; (1859):220–221, 229–232; (1861):239; 4: n.p.

39. Ibid., 4 (1907):28.

40. John Duffy, "The American Medical Profession and Public Health: From Support to Ambivalence," *Bulletin of the History of Medicine* 53 (Spring 1979):2; James H. Cassedy, *American Medicine and Statistical Thinking, 1800–1860* (Cambridge, Mass.: Harvard University Press, 1984), 200–201, 215–219.

41. Wilson G. Smillie, *Public Health, Its Promise for the Future: A Chronicle of the Development of Public Health in the United States, 1607–1914* (New York: Macmillan, 1955), 296–300, 331–339; Henry I. Bowditch, *Public Hygiene in America* (Boston: Little, Brown, 1877), 182–183, 256, 262, 269, 277.

42. Smillie, *Public Health,* 310; Cassedy, *American Medicine and Statistical Thinking,* 213.

43. Stanley K. Schultz and Clay McShane, "Pollution and Political Reform in Urban America: The Role of Municipal Engineers, 1840–1920," in *Pollution and Reform in American Cities, 1870–1930,* ed. Martin V. Melosi (Austin: University of Texas Press, 1980), 158.

44. John Duffy, *A History of Public Health in New York City,* vol. 1, *1625–1865,* vol. 2, *1866–1966* (New York: Russell Sage Foundation, 1974), 2:xxi; James C. O'Connell, "Technology and Pollution: Chicago's Water Policy, 1833–1930" (Ph.D. diss., University of Chicago, 1980), 78; Sam Alewitz, "Sanitation and Public Health: Philadelphia, 1870–1900" (Ph.D. diss., Case Western Reserve University, 1981), 42. For references to the urban South and Wilmington, Delaware, see n. 11, above. During the Progressive Era the medical profession became infused with the era's reform spirit and supported many government programs to improve the health of the American people, especially those that required the professional skills of physicians, such as campaigns against tuberculosis, infant mortality, and venereal disease. Leavitt, *Milwaukee and the Politics of Health Reform,* 43, 67–68, 74–75, 82, 200–203, 241, 246; Stuart Galishoff, *Safeguarding the Public Health: Newark, 1895–1918* (Westport, Conn.: Greenwood Press, 1975), 162–163.

45. Duffy, "From Support to Ambivalence," 7.

46. *Newark Annual Reports, 1904, Board of Health,* 71, *1915,* 674–675.

INDEX